Looking for Harlem

Looking for Harlem

Urban Aesthetics in African American Literature

Maria Balshaw

Pluto Press

LONDON • STERLING, VIRGINIA

First published 2000 by Pluto Press
345 Archway Road, London N6 5AA
and 22883 Quicksilver Drive,
Sterling, VA 20166–2012, USA

www.plutobooks.com

Copyright © Maria Balshaw 2000

The right of Maria Balshaw to be identified as the author of this work
has been asserted by her in accordance with the Copyright, Designs
and Patents Act 1988.

British Library Cataloguing in Publication Data
A catalogue record for this book is available from the British Library

Library of Congress Cataloging in Publication Data
Balshaw, Maria.
    Looking for Harlem : urban aesthetics in African American
literature / Maria Balshaw.
        p. cm.
    ISBN 0-7453-1339-6 — ISBN 0–7453–1334–5 (pbk.)
    1. American literature—Afro-American authors—History and
criticism. 2. American literature—20th century—History and
criticism. 3. Harlem (New York, N.Y.)—In literature. 4. City and
town life in literature. 5. Cities and towns in literature. 6. Afro-
Americans in literature. 7. Afro-American aesthetics. 8. Aesthetics,
American. 9. Harlem Renaissance. I. Title.
    PS153.N5 B285 2001
    810.9'327471—dc21
                                                                00–009743

ISBN 0 7453 1339 6 hardback
ISBN 0 7453 1334 5 paperback

09   08   07   06   05   04   03   02   01   00
10   9   8   7   6   5   4   3   2   1

Designed and produced for Pluto Press by Chase Publishing Services
Typeset from disk by Stanford DTP Services, Northampton
Printed in the European Union by TJ International, Padstow, England

For Jake and Lily

Contents

Acknowledgements

I should like to acknowledge the support of the AHRB Institutional Fellowship Scheme, which has allowed me to prepare this manuscript as part of the work of the *3 Cities* project, http://www.nottingham.ac.uk/3Cities. The support of the University of Birmingham is also gratefully acknowledged. Portions of Chapters 2, 4 and 6 have been published in earlier versions as essays: '"Black Was White": Urbanity, Passing and the Spectacle of Harlem', *Journal of American Studies*, Vol. 33, No. 2 (Summer 1999) pp. 307–22; 'New Negroes, New Women: The Gender Politics of the Harlem Renaissance', *Women: A Cultural Review*, Vol. 10, No. 2 (Summer 1999) pp. 127–38; 'Elegies to Harlem: *Looking For Langston* and *Jazz*', in Balshaw and Kennedy (eds), *Urban Space and Representation* (Pluto Press, 2000) pp. 82–98.

There are many people who have contributed to the making and shaping of this book. I would like to thank Peter Nicholls for his intellectual guidance through my postgraduate years and after. Anne Beech from Pluto has been a wonderful and very patient editor. I am profoundly grateful to all those who have offered ideas, support and critique over the years, particularly James Annesley, Peter Brooker, Helen Carr, Joshua Cohen, Dick Ellis, Emma Francis, Scott Lucas, Maria Lauret and John Phillips. Douglas Tallack, in his role as director of the *3 Cities* project, has always been an inspiring intellectual role model. All those who have participated in the Urban Cultures seminar at Birmingham deserve thanks both for giving up valuable Saturdays and for keeping lively intellectual engagement going even during busy teaching terms: Carol Smith and Jude Davies especially are a model intellectual partnership. Helen Laville is owed thanks beyond measure for intellectual inspiration, friendship, babysitting and wine drinking, without you I would surely be a lesser academic and a more miserable person. I owe an enormous debt to my parents, Colette and Walter Balshaw, for their love and support, to my brother Ian for ten years of computer trouble shooting and to my extended family for childcare duties, humour and solace beyond the call of duty. To Jake, Lily and Nathan Kennedy I offer love and thanks for cheering me up whenever I am down and for keeping academic work in its proper perspective, not forgetting the additional contributions of Ryan Lucas and Lauryn Laville (my lovely goddaughter) – it is truly a crime that Bob the Builder has no place in academia: can we write it? yes we can!

All my best thoughts come from conversations with Liam Kennedy, without him this book would not exist and I offer this thanks for everything his partnership brings to my life.

Introduction

They weren't even there yet and already the City was speaking
to them. They were dancing. And like a million others, chests
pounding, tracks controlling their feet, they stared out of the
windows for the first sight of the City that danced with them,
proving already how much it loved them. Like a million more
they could not wait to get there and love it back.

Toni Morrison, *Jazz* (1992).

Almost all of the fiction of recent black writers, even when its
theme is unequivocally pro-city, even when its mode and style
is urbane, hip, consistently reveals characters disappointed by a
marked and poignant absence of some vital element of city life
that is all the more startling because of the presence of this same
element or quality in their descriptions of rural or village settings
... What is missing in city fiction and present in village fiction is
the ancestor.

Toni Morrison, 'City Limits, Village Values' (1981).[1]

Which city is it that Morrison speaks of here in these passionately
articulated and utterly opposed utterances? The question is of
course redundant since one knows without needing to be told that
the City that Morrison eulogises in my first epigraph is Harlem,
Capital of the Negro world. Likewise, it is as obvious that her
earlier, pessimistic reading of urban space is also about Harlem,
even if she does not name it as such. In the history of twentieth-
century African American experience and letters it is Harlem that
has held pride of place as the urban locus for an African American
national imaginary. I start with these epigraphs as they pose for us
the paradoxical attitude to the city one finds structuring African
American urban literature throughout the twentieth century. On
the one hand we find a passionate urbanism, where the city stands
for the future and more particularly the future of the race. On the
other hand we see the city painted as the site of deprivation, squalor
and discontent, a version of racial urbanism we are perhaps more
familiar with in our contemporary era. Rudolph Fisher, the Harlem
Renaissance writer whose urban portraits have an important place

in this study, enunciates the paradox in suggestive symbolic terms: 'Harlem, land of plenty ... city of refuge ... city of the devil – outpost of hell.'[2] This book commences with the desire to explicate the paradox of the city of heaven that is also the city of hell.

The history of African American literary study has most often tended towards disparagement of the 'refuge' narrative, as a deluded hope of a promised land that is never fulfilled in America's not-so-melting-pot cities.[3] We see, indeed, the development of a critical anti-urbanism as strongly argued as any city advocacy one might find in African American writing. Morrison's 'Village Values' above emphasises this: the urban is the place where something is missing for African Americans; the site of a loss of cultural identity; of the dissolution of a prized sense of community. The problem with the city is that it is the site of the betrayal of racial feeling that for Morrison at least can only exist somewhere else, or in someone else, and is inevitably left behind in the journey from village to city. This is difficult to square with the writing I privilege in this book, for study of African American writing from the Harlem Renaissance onwards reminds one immediately just how central the city is, as a site of creativity and aspiration, to African Americans. Morrison's suspicion of urbanism is equally difficult to square with her own novel *Jazz*, which finds its aesthetic inspiration in the streets, buildings and sunsets of the city. What happens to her then, between 'Village Values' and *Jazz* prose?

In fact, it is not so much that Morrison changes her mind; the didactic lessons of *Jazz* are to mistrust the city and its wiles and to discover the self once again in a rural history that preserves the figure of the ancestor and an Africanist history and connection.[4] But her novel does catch, more powerfully than any other African American text, the utopian projection of the city as the promised land, even if that dream must be, in Langston Hughes's words, always the 'dream deferred'. It is in the tension between this projection of the dream and its failure, between the multiple varieties of urban writing in the African American literary tradition, and the residual suspicion of urbanism that characterises much study of this tradition that this book finds its subject. Taking inspiration from the work of Paul Gilroy on Black Atlantic modernity and drawing on the work of scholars who over the last few years have redrawn the urban dimensions of the Harlem Renaissance period I argue that it is the exploration of the paradoxes of the heaven *and* hell urbanism of African American writing that will allow us to see clearly the significance of the city to twentieth-century African American literature.[5]

As my point of departure I would suggest that twentieth-century African American literature presents us with a racialised urban aesthetic. What I see as a modern (and sometimes modernist) attitude to the city starts with 1920s writing of the so-called Harlem Renaissance – a body of work that takes its appellation from a city site but has less often been judged to have seriously engaged with the city as a site of representation. Writing about the city is not a phenomenon that begins in the 1920s; indeed, the city features in a number of key nineteenth-century texts from slave narratives such as Harriet Wilson's *Our Nig* (1859) or William Wells Brown's *Clotel* (1853) to early passing novels such as Frank Webb's *The Garies and Their Friends* (1857). However, the city as specific place, rather than generalised moral space, does not make its appearance until the beginning of the twentieth century, with perhaps the earliest example being W.E.B. Du Bois's *The Philadelphia Negro* (1899).[6] The 1920s see new forms of urban African American writing developing as new urban African American communities are formed. As Harlem, but also Chicago, Washington, Detroit and Philadelphia, draws migrants from the South, one gets the first insights into the city as modern space. This means engagement with the changing technological conditions of urban life, with the speed, noise and clutter of the new urban centres, with consumerism, with leisure, entertainment and crime. In short, all the characteristic features of the city in modernity. It is this city, as it is presented and interrogated by African American writers and artists, that is the subject of this book.

The book opens by analysing a number of lesser-known Harlem writers as well as some key documents such as Alain Locke's *The New Negro*. I move on to look at some later city texts that present a continuation of debates that structure the Harlem Renaissance period: debates about the meaning of urbanism for African Americans and the meaning of racial identity in an urban context. My approach stresses the centrality of gender, sexuality and class in the formation of urban race literature and explores how the inter-relation of race and urban space impact upon the formation of subjectivity in literary representation. I also stress the centrality of the image or the spectacle of urban space for the writing I examine, finding in the image of the city a useful ambivalence about urbanism and its pleasures and dangers for African American citizens. I explore the importance of ideas of urbanity to the writers analysed, and the manifold meanings of this term in an African American context. I touch on the extent to which African American authors draw on concepts of modernity and modernism and interrogate them in their work. I also touch on the special significance of Harlem as a site of representation for twentieth-century African American urban writing and suggest the extended geographical boundaries of 'Harlem' (in symbolic terms) as a site for African American aspiration and creativity in the first half of the twentieth century. Though the book moves beyond the physical boundaries of Harlem to look at a selected number of Chicago writings it holds on to the concept of a race capital that is clearly articulated in the writings of the Harlem Renaissance: a Harlem of the mind, a sensibility inspired by, but not confined to, a geography of Harlem.

I set out to examine a number of texts that seemed to me to raise interesting questions about African American representation, identity and history. The book deals primarily with texts produced from the 1920s to the 1940s. I make no attempt to trace the changes associated with the post-war passage into postmodernity – though I do take two contemporary texts that reflect back on this period as a point of closure for the study. Processes of social restructuring during and after the Civil Rights movement, the experience of de-industrialisation and the solidifying of the post-industrial ghetto as the site of an urban underclass, separate as never before the African American city from the life of the whole of the city. Writers such as Chester Himes, Louise Meriwether, Amiri Baraka, Claude Brown, Ishmael Reed, Gloria Naylor or Walter Mosley make fascinating case studies for the debates about the meanings of black city life and the presence of a racial urban aesthetic, which are central to this study. These must by necessity stand outside the scope of this study though texts such as Carlo Rotella's *October Cities* have in recent times begun this kind of analysis.[7] The work of these writers would complicate but not contradict the picture drawn here. As Charles Scruggs makes clear, urban aspirations still lay substantial claim to African American imaginative activity, a fact clearly demonstrated by the contemporary texts, *Jazz* and *Looking For Langston*, which do feature in this study.[8]

My study questions the ways in which the dominant literary histories of African American writing have been mapped out. Attempting to get around the back of these often overpowering debates I chose to draw on a number of different approaches, including feminist theory, cultural geography, psychoanalysis and cultural studies, with an eye to what my own orientation as a feminist cultural critic could bring to a project on African American literature.[9] These theoretical ideas make their presence felt as a kind of lens through which I read African American literature. In particular, work produced in the last decade under the auspices of cultural geography and cultural studies has developed study of urban space which stresses the psychological and subjective dimensions of city life, the micro-politics of urban agency and the psychic ordering of urban experience.[10] While this work does not ignore the political, economic and physical organisation of urban space, it does remind us that the psychological perceptions of cities will often exceed these facts of existence. This basic observation is a valuable one for consideration of urban African American writing. It allows one to appreciate the aspirations for the 'city of refuge' that are carried forward despite the brutal realities of the 'city of hell'. As Charles Scruggs observes: 'The city as a symbol of community, of home – this image lies beneath the city of brute fact in which blacks in the twentieth century have had to live.'[11]

Though the city of hell might at times appear to be the dominant mode of urban African American expression, especially if one confines ones attention to major canonical texts such as Richard Wright's *Native Son* (1940) or Ralph Ellison's *Invisible Man* (1952), viewed with these theoretical concerns in mind the picture looks rather different. None of the authors examined in this study project an idealised version of urban space, but even as they critique their city context they offer it as the only possible location for African Americans. Within this space oppressive realities are documented but resistant dreams are also elaborated. Even when the return to a pastoral idyll is contemplated (as for example in parts of Nella Larsen's or Marita Bonner's writing) the lost rural homeplace is not available as actual refuge, and indeed is often recognised as a still more dangerous place. In Larsen's *Quicksand* the South is offered as refuge to Helga only to turn out to be the place of her death due to unrelenting childbirth. In Bonner's work, life in the North is roundly critiqued but a return to the South is impossible because of its even more pronounced racism, economic hardship, and the threat of lynching. More to the point, in the majority of texts the ideal of the rural past only makes sense in the new urban context, as a site of memory rather than a location one might actually return to. As we see in *Invisible Man* (to pick one of the best-known examples of this trope) the yam that evokes Southern history for the invisible protagonist only carries mnemonic significance consumed on the city street. Or, to take another example, the wise women in Rudolph Fisher's stories draw wisdom not from the longing for a rural return but through the reordering of folk knowledge to suit their new urban context.

What I attempt here, then, is a series of related readings of key texts and moments that demonstrate the centrality of the city and the urban locale to African American writing. This may add up to an alternative mapping of the urban inspiration of much African American literature, as opposed to the frequently suggested folk/rural genesis of African American writing, though this is not a central aim of my analysis. What I would suggest is that the urban mappings I outline make up an important supplementary dialogue on, to echo Paul Gilroy, the dissident conditions of modernity for African Americans. I want to draw out the complexities of urban African American writing as they present themselves as dilemmas of racial, gendered, class and sexual location. By using the urban

as my initial category of analysis, rather than race, gender, class or
sexuality, the complexities of these identity formations reveal
themselves all the more clearly. These identity formations are at the
heart of an exploration of the meanings of urbanism and urbanity
for African Americans, at the heart of debates over issues of representation, throughout the twentieth century but particularly in
the Harlem Renaissance period, just as powerfully as they occupy
centre stage in our own time.

The Criteria of Negro Art

Any study that begins with the Harlem Renaissance immediately
raises complex issues of racial agency and appropriation, as well as
vital questions about the process of African American canon
building and what Richard Wright called 'The Criteria of Negro
Art'.[12] As seminal studies such as Nathan Huggins's *Harlem
Renaissance* (1971) or David Levering Lewis's *When Harlem Was
In Vogue* (1981) argue, Harlem was at least as much a construction of the white imagination as it was the site of black cultural
expression or freedom.[13] The Harlem presented in these texts is
shaped in part by the Black Arts movement that is the backdrop
to these important histories.[14] The Black Arts legacy has had
profound ramifications for what defines the Harlem Renaissance
and for what constitutes black writing. In a process which has
edited out much of the work central to this study, texts and writers
have often been measured according to the supposed authenticity
of racial understanding they evince. This generally means utilising
dialect and/or blues forms and working-class subjects, excluding
wide swathes of literature written by and for the burgeoning black
middle classes. Texts that dwell on the sexual, the spectacular or
the sensational are regarded warily because of their perceived
association with white primitivism. Further, anything that appears
to veer toward stylistic experimentation of a modernist persuasion
is regarded with deepest suspicion because of its perceived
complicity with white values and white writers.[15]

Although the assumptions of the Black Arts movement have
been widely questioned over the last two decades these attitudes
still persist in the assumptions made around issues of black authenticity that structure debates about black cultural production and
African American canon-building. Since the 1970s the African
American canon has been constructed and reconstructed and
expanded almost beyond recognition. If Henry Louis Gates Jr
could suggest in 1984 that African American scholars were only
just beginning to map the tradition of black literary development,
then the impact of his own work and the scholars associated with

him stands as a tribute to how far that process has come.[16] Gates's collection *Black Literature and Literary Theory* (1984), along with the monograph *The Signifying Monkey* (1980), proved profoundly influential in inaugurating what was perhaps the dominant mode of African American criticism in the 1980s, where critical theory (usually post-structuralism) came into signifying dialogue with African American texts. The development of this mode of African American critical practice has a controversial history (which goes beyond the scope of this book), but coupled with the so-called 'multicultural wars' and the impact of black feminism on literary study, the result is a literary field substantially richer in both textual and critical terms.[17] Yet, despite the diversity of texts that have been taken up by critics such as Gates, Houston A. Baker, Barbara E. Johnson and Hortense J. Spillers (to name a few of the critics whose theoretical work has been valuable to this study), and despite the immense body of scholarship fostered by black feminists such as Barbara Christian, Cheryl Wall, Mary Helen Washington or Valerie Smith (again to name only a few), the city has had rather muted treatment in this work. This is perhaps because despite the very great differences that separate these critics, and indeed separate them from their Black Arts predecessors, there is a shared element to their work that is worth drawing out before we move on.

An instructive example can be taken from the work of Houston A. Baker. His work, often allied with that of Gates, comes out of the Black Arts movement and finds rearticulation through the encounter with critical theory to produce what Baker calls 'soundings' of an Africanist African American tradition. Accordingly, Baker's trilogy of texts, *Blues, Ideology and Afro-American Culture* (1984), *Modernism and the Harlem Renaissance* (1987) and *Workings of the Spirit: The Poetics of Afro-American Women's Writing* (1991), construct a revisionary canon of African American letters based on idea of the trickster deformation of white philosophical and literary form. African American texts 'sound' on the white traditions that have so often sought to restrict their utterances, playing their rhetorical strategies back against the dominant culture and finding a vernacular expressivity that outwits the master's discourse. Baker's revisions of African American tradition produce some startling and illuminating readings but in a quite peculiar way they get hung up on the same question of authenticity that preoccupies his Black Arts predecessors.[18] The good African American text is one that displays a vernacular complexity, but more importantly it is one that connects with a sense of spirit, a word that carries a crucial significance for Baker. The blues, soul, dialect poetry and playing the dozens are all soundings that embody spirit for Baker in that they connect to an

African American exceptionalism and to an Africanism within African American culture that is the essence of the authentic for Baker (and for other critics like him).

What is troubling about this is not the residual essentialism; to point this out seems only to perform a deconstructive reading of a critic already involved in deconstructive critical practice (a nice example of 'what goes around comes around' to use the black idiom Gates and Baker are fond of). Rather, this vernacular definition of the good black text and authentic black expression leaves very little room for urban writings by African Americans that turn away from an Africanist spirit which is almost always articulated in rural terms. More problematically still it leaves little room for writings, like many Harlem Renaissance texts, which are comfortably located not in opposition to the (white) master's discourse but instead quite clearly in dialogue with it. Baker's *Workings of the Spirit* gives the best example of the problems that can arise with this approach when he categorises Jessie Fauset and Nella Larsen as ungrateful yellow-skinned daughters, who betray their soulful black foremothers and sisters (like blues singers Bessie Smith or Ma Rainey, or the folk-orientated Hurston) in their wanting-to-be-white narratives.[19] The problematic gender assumptions that underpin some of Baker's readings of African American women's texts have been roundly critiqued by black feminist writers; what I want to highlight is how this focus on the spirit often tips into a celebration of village values very close to the Morrison essay I took as an epigraph.[20]

What one loses in this version of the 'Criteria of Negro Art' are precisely the issues of gender, sexuality and class that complicate racial identity in the authors I examine in this book. Study of the ambiguity and conflict around the meanings of these different, and often contradictory, identity formations maps out another critical landscape that has been of vital importance to this work. If one element in the reshaping of the African American canon has been the debates over the nature and usefulness of theory, then an equally vital influence has been black feminist work to rediscover, reread and revalue the literary production of African American women: indeed, it would be a mistake to separate these two influences from one another as their trajectories cross often and in important ways. The debt this study owes to the work of black feminist critics is registered in the extensive discussion of the essays and books produced over the last two decades in the body of my study and its footnotes. Even here though I must mark a divergence in approach, as within this tradition too one can see the workings of a kind of 'spirit' that results in the sidelining of the city as a site of representation for African American women writers. Within black feminist study there has been a powerful desire to locate the ancestor, or literary foremother; which has very often meant the valorisation of a positive maternal, often rural, history as the means to the regeneration of the self in the present. To cite what is perhaps the most moving usage of this trope, 'In Search of Their Mothers' Gardens', many feminist writers, black and white, have found their own. The phrase, of course, is Alice Walker's from the collection that bears it as a title, *In Search of Our Mothers' Gardens: Womanist Prose*.[21]

This womanist impulse (to use Walker's term) brings with it, however, a seeming distrust of urban writing rather similar to Morrison's misgivings in her 'Village Values' essay. Hazel Carby has critiqued the unquestioning adoption of Zora Neale Hurston as literary godmother of choice by white and black feminist writers, pointing to the complicity of the publishing industry with a putative multiculturalism that is willing to reintroduce texts to the classroom while ignoring institutional structures of racial exclusion in education and in culture at large.[22] I can only echo her misgivings, and also suggest that many of the authors discussed in this study would, by virtue of their ambiguous loyalties to notions of community, family, race and gender, necessarily fall outside a womanist-inspired critical project. In the urban representations that are the subject of this text I examine the not-so-positive literary foremothers, for whom gender and race (as well as class and sexual identity) are addressed as problematic, and often insurmountable, social formations. Furthermore, as this study will reveal, the urban literary communities of Harlem – or Chicago – suggest one should explore the ways in which these identity formations are manifested in the writings of African American male as well as female authors. If we are to challenge, as Carby suggests we must, the extent to which the work by black women and gay men is still seen as peripheral to the African American (male) establishment then the questions raised by the female authors whose work makes up the bulk of this text must also be applied to the key (male) texts that have historically represented the Harlem Renaissance and African American literary history.[23] This book goes some way toward this task, and in taking some time over lesser figures from the annals of African American history (male and female) suggests that a rather different (less masculinist) tradition emerges in the urban engagements we see here. I set myself within and to some degree against the critical debates I have mapped out here. As I select my own narrative of African American writing I privilege the urban not as the definitive marker of some form of 'spirit-work' so much as a contradictory site for the continuing debates over the meanings of racial identity and race writing.

The Race Capital

Chapter 1 takes as its starting point the hugely influential 1925 *Survey Graphic* Special Issue edited by Alain Locke, which became *The New Negro*, foundation text of the Harlem Renaissance. Though urban migration and the expansion of Harlem, both geographically and culturally, starts substantially long before Locke's text, *The New Negro* develops a particular self-consciousness about what it means to be an African American artist, which can be read as a creative engagement with debates about the meanings of urbanity for African Americans. Highlighting the significance of Locke's definition of Harlem as a 'race capital' the chapter examines the centrality of urban experience to definitions of the so-called New Negro. I argue that the understanding of urban culture as civic culture, drawn from the contemporaneous work of the Chicago School sociologists, is crucial to understanding the cultural and philosophical context of the debates over the New Negro. I then discuss *Fire!!* magazine, published in the same year as *The New Negro*, to argue that this text's modernist avant-gardism should be read as an extension of the critical positions adopted by Locke, as typical of and congruent with New Negro aesthetics, rather than (as critical opinion would usually have it) antithetical to them.

Chapter 2 examines the rarely studied work of Rudolph Fisher. His writing develops ideas of racial urbanity as a means to capture the multiple, conflicting discourses that structure African American urban space. Fisher's short stories and novels develop a critical cosmopolitanism where mastering the rules of social interaction in the city – becoming urbane – is seen as the most productive means of mastering city space. The chapter concludes with Fisher's usage of the conventions of detective fiction in his 1932 novel *The Conjure Man Dies*. As much as solving a crime, *The Conjure Man Dies* is concerned with the meanings of racial identity in an internally divided city space. I draw out the connections between these discourses of racial identity and the broader debates that structured literary and cultural experimentation in this period, seeing Fisher's work as an example of inter-cultural dialogue on these issues and as a critical commentary on the debates which helped foster the New Negro Renaissance.

Chapters 3 and 4 turn to focus on issues raised by the literary production of African American women in 1920s Harlem. If the city has conventionally been seen as a place of disappointed dreams for African Americans, then its potential for black women has been judged still more negatively. Carrying the double burden of structures of racial and gender oppression women writers have rarely been considered as productively engaged with the city as a site of representation. Yet when one looks at the Harlem

Renaissance the role of women artists is crucial and the influence of women as organisers and proselytisers for the New Negro Renaissance has been systematically underestimated in studies of the Harlem Renaissance. The significance of literary production by African American women in the decades prior to the 1920s has been traced by a number of scholars.[24] Certainly, one should see the literary and cultural activity of groups of women artists as continuing the traditions of turn-of-the-century women's clubs and anti-lynching campaigning. However, the 1920s see a significant shift as women artists, living in the major cities, work at their art for a living, and find their artistic and social contexts within the social and economic fabric of the city and within the worlds of work and leisure. The contribution of women to the urban aesthetic I am tracing in this book expands the boundaries of Harlem, to embrace Georgia Douglas Johnson's literary salon in Washington and Marita Bonner's presence in Washington and Chicago, as well as those better-known writers who found their artistic home in Harlem.

Chapter 3 looks at the passing fictions of Nella Larsen. Unlike many of the writers in this study Larsen's work has been the subject of considerable critical attention over the last few years, with a number of essays analysing her peculiar, angst ridden representations of racial and gender identity. This chapter resituates her work within the broader context of Harlem women's writing, and Harlem Renaissance modernism. The passing women in Larsen's novels can be seen as a figures for cultural anxieties about racial identity, which are more pointed in an urban context that offers the promise of racial and sexual anonymity. Written by and for the burgeoning black bourgeoisie, the racial conservatism of these and other passing fictions has allowed them to be too easily dismissed as peripheral to the Harlem Renaissance and to African American literary history, with the result that the complex interdependence of racial, gender and sexual identity they evidence has been overlooked. Taking up a focus on consumer culture, I argue that it is city life that is central to understanding Larsen's versions of the passing narrative, particularly in the texts' dependence on scenes of visual spectacle and conspicuous consumption. This chapter argues that we should see the racial and class conservatism of the passing woman as the necessary counterpoint to a sexual radicalism which is possible only within the city. Furthermore, the passing woman can be seen as a quintessentially modern figure – characterised by her anonymity, her restless pursuit of pleasure, disavowal of family and racial belonging as well as her enthusiastic embrace of the material experience of modern life.

Chapter 4 turns to works most usually passed over in studies of Harlem Renaissance writing. The writings of Marita Bonner and

Angelina Weld Grimké add considerable richness to our conceptions of the period. Their work looks at the effects of urban life on African American women in the first half of the twentieth century. They focus on the difficulty of reconciling the demands of motherhood and family with a rapidly shifting urban scene. The despairing urban narratives examined in this chapter counterpoint Larsen's glamorous city scenes, but they are nevertheless engaged with a very similar constellation of cultural and discursive forces. Of particular interest is how the subject of inter-racial relationships, and the threat of miscegenation, is reformulated in this urban context. Here we see African American women, and women writers, awkwardly caught between competing discourses of New Negro aesthetics, burgeoning feminism, racial uplift and eugenics, a difficulty which often manifests itself in anxiety around motherhood and the black woman's relationship to (and responsibilities toward) her race. I move on to examine how working-class urban life becomes of key interest to Bonner as she constructs a geography of racial disaffection and confinement in her little-known Frye Street stories. Analysis of these short stories, which construct a fictional urban neighbourhood (based on an area of Chicago), reveals a transition from the optimism of 1920s Harlem toward the harshness of 1940s examinations of urban life that are the focus of Chapter 5, a transition most clearly measured in Bonner's work through the dispiriting impact of the city on the lives of women and children.

The impact of urbanism on the lives of women and children also marks out the concerns of Chapter 5. I now turn to a group of post-Harlem Renaissance texts, examining urban representations of Harlem and Chicago from the late 1940s. This chapter and the next are critical reflections on the texts and issues mapped out in the first three chapters and this section in particular tests some of the assumptions and ideas drawn out in earlier readings against texts and contexts considerably less favourable to African American life and cultural expression. The exotic urban scene of the passing novel is substituted for the harsh negativity of urban space in Ann Petry's novel *The Street* (1946), Gwendolyn Brooks's poetry sequence *A Street in Bronzeville* (1945) and, as counter-text, Richard Wright's *Native Son* (1940). These texts stress important qualifications to the putative freedoms of the city for African Americans. Nevertheless, I argue that even in these texts the city is the site of ambivalent experiences, which integrate African Americans into the fabric of the city even as the texts stress the spatial confinement of race. Emphasising the importance of commodity culture to all these texts and stressing the gendered as well as racial dimensions of urban experience, the chapter highlights a tracing of alternative life practices mapped across the city, inscribed in and between the official story of racism. Taken together these three central chapters of the book outline an alternative tradition of female social protest by African American writers: a model of protest more tentative and equivocal than those rather more strident voices (like Wright or Ellison) which have played such a significant role in defining the African American literary tradition. This equivocal protest stands as testament to the complicating role of gender and sexuality on the experience of race in American culture. That the significance of these dissident voices has rarely been noted testifies to the persistence of a fundamentally masculinist tradition of African American letters.[25]

Interest in the racialised life practices which structure a prosaic and contingent but nonetheless powerful 'geography' of the city can also be seen in contemporary African American literature and film. The final chapter of the text looks at Toni Morrison's novel *Jazz* (1992) and Isaac Julien's film *Looking For Langston* (1989). These texts take the city, and in particular the legendary Harlem of the 1920s, as central to their understanding of contemporary African American identity. They exhibit marked attention to the significance of gender, sexual desire and spectacle in the formation of racial subjectivity, tracing counter-histories of fantasy, desire and longing presented as meditations on urban space. They also bring together key issues for the text as a whole through a sustained commentary on African American urbanity, history and identity, which it is their critical intention to reformulate. Each text exhibits an unstable 'passing' structure to emphasise the contingency of urban African American experience, and they present new New Negro philosophy, linking contemporary debates about identity politics and multiculturalism with the texts and arguments of 1920s Harlem. The female-voiced narration of Harlem in Morrison's text and the multi-voiced speaking of homosexual desire in *Looking For Langston* make explicit the implicit coordinates of urban African American literature that have been traced throughout the book. As such these texts self-consciously reflect on the major themes of this text and bring it to a close as they re-place the city at the heart of an African American urban imaginary it is the object of this study to locate.

CHAPTER 1

New Negroes, New Spaces

Huh! de wurl' ain't flat,
An' de wurl' ain't roun',
Jes' one long strip
Hangin' up an' down –
Since Norf is up,
An' Souf is down,
An Hebben is up,
I'm upward boun'.

Lucy Ariel Williams, 'Northboun', *Opportunity* (June 1926).

Lucy Williams's celebration of the heaven that is the North echoes a utopian strain to be found in much African American writing of the 1920s, particularly in the sense that the reputation of Harlem draws writers to this famed 'city within a city'.[1] This sense of excitement can be found in a wide variety of Harlem Renaissance writers and cultural commentators, from Alain Locke's celebration of the new spirit in Negro life in *The New Negro* (1925) to James Weldon Johnson's *Black Manhattan* (1930), the controversial avant-gardism of *Fire!!* magazine and the sophisticated wit of Rudolph Fisher's urban tales. For these and many other Harlem writers the definitive changes brought about by large-scale migration to the Northern urban centres by African Americans after the First World War, and the subsequent expansion of Harlem, are registered as a barely contained excitement with the city these writers situate themselves in.[2]

We see a very good example of this thrill of the urban in a story by Rudolph Fisher called 'City of Refuge', published in 1925 in *Atlantic Monthly*.[3] This shows us the shocking newness of Harlem through the eyes of a typical urban ingenue, a migrant from rural Georgia, King Solomon Gillis. 'City of Refuge' demonstrates that despite the economic hardships, racism and exploitation which existed at the time, Harlem does act at this point as a fantasy space of freedom, pleasures and opportunities for African American citizens (as well as acting as the legendary space of exoticism and license for the white imagination). Gillis, the putative hero of Fisher's story, is on the run from the South after killing a white

14

man and comes to Harlem 'with the aid of a prayer and an automobile' (p. 3) to escape being lynched. His arrival sees him propelled into a carnivorous city of disorienting sounds, speed and subways until, like Jonah out of the whale, he is burped up into a sunny, calm and all-black Harlem:

> Then slowly, spreadingly, he grinned at what he saw: Negroes at every turn; up and down Lenox Avenue, up and down 135th Street; big, lanky Negroes, short, squat Negroes; black ones, brown ones, yellow ones; men standing idle on the curb, women, bundle-laden, trudging reluctantly homeward, children rattle-tapping about the sidewalks; here and there a white face drifting along, but Negroes predominantly, overwhelmingly everywhere. There was assuredly no doubt of his whereabouts. This was Negro Harlem. (p. 3)

As the quotation aptly demonstrates Gillis is dumbfounded at the sight of so many African Americans gathered together and it catches very well the Harlem street scene; a feature of many of Fisher's short stories. Part of the newness of Harlem for Gillis is the comfortable occupation of public space by African Americans and the experience of Harlem as mass phenomenon. The sense of shock at the all-black space Gillis experiences is perhaps a little deceptive, since his Southern home will have assuredly been a segregated community. What is remarkable to him about Harlem is the occupancy of *urban* space as racial space. The story conveys his shock that the social organisation of the space, from shops to landlords to traffic cops, is in the hands of African Americans and he cannot get over the sight of a thoroughly developed, socially progressive urban race capital. In terms that will be developed through this chapter, Gillis is profoundly disturbed and deeply delighted at African Americans pursuing the practice of urbanity.

For Gillis, Harlem offers all the opportunities conventionally associated with the modern city: anonymity, entertainment, work, pleasure and mobility. It is, furthermore, a place of safety, because the modernity of Harlem offers the possibility that Gillis will be able to disappear into the mêlée:

> In Harlem, black was white. You had rights that could not be denied you; you had privileges, protected by law. And you had money. Everybody had money. It was a land of plenty ... The land of plenty was more than that now; it was also the city of refuge. (p. 4)

The city eventually consumes the naive Southerner, but not before the story catches the elation of arrival to this turned around, 'black is white' world of Harlem, registered in Gillis's amazed exclamation: 'Even got cullud policemen' (p. 5). This elation underlines the extent to which Harlem is not simply Gillis's port of refuge but is a projection of a state of mind about urban aspirations for African Americans. Fisher uses indirect discourse to allow Gillis's amazed perceptions to in part take over the narrative voice of the story to convey a larger-than-life perception of Harlem. We see, for example, the policeman directing traffic as 'a handsome brass-buttoned giant' (p. 4). The story ends with Gillis being duped by a rather more street-wise Harlemite into trafficking drugs, but the apparent failure of the 'city of refuge' to save Solomon Gillis is presented by Fisher in complex terms. As he is seized by policemen in a night-club Gillis finds himself face-to-face with the gigantic apotheosis of his Harlem aspirations, an African American policeman. Instead of continuing to fight: 'Very slowly King Solomon's arm's relaxed; very slowly he stood erect; and the grin that came over his features had something exultant about it' (p. 16).

This strange ending underlines the most notable feature of the story, that the urban space in which Gillis finds himself is a utopian projection of his own psyche, at least as much as it is a reflection of the conditions of Harlem life at the time. In this sense the ending represents not the failure of urban promise but the limits of powerful psychic and social realities for African Americans in this period when Harlem comes to be claimed as a 'race capital'.[4] The attitude to the city in Fisher's story sees African Americans as part of a narrative of modernity associated with movement away from the perceived backwardness of the South and the (premodern) history of slavery and Southern racism; a narrative which sees the South as an anachronism which will be replaced by a new age, represented particularly by Harlem. To echo Paul Gilroy's suggestions in The Black Atlantic, this clearly places African Americans as insiders to an essentially Enlightenment narrative of modernisation and progress.[5] It critiques the myths of modernity not through asserting that African Americans are outside or exiled by these myths, but by pointing out how the experience of migration to the North, and the subsequent narratives of urban life generated by these migrants, place African Americans as players in the story of the making of America and the American city despite the material and racial prohibitions encountered in the urban environment.[6]

The Harlem presented in the texts that form the basis of this chapter is a city of urbanity and urban sophistication, particularly as this defines a race capital in Harlem in opposition to the rural or Southern history of African Americans. This raises important questions about the centrality of urban experience in understanding the meanings of race in the writing of this period. It also implicitly raises questions about the relationship between African American writing and critical conceptions of modernity and of that

problematically related term, modernism.[7] While the 'discovery' of
African American modernism in the writers and writing I examine
functions as little more than academic name calling, I do want to
suggest that the Harlem writing privileged in this chapter (and at
other points in this book) demands consideration in terms which
we might *loosely* categorise as modernist: that is, defined through
its fascination with urbanity as a key shaping element in the
development of a racialised aesthetic commensurate to the
experience of African American life in Harlem.[8]

This race aesthetic presents African American subjectivity as
mediated by the impact of new forms of urban organisation that
develop in the Northern urban centres and most typically and substantially in Harlem. Representations of Harlem typically articulate
the dislocated and unsettling aspects of urban life as a characteristically modern fragmented subjectivity. There is a fascination
with the visual impact of Harlem and with the imbrication of race
and sexuality in the formation of subjectivity. This writing often
features the spectacular experience of Harlem night-life, a
primitivist celebration of racial and sexual exoticism, or Africanist
otherness, but I do not want to move too quickly to dismiss these
representations of Harlem's legendary exotic spaces. To condemn
them as irretrievably compromised by the taint of white influence
is to impose an after-the-fact self-consciousness about the politics
of the black liberation struggle.[9] This does a disservice in both
cultural and literary terms to the aims and agendas of the New
Negro movement, as I have already outlined in my introduction.
It is also very important to weigh things carefully when one
considers the kinds of sexual freedoms offered in Harlem's largely
unlicensed and unregulated entertainment economy. The work of
Lillian Faderman and Eric Garber points out the importance of
Harlem as a gay scene at this time and the position of women
within the burgeoning race capital is as interesting as it is
problematic.[10] It would be a mistake to underestimate the significance of the exploration of sexual identity in the shaping of African
American urban identity merely because the writing often does
not conform to conventional ideas of authentic black expression.[11]
These issues will be explored as the study unfolds, for now we
must simply note that while Harlem was not by any means a free
expressive space, interesting configurations do emerge out of the
conscious understanding in the period of its status as an urbane
and cosmopolitan race capital.

Racialised Urbanity

The notion of urbanity as the expression of a peculiarly modern
form of urban consciousness – the projection of an urban mode of

being and self-awareness of what it means to be a citizen in a rapidly changing urban polis – has been the subject of much critical analysis.[12] The modern origins of this concept can be traced back to the writings of Robert E. Park and his contemporaries (particularly Louis Wirth) and the foundations of the Chicago School of sociology.[13] The meanings of urbanity are manifold, but what emerges most clearly from the writings of Park and his contemporaries is that it refers to the evolution of civic consciousness and responsibility and stresses the importance of the life of the mind, in terms of everyday customs, artistic endeavour, human communication and philosophy, in the construction of what it means to live in the city. It is also crucially dependent on the idea of the coming together of strangers who construct the city through social interaction that is not based on kinship or group membership.[14] In Park's most famous formulation the city is,

> a state of mind, a body of customs and traditions, and of the organised attitudes and sentiments that inhere in these customs and are transmitted with this tradition. The city is not, in other words, merely a physical mechanism and an artificial construction. It is involved in the vital processes of the people who compose it; it is a product of nature, and particularly of human nature.[15]

This notion of the civilised and civilising human organisation of the city is one which has been questioned profoundly in the years since Park wrote, both in terms of the subsequent development of the cities he wrote about and his theoretical conception of it. The concept of urbanity has also accrued rather different meanings as the twentieth century has progressed, coming to stand less for the active striving toward civic responsibility and more for a social and cultural sophistication, a self-consciousness about how to project the manners and mores of urban living: being urbane rather than practising urbanity.[16] It is useful though, at least for this study, to remember the connections between urbanity and civic consciousness, and being urbane as self-consciousness, because the Parkian stress on the importance of communication and social interaction, with the arts as an integral part of this urban social interchange, does connect importantly to the other sense of urbanity as proficiency in negotiating cultural capital. These connections can provide us with one way of understanding the motivations and aspirations of at least one strain of New Negro writing.

Tracing the importance of urbanity to New Negro writing might at first seem a rather odd task given that it is not a concept held to have much relevance to African American urban experience. This is understandable given that the subsequent history of African American life in the northern urban centres such as New York or Chicago might be cited as the antithesis of the experience of urbanity. The optimism of Park's understanding of urban space is most easily undermined if one considers the lack of progress in cultural, economic or political terms that has characterised black urban experience in the decades since the 1920s. This is borne out if one looks at the 1922 Report of the Chicago Commission on Race Relations, *The Negro in Chicago*, which featured a Parkian stress on the eventual resolution of urban strife through social cooperation and the civic-minded behaviour of Chicago's different communities.[17] The Report, steered by the dynamic Charles S. Johnson, a student of Park and one of the foremost African American sociologists of his age as well as the editor of *Opportunity* magazine in the New Negro years, makes depressing retrospective reading, especially if one considers that more than half of its recommendations refer directly to the responsibility on the part of Chicago citizenry to cultivate a fair-minded tolerance between racial groups.[18] That these hopeful admonitions toward a racially tolerant urbanity do not materialise in Chicago or anywhere else is the subject of any number of historical and sociological analyses; for the purposes of this text we shall see the unfulfilled promise of urbanity marked clearly enough in the texts of Marita Bonner, Ann Petry and Richard Wright analysed in later chapters.

Yet, urbanity does have key significance to African American writing, particularly during the 1920s. The influence of Parkian thinking on the key players in the Harlem Renaissance can be traced in direct terms through figures like Charles S. Johnson, as George Hutchinson and others have shown.[19] It has a broader influence, however, if one sees that the particular mode of 'uplift' or racial improvement that leaders of the New Negro movement like Alain Locke advocated was one which was plainly concerned with the cultivation of urbanity as both civic responsibility and as an artistic attitude of mind. In this sense the race aesthetic advocated by New Negro philosophers could be termed racialised urbanity. Furthermore, the stress in Chicago School work on the significance of the coming together of strangers in the public spaces of the modern metropolis gives us a useful context for understanding the fascination with racial spectacle, in the form of cabarets, balls, dances and bars, in the work of many Harlem Renaissance writers. While one must allow that this in part reflects awareness of what white (and black) readers expected of Negro Harlem and its writers, one should also see these representations as part of an urge toward urbanity which is an important element of African American thinking about the city.

From the Harlem Special Issue to The New Negro

I want to trace the construction of this racial urbanity by looking first at the most famous of all Harlem Renaissance texts, Alain Locke's collection *The New Negro*.[20] This text developed from the *Survey Graphic* Special Issue on Harlem which Locke had edited and it has come to stand as the apotheosis of the New Negro Renaissance (indeed to a large degree it was regarded as such at the time).[21] It included stories, poetry, essays and polemic and featured virtually every black writer of note in the period. For commentators of all theoretical and political persuasions Locke's collection stands as *the* New Negro document, representing (variously) the most definitive statement of black modernism, a trickster mastery of form, the highpoint of the Negro vogue, a pragmatist expression of desires for social change through artistic excellence, as well as the first seeds of the eventual compromise of New Negro hopes.[22] To paraphrase George Hutchinson, it is likely that all these views are mostly right but partly wrong.[23] While I do not want to knock *The New Negro* from pride of place in the pantheon of Harlem Renaissance texts, I want to draw attention to elements of the collection that reveal an abiding concern with the construction of urbanity as a racial attitude and as an artistic impetus.[24]

The genesis for the *Survey Graphic* Special Issue came from the famous Civic Club dinner in March 1924 organised by Charles S. Johnson and hosted by Alain Locke. This event, which has been as much studied as the collections which grew out of the meeting, gathered together most of the younger African American writers and artists of note for a kind of launch party for the New Negro, ostensibly in celebration of the publication of Jessie Fauset's novel *There Is Confusion*.[25] The speeches at this gathering, the essay which Locke himself wrote as introduction to the *Survey* collection, and the more numerous essays which punctuate *The New Negro*, make it clear that the cultural awakening that these collections herald is one which breaks with the tradition of genteel fiction that was associated with Fauset's work. Indeed, as George Hutchinson points out, Fauset was explicitly sidelined by Locke because he saw her conservatism as being at odds with the new spirit that he wished to capture in his anthologies.[26] In Hutchinson's view this new spirit, or cultural racialism, was part of more general cultural tendencies that saw New Negro writing as part of a resurgent cultural nationalism, which drew out racial and ethnic distinctiveness at the same time as articulating American values as they were being shaped in the work of philosophers like William James and ethnographers like Franz Boas, developing what Hutchinson calls a 'rhetoric of Americanism'.[27] The idea of a race spirit, and the racial aesthetic which forms the basis of Locke's *New Negro* essays and gives critical shape to this incredibly diverse (some would say antagonistic) collection, should undoubtedly be viewed in this light and Locke makes explicit claims about the New Negro's American credentials. He argues, 'the choice is not between one way for the Negro and another way for the rest, but between American institutions frustrated on the one hand and American ideals progressively fulfilled and realized on the other' (p. 12).

The modernist aspirations of the collection are also clearly evident in Locke's essays. In a preface to the fiction in the collection he says: 'It has been their achievement also to bring the artistic advance of the Negro sharply into stepping alignment with contemporary artistic thought, mood and style. They are thoroughly modern, some of them ultra-modern, and Negro thoughts now wear the uniform of the age' (p. 50). Whether one chooses to go along with Locke's assessment of the fiction (and not all of it fits this 'ultra-modern' description), or for that matter whether one sees Locke's integrationist modernism as a useful strategy for African American artists in this period, was the subject of at least as much comment in Locke's time as it has been in the decades since the collection was published. Documenting the intensity of contemporary or subsequent spats over Locke's rather programmatic shaping of the collection goes beyond the remit of this study, even if this had not already been the subject of excellent and extensive scholarly debate.[28] What I want to draw out is the extent to which Locke draws on a notion of urban civic culture as a means to articulate a national and racial identity and literature.

Locke undertook substantial revisions between the *Survey Graphic* issue and the expanded collection. While the first collection bears Locke's imprint in terms of the fiction and poetry he solicited as well as in his own keynote essays, it is also shaped by the social work agenda of the *Survey*. So, a number of the pieces have a sharp sociological edge rather at odds with the broader artistic and cultural optimism that underpins Locke's framing pieces. He subsequently found himself subject to a number of critiques about the negativity of some of the essays in the *Survey* issue as well as to lobbying from powerful middle-class interest groups (who wished to see the race represented by institutions such as Howard University rather than through the bars and tenements of working-class Harlem). Locke also harboured his own agenda about what should be projected as a representative image of the race and his response was to remove many of the pieces which reflected the mass urban phenomena of Harlem when he expanded the edition on the grounds that they might confirm the worst (white) preconceptions about Harlem and its citizenry. So Winthrop Lane's article 'Ambushed in the City: The Grim Side of Harlem', as well as Kelly

Miller's 'The Harvest of Race Prejudice' and Eunice Roberta Hunton's 'Breaking Through' (which drew out an interpretation of Harlem as a modern ghetto very close to the picture we will see later of Chicago in Marita Bonner's work) were all excluded from the later collection.[29] However, contrary to criticisms of Locke's collection offered by scholars such as Charles Scruggs, I suggest that while pieces which foreground African American social problems in the race capital are excised, the collection retains a focus on the social organisation of African American urban life. This is reflected in the fiction and the poetry but also, at a deeper rhetorical level, in essays by Locke, James Weldon Johnson, J.A. Rogers, Melville Herskovits and Elise Johnson McDougald, which draw on urban experiences as the foundation for a new race aesthetic and for renewed race pride.[30]

In a passage which survives the transition from *Survey* to book edition Locke lays claim to a series of international precedents which allow him to formulate the spirit of the New Negro as well as to place African American artistic renaissance in line with other national cultures the *Survey* had taken as subjects in the preceding years.[31] Following his claim that Harlem is a race capital he goes on to say: 'Harlem has the same role to play for the New Negro as Dublin has had for the New Ireland or Prague for the New Czechoslovakia' (p. 7). What is interesting in terms of this study is the way in which Locke sees cultural renaissancism, or the building of a race spirit, as part of the development of urbanity as a key marker of progressive national identity. Caught up with this is his understanding of African American modernism as a projection of New Negro aspirations toward cultural renewal as well as a reflection of the changing conditions of black urban life. This places the Negro as the most forward looking of American citizens at the same time as claiming a kinship with artistic and cultural innovations in an international frame.

This can be seen if one looks again at Fisher's 'City of Refuge'. Locke supplemented 'The South Lingers On', Fisher's original submission to the *Survey* issue, with 'City of Refuge', previously published in *Atlantic Monthly*. As the first piece in Locke's fiction section it sets a dynamic urban tone for the rest of the collection, as well as most adequately fulfilling Locke's grand statements about the ultra-modern tendencies of the writing.[32] This urban tone is continued in the second Fisher piece 'Vestiges' (a revised version of 'The South Lingers On'), which presents a number of short snapshots of African American urbanism, highlighting episodes that were to become key issues in Fisher's writing: night-life, sexual relationships, the significance of the church to African American urban life and the peculiar persistence of superstition within city culture. These are in many ways precisely those issues that disappear in sociological form between the *Survey* issue and *The New Negro*, but are maintained in a more attenuated yet still powerful way in the fiction, poetry and drama. While one might note that the majority of the pieces which make up the official poetry section is of the Countee Cullen mode of traditional lyric expression of African American spiritualism, one can see a more populist and urban driven poetry interspersed through other sections of the collection, for example in Langston Hughes's 'Jazzonia' and 'Nude Young Dancer', in Gwendolyn Bennett's 'Song', or Claude McKay's 'Negro Dancers', which precedes an essay by J.A. Rogers on jazz and its urban locale.[33] This attention to the material urban scene surfaces only intermittently through the entire document but it powerfully connects to the ideas of urbanity and racial progress which Locke seeks to foreground as the primary mode for New Negro literature and culture.

In revising the collection Locke works hard to foster a self-conscious urbanity as the characteristic tone of the pieces. He, in essence, presents a collection fit for Harlem as the 'race capital' he wants to claim. The essays and stories in the collection have always offered ammunition to those who wish to damn the Harlem Renaissance for its capitulation to white dictated norms and values (particularly in terms of the largely middle-class orientation of the pieces).[34] These charges are true in part but also substantially misleading. In the changes Locke made between the two collections one can see a striving after an urban self-consciousness. If one holds this in mind and entertains the idea that urbanity is the central note that runs through the collection then the manifold and diverse opinions contained within it seem to make more sense. This would also make explicit the influence of progressive sociological narratives of urban space, drawn from the work of Robert E. Park and filtered through Charles S. Johnson, as an important background to Harlem Renaissance urban optimism.

Fire!! *Magazine*

Viewing *The New Negro* in this light places it in line with another 1926 text, *Fire!!* magazine – a text it is usually held to be in direct opposition to.[35] *Fire!!* was edited by one of Harlem's more controversial figures, Wallace Thurman, whose disparagement of Harlem's intelligentsia almost certainly led to his not being asked to contribute to *The New Negro*.[36] This magazine represents the most deliberate attempt during the Harlem Renaissance to foster an African American modernism. It attempted to emulate the style of modernist little magazines like the Greenwich Village-based *Quill*, and was a self-conscious attempt to break with the orthodoxy of race writing in the period in thematic and stylistic terms. Thurman clearly believed that the magazine should be a statement of aesthetic position taking, commenting: '*Fire!!* would burn up a whole lot of old, dead, conventional Negro-white ideas of the past, *épater le bourgeoisie* into a realisation of younger Negro writers and artists.'[37] This idea of a flaming intervention became a rather lamentable reality for the magazine. The financing of the venture was always insecure and Thurman was forced to leave the majority of the issue with the printer until he could raise the required funds. This didn't happen quickly enough unfortunately, as before he could get the copies released the printer's store went up in flames.

The contributors to the magazine included most of the notable younger Negro writers: Thurman, Fisher, Zora Neale Hurston, Countee Cullen, Arna Bontemps, Gwendolyn Bennett, Langston Hughes, Aaron Douglas and Bruce Nugent amongst others, but excluded many of those older, more established (and more conservative in Thurman's opinion) writers who featured in *The New Negro*. The subject matter was resolutely and rigorously urban in focus, and dealt with elements of working-class life that are largely absent from *The New Negro*, particularly in Wallace Thurman's short story of the encounter between a naive New Negro and a young potential prostitute; Langston Hughes's poems, including his wonderful but much reviled 'Elevator Boy'; and Gwendolyn Bennett's 'Wedding Day', which dealt with a relationship between a black boxer and a white prostitute.[38] The front page of the magazine designed by Aaron Douglas featured a stark geometric representation of a Sphinx in blocks of red and black. Viewed across its vertical axis the design revealed a stylised man's face adorned with an Africanist earpiece. The design is a more clearly abstract version of the African-inspired artwork Douglas produced for *The New Negro* and shows a style he was to develop more fully for covers for *Opportunity* magazine during 1926 and 1927.[39]

The Sphinx-face of Douglas's design underlines the magazine's central premise, that this challenge by 'Younger Negro Artists' to accepted models of African American writing was conceived as a stylistic break as much as a change in subject matter. Douglas's motifs ran throughout the magazine, a technique that was adopted intermittently by *The Crisis* and *Opportunity* in the later 1920s as well as being a feature of Locke's collection. In the case of *Fire!!*, the integration of typeface, story and poetry layouts, page headers and portrait pieces is a much more thoroughgoing design principle and one which deliberately fosters the integration of avant-garde form and content and works away at the distinction between the two. The foreword which takes up the first page proper continues this stress on aesthetic innovation adorned as it was with a credo which began: 'FIRE ... flaming, burning, searing, and penetrating far beneath the superficial items of the flesh to boil the sluggish blood.' It also echoes key modernist motifs of primitivism and exoticism, reconceptualised from an African American perspective, as the polemic goes on to dissolve boundaries between material, flesh and action in crusading modernist abandon as well as taking up a distinctly pagan African style and an African American blues-inflected spiritualism. As the last passage of the foreword proclaimed:

> FIRE ... weaving vivid, hot designs upon an ebon bordered loom and satisfying pagan thirst for beauty unadorned ... the flesh is sweet and real ... the soul an inward flush of fire ... Beauty? ... flesh on fire – on fire in the furnace of life blazing ...
> Fy-ah
> Fy-ah, Lawd,
> Fy-ah gonna burn ma soul! (p. 1)

A good example of how *Fire!!* stands in relation to the aesthetic strategies of Locke's *Survey* issue and *The New Negro* can be seen in the drawings that feature in each of them. The *Survey* issue included a number of portraits by the German artist Winold Reiss which made up a kind of roster of African American urban types, including a picture of a mother and child and of two African American school teachers. These pictures of Negro women caused something of a furore, with many of the middle-class black readers of the issue objecting that the naturalistic style adopted by Reiss was not representative of Negro womanhood as they saw it.[40] The dark skin and natural hair depicted were rather far from beauty ideals of the period however beautiful they may appear to us now. It is perhaps not the images themselves that caused offence so much as the suggestion that they should be considered representative of Harlem's model citizens – the new urban African American. This drive toward urban typing through the artwork is something picked up directly in *Fire!!* as we shall see in a moment, and both magazines stand as useful examples of the racial urbanity I am tracing.

In *The New Negro* the issue of representativeness is taken up in a slightly different fashion. Reiss's artwork is replaced by that of Aaron Douglas, who had studied under him for some time.[41] He moves the idea of urban typing in a different direction, drawing on African motifs and designs to thematise the collection as an Africanist urban celebration. This is entirely in line with Locke's internationalist framing of the collection, as well as providing a working example of the relationships between the ancestral arts of Africa and African American culture, which are the subject of a number of the essays in the collection.[42] Douglas's striking illus-trations provide the most concentrated example of the aesthetic tendencies I have been highlighting in that they present an urban scene mediated through an international context of black history and culture *and* modernist interest in primitivism. Douglas was to go on to paint large-scale murals for the walls of the 135th Street library (now the Schomburg Library) which utilised the technique he initiates in these drawings to portray the journey of Africans to the New World and into modernity. His work provides one of the best examples of a simultaneous dialogue with African traditions and white modernism, which produces a unique and dynamic representation of African American culture.[43] His figuration of the black body in these pictures is very far from the naturalism of Reiss's portraits, utilising a semi-abstract style of symmetrically organised extended limbs, angular head and torso shape and blocks of colour, notably black against white or cream. Presumably, the Africanism of the art didn't offend in the same way as Reiss's portraits since it was not assumed to represent anyone actually residing in Harlem. What is interesting is that Douglas's style, which captures movement and energy very well, especially in the 'Emperor Jones' and 'Music' drawings, clearly goes on to influence the ways in which Harlem's cabarets and street life become codified in painting by subsequent white and African American artists, forms of representation to which the better class of New Negro would surely have objected.[44]

In *Fire!!* Douglas provides another set of urban figures, rather different from those already examined. Douglas's caricatures of urban figures in the magazine extend the principle of urban typing – his pictures are of the race leader, the artist and the barmaid – but they break with the representational mode, this time drawing aesthetic inspiration from popular urban experience to construct a line-drawn jazz style.[45] The drawings also break with the noble tradition of representative portraits of these New Negroes as Douglas develops black-qua-black stereotyping, emphasising big lips, long limbs and styled-out posing in an attempt to catch the mood of the high and low cultural elements of Harlem life. The other drawings in the magazine, by Bruce Nugent, were still more provocative as they featured nude black women with the lithe bodies of dancers and kinky hair in a stylised African setting of palm trees and abstract patterned black and white surrounds.[46] While this is in line with Douglas's drawings in *The New Negro* they go considerably further than he does toward a celebration both of African primitivism and exotic sexuality. Although it is almost too easy to seize on those recorded comments by rather conservative African American critics like Benjamin Brawley and Rean Graves, we should note that neither Douglas's nor Nugent's pictures pleased them at all – both felt that the drawings were not worth the paper they were printed on.[47] Moreover, the difficulty around the question of representation is precisely that which Thurman would take up in his bitingly satirical editorial commentary, which closes the magazine.[48] Taking issue with the responses by black intellectuals to Van Vechten's *Nigger Heaven*, which Thurman believed showed the fundamental hypocrisy of those figures who promoted the uplift message, he argues that to claim that a jazzer or con-man misrepresents the New Negro is as fatuous as claiming that all African American women resemble the heroines of Jessie Fauset's novels. Of course, he intends to provoke by defending the most vilified of white-authored Harlem novels, but at the same time the editorial is a defence of the content and formal aesthetic of the magazine which it concludes.

The magazine's combination of art, poetry, polemic and distinctly salacious fiction certainly provoked reaction from the African American intelligentsia, though not generally a favourable one, and this extended beyond a few reactionary complainants.[49] The *Fire!!* philosophy was one that presented itself as avant-garde radicalism, even if it now seems rather overblown and pretentious (particularly since the magazine only survived one issue). The controversy generated by the magazine seems to justify Thurman's feeling that things needed radically shaking up. What is interesting in terms of the writing examined in this book is the stories which caused most offence among the African American establishment and media were those which were concerned with urban sexuality, particularly Thurman's 'Cordelia the Crude', the story of a young prostitute, and Bruce Nugent's 'Smoke, Lilies and Jade'. Nugent's piece caused the greatest fuss when *Fire!!* was published and was hailed by some as the most signal evidence of the magazine's degenerate tendencies.[50] The delight the text exhibits in Alex's idleness and the frank celebration of inter-racial homo- and bi-sexuality was a step too far for many contemporary commentators. Rean Graves, of the *Baltimore Afro-American*, in an article headlined 'Writer Brands *Fire!!* As Effeminate Tommyrot', documents his pleasure at tossing the first edition of the magazine into the fire.[51] Complaints about the piece, and about *Fire!!*, were however rarely kept to moral objections at the level of content. The pursuit of what we might recognise as modernist experimentation with literary form also seemed to cause offence. The following comment by Benjamin Brawley in *Opportunity* magazine makes it clear that stylistic transgression ranks high on the taboo list for the responsible African American artist:

> Another matter is that of the jerky, hectic, incoherent composition that some people are cultivating today, but that is nothing more than the workings of the Bolshevistic spirit in literature. With some people the sentence has lost its integrity

altogether, and writing is nothing more than a succession of coarse suggestive phrases.[52]

We can only speculate on who these 'people' were, but evidence such as 'Smoke' would give one a pretty good idea.

'Smoke' concerns the story of the hero Alex's affair with a white man, referred to as Beauty, and a black woman called Melva. It is written in free indirect discourse and eschews conventional punctuation, joining fragmented observations through sets of ellipses. There is little narrative progression, the text working instead through the repetition of key phrases, colours, and feeling, forcing a synathesic attention to the words as they construct a kind of empty artificiality conveying a decadent and delirious city scene. The story's fragmented meanderings are, it becomes clear, the disconnected musings of the superbly camp Alex, as he pursues a night-time existence and sexual relationships with Beauty and Melva. Alex's bisexual and inter-racial relationships are made possible by an attitude to the city that insists on the pleasures of this urban environment. Awareness and indeed exploitation of the spectacle of Harlem finds its most outrageous expression in the story as it cultivates an obsessive fascination with looking relations, decadence and the city scene.

Alex rarely gets off his couch, where he puffs contentedly on a cigarette held in a red and green jade inlaid cigarette holder; when he does it is to move through the anonymous modernist city space of the flaneur. Moving from one briefly articulated bohemian scene to another, he encounters various members of Harlem's literati, all presented as endlessly substitutable names which flicker across Alex's consciousness; an errant progress which leads him to a chance street encounter with a stranger, whom he christens Beauty,

> ... the echo of their steps mingled ... they walked in silence ... the castanets of their heels clicking accompaniment ... the stranger inhaled deeply and with a nod of content and a smile ... blew a cloud of smoke ... Alex felt like singing ... the stranger knew the magic of blue smoke also ... they continued in silence ... the castanets of their heels clicking rhythmically ... Alex turned in his doorway ... up the stairs and the stranger waited for him to light the room ... no need for words ... they had always known each other .... [sic] as they undressed by the blue dawn ... Alex knew he had never seen a more perfect being ... his body all symmetry and music ... and Alex called him Beauty ... (p. 35)

Nugent's piece depends most crucially on the elaboration of desire as the exchange of looks between characters in a city space that is both commodified and aestheticised; being and looking urbane is Alex's primary goal. In its obsessive cultivation of the rare, the beautiful and the artificial, and its understanding of identity as nothing more than the chance encounter or the surface apprehension of difference, Nugent's story is exceptional within Harlem Renaissance writing. Indeed, we might say thankfully so, in that Alex's exceptionalism seems to offer little except a rampant snobbery and intellectual one-upmanship. However, I am unwilling to let the story go that easily. Perhaps the fact it was so vilified at the time (and since) is what appeals to me, and perhaps also I'm unwilling to dismiss one of the only explicit representations of homosexuality generated within Harlem Renaissance culture (despite the number of central figures who were gay).[53] We see attention to a cultivated scene of urbanity, and the cultivation of a decidedly rarefied form of urbane behaviour, in the development of a race literature worthy of a rapidly expanding race capital. But more than this, the spectacular urban playground so fundamental to Nugent's story is refracted through a range of writings and writers in variously provocative ways, as we shall see in the following chapter.

CHAPTER 2

Space, Race and Identity

If one can see a cultivated urbanity characterising *The New Negro*, and a rather hectic thrill of the new combined with a celebration of the déclassé elements of urban life as the key note to *Fire!!*, then we provide a useful framing context for a number of 1920s writers who are usually played off against one another, as falling into the traps of either New Negro gentility or primitivist coarseness. Claude McKay, Wallace Thurman, Bruce Nugent and Nella Larsen, to name just a few, can be read across this urban (and urbane) spectrum. In this second chapter I want to trace the peculiar urban engagements presented in a number of these key Harlem writers, focusing primarily on the writing of Rudolph Fisher – whose 'City of Refuge' provides *The New Negro* with perhaps its most potent image of the energies of the 'race capital'. Fisher is the most unjustly neglected of contributors to *The New Negro* particularly given his persistent focus on the modes and conditions of urban life in Harlem, and this chapter will go some way to correcting this situation. I shall also point up the significance of debates about urbanity, modernity and racial identity in his work, issues that underpin the work of his better-known contemporaries such as McKay and Thurman. These writers – too often dismissed as coarse sensationalists, or primitivists pandering to white tastes for the exotic – would provide useful comparison to Fisher's work, though space prevents such an analysis here. Suffice it to say that Thurman's *Infants of the Spring* (1932) or McKay's *Home to Harlem* (1932) could stand in productive dialogue with Fisher's race satire *The Walls of Jericho* (1928) and McKay's *Home to Harlem* would make a rich countertext to his *The Conjure Man Dies* (1932). In Fisher's writing we see the development of a critical cosmopolitanism – an urbane attitude which is formulated as the ideas of race pride, aesthetic excellence and civility meet the contradictory demands of a class-differentiated and multi-ethnic urban polis – and we see the shaping of Harlem as a race capital and a ghetto occurring simultaneously. The backdrop to his work is the ongoing New Negro argument about what it means to be black, modern and urban.

Rudolph Fisher published fifteen short stories between 1925 and 1935 as well as two novels and a number of journalistic pieces and scientific articles. He was in many ways an exemplary New Negro, being both a successful writer and a doctor who specialised in the newly developing science of x-rays. Langston Hughes recorded that Fisher was 'the wittiest of these New Negroes of Harlem, whose tongue was flavored with the sharpest and wittiest humour' and went on to say, 'he always frightened me a little, because he could think of the most incisively clever things to say – and I could never think of anything to answer'.[1] Fisher's work was popular in the 1920s and received extensive notice in the African American press as well as being one of the very few black writers who consistently published in mainstream white magazines, particularly *Atlantic Monthly* which published four of his pieces, but also *McClure's Magazine* and *Story*.[2] In subsequent decades, however, he has been ill-served by literary and cultural histories of the Harlem Renaissance period, as John McCluskey Jr points out.[3] While most discuss 'City of Refuge' and its place within *The New Negro*, there is precious little discussion of his other short stories, and even less of his two novels.[4]

Explanations of this lack of attention may be bound up with a perception that he published 'local colour' stories for white magazines, a rather unfair assessment of his rich and complex body of urban stories, but may also be to do with his untimely death in 1934 which, as Levering Lewis comments, robbed Harlem of one its most exciting developing voices.[5] Fisher died of intestinal cancer contracted through exposure to the x-rays with which he worked and his premature demise is cited as one of those episodes which symbolises the death of the New Negro movement.[6] In rather more prosaic terms the lack of a collection of his stories before his death meant that for a long period his stories were unavailable to anyone but those willing to trawl through the archives of the magazines which originally published his work. The novels too went out of print, until the revival of publishing interest in African American fiction in the 1980s, and so for most of the twentieth century African American scholars have missed not just the promise a mature Fisher might have provided, but the work of the most engaged urban interpreter of 1920s Harlem and a key antecedent to those later writers like Chester Himes or Ishmael Reed who deal with key Fisher themes of crime, detection, the black inner-city and popular culture. Comparison of Himes's detectives Gravedigger Jones and Coffin Ed with Fisher's Dart and Archer moves one from the gentleman sleuth to the hard-boiled 'tec, in African American terms, such is the difference between them. In other ways, however, there are important connections; both deal with the racial organisation of urban space, and with the different orders of knowledge, insider and outsider, local and general, vernacular and high-brow that are variously required to negotiate urban space. Both also share a fascination with voodoo and African superstitions as they are reformulated in the American city scene. One also sees a shared interest in *The Conjure Man Dies* and Ishmael Reed's *Mumbo Jumbo* in the multiplicity of voices that make up an alternative Africanist tradition of vernacular history, what Reed calls 'Jes Grew'. For the purposes of this study Fisher is a vital figure to retrieve from the lesser annals of African American literary history because taken as a whole his writing presents the most sustained conversation about the multiple dimensions of New Negro urbanity.

The H of Harlem

Negro Harlem's three broad highways form the letter H, Lenox and Seventh Avenues running parallel northwards, united a little above their midpoints by east-and-west 135th Street.

Lenox Avenue is for the most part the boulevard of the unperfumed; 'rats' they are often termed. Here, during certain hours, there is nothing unusual in the flashing of knives, the quick succession of pistol shots, the scream of a police-whistle or a woman.

But Seventh Avenue is the promenade of the high-toned dickties and strivers. It breathes a superior atmosphere, sings superior songs, laughs a superior laugh. Even if there were no people, the difference would be clear: the middle of Lenox Avenue is adorned by street-car tracks, the middle of Seventh Avenue by parking.

These two highways, frontiers of the opposed extreme of dark-skinned social life, are separated by an intermediate any-man's land, across which they communicate chiefly by way of 135th Street. Accordingly 135th Street is the heart and soul of black Harlem; it is common ground, the natural scene of unusual contacts, a region that disregards class. It neutralises, equili-brates, binds, rescues union out of diversity.[7]

This is the opening of 'Blades of Steel', published in *Atlantic Monthly* in 1927. This mapping of the H of Harlem is an oft-used trope in Fisher's work, and in 'Blades of Steel' it introduces a powerful representation of Harlem as geographical location and hierarchised social space. As Fisher traces the shape that is Harlem's physical reality and signature he marks out the cultural and class dimensions of the race capital and marries social insti-tutions, material location and social aspirations. If bars and speakeasies are the provenance of Lenox, and high-class residential accommodation the most notable features of Seventh, then the characteristic feature of the 'common ground' between them,

135th Street, is the infrastructure of social interaction as it is expressed in the built environment, 'every institution necessary to civilization' (p. 132). To 135th Street belong the Carnegie Library, the public school, the police station, the church, the undertaker and, central to 'Blades of Steel', the barbershop.

'Blades of Steel' tells of a conflict over a woman between Dirty Cozzens and Eight-Ball, the first a vicious representative of Lenox Avenue's worst tendencies and the second the everyman hero of 135th Street. Though the story of competitive love interest moves the plot along, what is really debated in the story, as in so many Fisher pieces, are modes of urban behaviour and the relationships between Harlem's inhabitants and the social institutions which make up the 'H'. Characters like Eight-Ball, or Dave in 'Miss Cynthie', or Sam and Judy in 'Guardians of the Law', formulate modes of urban being which negotiate between tradition and modernity, between older generations and the fast New Negroes, between a cultural history drawn from the South and its reformulation to suit the rhythm of urban life.[8] This negotiation between tradition and modernity is often affected by contact with an ancestor figure. That these figures, such as Miss Cynthie or Grammie in 'Guardians of the Law', are gifted with bucket loads of mother-wit makes the process of urban acculturation easier. It also suggests that for Fisher the division between old and new and between urban and rural is not strictly drawn since the wise newcomer is not only the carrier of history left behind by too many of Harlem's city dwellers, she (and it is almost always a she) possesses a linguistic talent and flexibility that is seen in other places as the defining characteristic of urban being.[9] As Miss Cynthie observes: '"Always like to have sump'm in my hand when I walk. Can't never tell when you'll run across a snake." "There aren't any snakes in the city." "There's snakes everywhere, chile."'[10] The figure of the grandmother provides grounding for urban assimilation, but she represents not so much a Southern or rural history kept alive as the redrawing of tradition within the urban context. As we shall see, the traditions that urban African Americans may draw on to structure urban being are most profoundly debated in *The Conjure Man Dies*. For now we should note for future reference that Fisher's wise women answer one of the dilemmas which preoccupies Toni Morrison in *Jazz*: how to maintain a sense of history in an urban scene where, to quote Mammy from 'The Promised Land', one must accustom oneself to 'the philosophy of the metropolis, its ruthless opportunism'.[11]

Fisher develops across his stories a writing style that expresses itself as urban populism. In 'Blades of Steel' success is exemplified by the ability to negotiate a divided racial space by recognising that community and, in Locke's terms, 'race spirit' is constructed not

simply through elite institutions such as the library or the public
school, or through the actions of an artistically minded 'talented
tenth', to use Du Bois's famous phrase, nor through a supposedly
authentic street culture, but in the negotiations between and across
these spheres. Certain figures come in for a great deal of criticism,
for example dicty snobs in a number of pieces, but also con-men,
thugs, or 'fast' city girls in other pieces. Fisher does not want a city
polarised along genteel versus primitive lines. His urban aesthetic
is unique in that it draws life-blood and inspiration from across
the Lenox/Seventh Avenue divide, drawing together usually divided
realms of popular and high-brow African American culture. In
'Blades of Steel' it is the barbershop that stands as the symbol for
progressive urban culture, a 'common ground' that maintains a
tradition of African American vernacular culture, as well as a com-
mercially inflected race pride, 'of, for, and in spite of the people'
(p. 137).

'Blades of Steel' develops a sense of progressive urbanism and
African American cultural dynamism through attention to
vernacular performance and a keen sense of the spectacle of racial
urbanity that it takes as its subject. Fisher uses the vernacular as
reported speech to give a sense of Harlem specificity: '"You means
to grace our function wid yo' attendance?" The other's assent was
typical Harlemese: "I don't mean to attend yo' function with my
grace."' (p. 133). It also gives an energetic quality to his writing in
this and other stories as the verbal sparring between characters is
more significant than the movement of the stories, which are often
only weakly plotted. As is apparent in the above quotation the
writing moves in and out of the vernacular, with the narratorial
voice usually remaining in standard English, but at certain points,
and in nicely subtle ways, vernacular perceptions leak into the
narrative tone. This is certainly the case in 'City of Refuge' where
the rapid movement of the impressionistic prose gives a sense of
the bewilderment of the city that is clearly the provenance of the
confused Gillis. This technique develops through Fisher's work to
become a racially inflected urban reportage. 'Fire By Night',
published in 1927, is an excellent case in point. The story oscillates
between Harlem's symbolic heights and depths with the pull of
the church being played off against the speakeasy; the story
ultimately finding its common ground in the chaotic disruption of
a dicty Ball by speakeasy customers who see the unmanned
cloakroom as 'a gravy-train'.[12] The story navigates legitimate and
illegitimate Harlem in ways that exceed the movement of characters
between the two spheres, drawing on the language of the bar and
the language of the church to find a voice to match the competing
attractions of a class-divided racial space. In the central scene at
the So-and So's Ball this allows Fisher to experiment with a verbal

free-for-all as violent as the fight he represents. This verbal dynamism finds its fullest expression in *The Conjure Man Dies* with the extended performance of vernacular competition between Bubber and Jinx, two of Fisher's most engaging creations. For now we should note that this vernacular display is matched by a fascination with the spectacle of public gatherings, situating populist urbanity as a key mode of African American urban expression.

In 'Blades of Steel' this populist urbanity is developed in a slightly different way; one that is highly significant to Fisher's overall style. While the denouement of the story is rather obviously signalled, with Eight-Ball triumphing over Dirty Cozzens with the help of his resourceful girlfriend Effie, the story also finishes in a more open-ended fashion with a repeated blues record playing on the phonograph – 'Tessie' Smith's 'Lord Have Mercy Blues'. The blues refrain shades the story with tragedy and draws from black music a more ambivalent reading of the urban scene: 'Grief, affliction, woe, told in a tone of most heartbroken despair' (p. 141). John McCluskey Jr has argued the jazz and blues music featured in many Fisher stories often represents a folk wisdom, which Fisher suggests has been lost in the migration northwards.[13] This is true in part, but as I have already suggested the picture is a little more complex than this. Music features in Fisher's work in commodified form as part of the urban scene – indeed as characteristic of Harlem – whether it is played on records as in 'Blades of Steel' or 'The Promised Land', or performed at a dancehall or theatre as in 'Common Meter' and 'Miss Cynthie'. 'Common Meter' tells of a play off between two rival jazz bands. Despite being hijacked by the cheating Fess Baxter, the crowd's favourite Bus Williams wins out by performing an old-style shout in a new jazz setting, bearing out my earlier point about the incorporation and reformulation of tradition in the new urban setting.[14]

The musical forms give a counter-reading of the urban scene allowing that the story may move in more than one direction at the same time. In 'Blades of Steel' the blues falls as a shadow or warning across the piece, whereas in a story like 'Miss Cynthie' music stands in dynamic relationship to a city scene which Miss Cynthie initially sees as corrupting and amoral. In the Lafayette theatre, 'the stronghold of transgression' (p. 75) as far as Miss Cynthie is concerned, she sees the audience transformed from a 'mob of sinners' to childish innocents as the crowd respond to her grandson Dave Tappen dancing to a tune she taught him as a boy:

> Her bewildered eyes turned on the crowd, on those serried rows of shriftless sinners. And she found in their faces now an overwhelmingly curious thing: a grin, a universal grin, a gleeful and

sinless grin such as not the nakedest chorus in the performance had produced. In a few seconds, with her own song, David had dwarfed into unimportance, wiped off their faces, swept out of their minds every trace of what seemed to be sin. (p. 77)

The sinful story Dave Tappen and his troupe have been performing in the theatre tells of a young man's journey to Harlem and the trials and temptations that he must come through. That it ends with this syncretic dance of old and new racial expression underlines the double-voiced complexity of Fisher's urban narratives.

Harlem Hierarchies: Racial Performance, Social Space

Fisher's 1928 novel *The Walls of Jericho* takes on with great satiric fervour prominent New Negro narratives of racial uplift and improvement, drawing out the way in which uplift depends on two contradictory senses of urbanity.[15] The sense of urbanity as the gathering together of strangers and the pursuit of urbanity as a mode of self-projection (being urbane in the Nugent sense) are at the heart of Fisher's dissection of the manners and mores of high and low Harlem culture. The novel was a popular success, going on to be transformed into a play, and is a sharp account of the racial and class composition of Harlem, 'from the rattiest rat to the dictiest dicty' (p. 27). It gives us the story of a 'passing' light lawyer's move from Striver's Row to an exclusively white neighbourhood, paralleled with the story of Shine, a down-to-earth, dark-skinned furniture removal man, and his romance with the beautiful brown 'Sheba' Linda. This slight story provides occasion for numerous set-pieces of racial display played out across a clearly hierarchised and internally divided racial community, and in the longest section of the novel Fisher presents the performance of racial urbanity at a grand ball; pointing up just how easily aspirations toward civic progress tip into the display of social hierarchy. This runs across five chapters, but I shall quote just a section here:

> There is at least one occasion a year when Manhattan Casino requires no decoration – the occasion of the General Improvement Association's Annual Costume Ball. The guests themselves are all the decoration that is necessary.
>
> This is not only because many of the guests attend in costume, but also because, of all the crowds which Manhattan Casino holds during the year, none presents a greater inherent variety. There is variety of personal station from the rattiest rat to the dicktiest dickty ... the bars are down. This is for the Race. One great common fellowship in one great common cause ... So swept the scene from black to white through all the shadows and

shades. Ordinary Negroes and rats below, dickties and fays above, the floor beneath the feet of one constituting the roof over the heads of the other. (p. 27)

The novel deals with the proto-eugenic structuring of social relations in Harlem, where 'light equals right' (to quote from Fisher's story 'High Yaller') – a subject taken up with greater venom in George Schuyler's satire *Black No More* (1928), discussed in Chapter 3.[16] The scenes documented across these central chapters lampoon white racist understandings of blackness. The text identifies three types of 'white folks': those who come to enjoy themselves, and just get on with it; the 'professional uplifter' determined to be broad minded; and the newcomers, drawn by Harlem's legendary licence, hence giggling and ogling with barely concealed racism. More significantly, as we can see from the section above, the spectacular scene presents race as something which is crucially mediated by class and gender location, and as something which is understood by the narrator to require the performance of racial identity as well as understanding of class and gender location within an inter- and intra-racial urban hierarchy. So, what is fascinating is the heterogeneity of Harlem, but also the understanding of this heterogeneity as spectacle and performance: 'The guests themselves are all the decoration that is necessary' (p. 27). Most importantly these scenes demonstrate an acute awareness of the spectrum of reactions to this scene on the part of black and white spectators, which runs from nonchalance to unease. These reactions to Harlem, at one level documenting class-bound snobbery and the appropriative presence of 'white folks' who construct the scene as exotic and erotic spectacle, are simultaneously a part of the performance of a great Harlem event. The text also notes the shifting markers of blackness used by each type of white participant, from the epithet 'Negro' used by the dedicated dancers, to the uplifters' use of 'darker brother' and 'nigger' used by the ogling newcomers. This registers an internal diversity (and implicit racialising) of whiteness which matches the spectrum of colours of blackness the novel insists upon, divisions which speak of class, gender and political arrangements as they also mark the context dependent meanings of race – whiteness as well as blackness.

This complex reaction to Harlem as a commodified and spectacular site of desire for both black and white spectators/performers facilitates the text's *ironic* performance of urbanity and emphasises the contingency of racial identity which underpins this city spectacular. Fisher's attention to the spectacle of Harlem and its structuring in racial, class and gendered terms alerts one to the 'inherent variety' (or power relations) that always undermines the fiction of urban unity. Yet, this is also a space where race, class and gender lines are transgressed because of the anonymity of strangers who make up the whole. In critiquing the urban spectacle Fisher's novel still maintains that the practice of urbanity (in its variety) is crucial for understanding the workings of the race capital.

Fisher was not naively celebratory about the possibilities and pleasures of city life for African Americans. Indeed, in pieces such as the journalistic 'The Caucasian Storms Harlem' he shows considerable disdain for the presence and behaviour of certain kinds of whites.[17] He explicitly critiques white appropriation of many of Harlem's black cabarets and dance halls, but even so demonstrates a highly mobile sense of racial identity. He observes: 'The time was when white people went to Negro cabarets to see how Negroes acted; now Negroes go to these same cabarets to see how white people act.'[18] This inversion of looking relationships suggests an active position for the black subject within the urban scene, in spite of the appropriative presence of white people it is they rather than the black performers who are objectified by this gaze. In closing the piece Fisher again undermines conceptions of authentic black experience, when he admits to being jealous that these white folks are able to perform black dances better than he has ever been able to, and he finishes with a wry suggestion that perhaps he is witnessing a spectacular 'browning' of the 'Nordics'. Without falling into utopian celebrations of the city (he certainly documents in some detail the constrained material circumstances of the large majority of urban African Americans) Fisher still insists upon the powerful excitement generated by the spectacle of Harlem as a site of desire and imaginative possibility for African Americans.

The Conjure Man Dies

Fisher's last novel, *The Conjure Man Dies*, is a fascinating case study for this book since it plays fast and loose with tradition, urbanity, high and low culture, rationalism and primitivism: all the key terms of this chapter's discussion.[19] This curious novel is the most overlooked of Fisher's texts, perhaps because there seems so little context for understanding an African American detective novel in this period; perhaps more because its 'inherent variety' of form makes it a difficult text to classify or respond to. For my purposes the novel is extremely useful since it deliberately constructs African American urban culture as a series of conversations about the nature of racial being. The dimensions of racial being are explored through drawing on competing philosophical and popular traditions; ranging from African myth and African American spiritualism, to American pragmatism, applied determinism, scientific rationalism, psychoanalysis, popular science and vernacular street culture. This rather heady mixture is yoked together through a classic detective plot where the conundrum of an impossible murder resolves itself as down-to-earth revenge for sexual infidelity. The convoluted plot is worthy of some outlining, although it will become clear that what happens is almost beside the point in this tale of Harlem's darker and more exotic depths.

The novel opens with another example of the mapping of the divided dimensions of Harlem's racial spaces as they run along Seventh, 135th and Lenox Avenue, here more radically subjectivised as Fisher describes the winter cold intensifying and waning in response to the relative energies of the Avenues. We arrive at the house of Samuel Crouch, Undertaker, and N. Frimbo, Psychist, the primary locus of the unfolding events and the residence of the text's central protagonist, Frimbo, the conjure man of the title. Frimbo is an African prince, trained in philosophy at Harvard and settled in Harlem as a perfect testing ground for his experiments in evading the deterministic force of linear time and history as well the constraints of racial being. There he predicts the future for clients who come to him with problems ranging from luck on the numbers to unfaithful wives and ailing relatives, but his method is less conjure than talking cure as we see him sit in the darkness reading the future from the narratives the clients share with him. It is in Frimbo's consulting room that the first murder occurs as he predicts the future for Jinx Jenkins, one half of an Amos and Andy-style double act who represent Harlem's Lenox side in the novel.[20] Frimbo is apparently killed and the blame falls on the hapless Jinx, but this proves to be only the beginning as we find that Frimbo returns from the dead to participate in the pursuit of his own murderer.

We are introduced to Sergeant Perry Dart, one of Harlem's first black detectives (and certainly Harlem's first literary one), and his friend and fellow sleuth Dr Archer, whose scientific rationalism is played off against the pragmatism of the down-to-earth Dart. Added to this already complex roster of detectives we also have Jinx Jenkins and Bubber Brown, whose desperation to get work has led them to set up a detective agency, specialising in marital infidelity and money suits. The dead body turns out to be that of Frimbo's servant, which Frimbo must dispose of himself in accordance with the ancient laws of his African tribe. Frimbo insists, however, that he will indeed die, and though he can predict this occurrence he cannot stop his own murder nor name the perpetrator. His words are fatally borne out when Dart and Archer stage a reconstruction of the night of the murder. On the way to this denouement we find out that the mystery is caught up with the 'rite of the gonad' of Frimbo's African tribe, whereby the history of the tribe and the virility of its male leader are bound together in the ingestion of an extract of the gonad of the tribal ancestors. This outlandish practice, combined with Frimbo's investigations into the philosophical dimensions of determinism, has led him to be capable of evading the strict laws of cause and effect, something not lost on the reader as Fisher slyly mirrors his conjure man by playing around with the conventional cause-and-effect organisation of the detective form. As this summary suggests the novel rather over-runs its murder-mystery frame. What is pursued with some assiduousness, however, is the principle of detective work as a mode of urban operation. Fisher's novel is a tour-de-force of Harlem ways of being, and as we follow the clues to the double murder of Frimbo we discover certain clues to the populist urbanity that Fisher articulates through his fiction.

On the first page of the novel we see a characteristic Fisher trait, the overheard blues refrain on the city street. The blues fragment relays for us the subsequent narrative course as a clue we have to hold in mind even as we are confused and dazzled by the competing sounds of urban experience. The blues tells us:

I'll be glad when you're dead, you rascal you
I'll be glad when you're dead and gone, you rascal you.
What is it that you've got
Makes my wife think you're so hot?
Oh you dog – I'll be glad when you're gone. (p. 3)

The song drifts in and out of the text a number of times as 'the moment's most popular song' (p. 3) and sounds a note to the wise that the apparently complex tale will be revealed as a simple blues refrain of sexual jealousy. The transparency of the blues works subtly against the more complicated ways of solving the crime that are debated as the text moves through a series of deductive and inductive possibilities. The ways in which the crime might be solved are always also the ways in which we might understand the urban scene that frames the narrative. Understanding urban African American identity is the true puzzle for the text and reader, as the prescient Frimbo observes about his own apparent murder:

Archer: 'You don't think the causes of a mere death a worthy problem?'
Frimbo: 'The causes of *a* death? No. The causes of death, yes. The causes of life and death and variation, yes. But what on earth does it really matter who killed Frimbo – except to Frimbo?'...
... 'The rest of the world would do better to concern itself with why Frimbo was black.' (p. 230)

The blues gives us, then, not a simple expression of the truth of the tale so much as one way of reading the urban scene and the puzzle of urban black identity. When we see the fascinating conjure man outwitted by the powerful inevitability of death we come to understand the complexity of the apparently straightforward lyric and appreciate the embedded vernacular histories that music carries in the novel. There are, however, many other forms of urban knowledge that work alongside the bitter-sweet sexual story of the music, as the story teases out not Frimbo's murderer so much as the meaning of his blackness.

Conjure and superstition hold sway in the novel as the most forceful vernacular reading of urban space and identity alongside the blues. The pernicious influence of superstition, as a regressive form of folk knowledge, is also the subject of Fisher's only other detective story, 'John Archer's Nose' (1935).[21] Dart and Archer reappear in this story which features the deaths of a child and a young man, Sonny Dewey, because their families rely on conjure charms instead of conventional medicine to treat the tuberculosis they are both suffering from. As Archer observes at the end: '"Superstition killed Sonny." He sighed. "But I doubt that we'll ever catch that."' (p. 194). The significance of superstition as a form of urban knowledge are confirmed not by the conjure man himself but rather by his clients, pre-eminently Bubber and Jinx who present a counter-history of philosophical determinism as they discourse on the inevitable consequences of the signs they see in their Harlem surroundings. Clouds across the moon, deaths in threes, and the predictive force of conjure are all taken and debated as lore of the street in the interchanges between Bubber and Jinx. In fact, none and all of their predictions come true as we find that their function is not so much as source of folk-knowledge as the performers of urban-folk identity. It is true that this tips almost into stereotype at points, but the vernacular stand-offs that the two continually practice go further than simply providing comic relief. In the end, rather like the blues, Bubber and Jinx's vernacular discussions on their relationship to Africa (or lack of it), or their respective competence in negotiating the complexities of urban life, are offered as a counter-commentary to the much more high-brow (but equally ridiculous) postulations of Frimbo, Archer and Dart:

> [Bubber] 'Red moon mean bloodshed, new moon over your right shoulder mean good luck, new moon over your left shoulder mean bad luck, and so on. Well, they's one moonsign my grandmammy taught me befo' I was knee high and that's the worst sign of 'em all. And that's the sign I seen tonight. I was walkin' down the Avenue feelin' fine and breathin' the air – '
> [Jinx] 'What do you breathe when you don't feel so good?'
> (p. 30)

This 'suprastition' (p. 29), as Bubber calls it, is not discredited so much as proved in the novel, as Bubber and Jinx go on to see the three deaths predicted by the 'moonsign'. This knowledge, or way of reading the signs in the city, is set into competitive dialogue with other modes of understanding. Perry Dart believes that conclusions must be drawn from facts, rather than facts from conclusions, a deductive strategy repeatedly undermined by his scientist partner Archer, who understands that facts must be found to justify impossible conclusions. Frimbo, on the other hand, eschews cause and effect altogether for an assertion of will that shapes history and the future predictively. Each character draws on a set of authorities to justify his position: police-procedure, inductive rationalism and applied determinism to cite each man's credo. Each, however, must face the insufficiency of his mode of understanding the crime and the racial scene that is the novel's larger topic. What does work as a strategy of urban interpretation is the eclectic engagement of each of these modes of understanding with one another, in a dialogue that a later African American writer calls 'vicious modernism. Bang Clash': a phrase well suited to Fisher's Harlem.[22]

This can be seen clearly if we devote a little more attention to the delightful rite of the gonad. This apparently crazy plot innovation seems less peculiar if one considers it as one form of urban discourse amongst the many that circulate in the novel. As Ann Douglas observes, the fashionableness in urban circles in the 1920s of ingesting monkey and goat glands for virility, and specifically in order to ward off the enervation of urban living, was simply one of many mad urban crazes of the time, to be substituted with psychoanalysis the next week, and reading tarot the week after that.[23] Reading the text it becomes clear that Fisher strives to include as many strange crazes as he can fit within the pages of the novel. The novel is also full to the brim with stereotypical urban figures: so we see Pullman porters, undertakers, detectives, numbers runners, religious evangelists, night-club singers and conjure men (and the novel starts to seem more and more like one by Chester Himes). Cultural fads vie for position with rather more high-brow modes of cultural authority as conjure work is revealed to be something close to Freudian analysis and Frimbo's African primitivism is revealed to be the radical relativism of a Harvard-trained philosopher. In fact, Fisher's novel offers itself as a model (at least in humorous form) for the encounter between psycho-analysis and philosophy and the developing sciences of ethnography and anthropology as white forms of cultural authority that derive their insights from the observation of supposedly primitive tribes. This is a crucial part of debates in the period that helped to define each of these disciplines, as Robyn Wiegman points out.[24] One can only surmise that Fisher's scientific training as much as his immersion in these debates as they touched on New Negro discussions of racial being facilitates his populist reading of these so-serious issues. What there is no doubt about is that the novel, at both implicit and explicit levels, takes on board the weighty philosophical issues of the age – the meanings of time and the determination of history, the meanings of racial identity and the origins of man – and poses them as part of the fashionable discussion of what it means to be modern and a city dweller.

These competitive modes of urbanism find their most potent symbol in Frimbo, the African prince, conjure man, psychoanalyst, quack doctor, philosopher, ladies' man. Frimbo acts as a node around which the conflicting interpretations of African American city life circulate. The most exaggeratedly urbane of Rudolph Fisher's city dwellers, Frimbo is also the primitive within the city and the outsider figure who can most perceptively read the dynamic urbanism that characterises his Harlem setting. He fulfils a clutch of paradigmatic urban figures all at once: being the flaneur, able to move in and out of his house and around the city all seeing but unseen; the intellectual, whose disinterested investigation into the social make-up of Negro Harlem has led him to understand both the nature of urbanism and racial being; the primitivist, whose African otherness is a thrilling and compelling draw to women; and the psychist, whose ability to predict the future is bound up with his ability to see the city as the future. Why, Archer asks, would anyone give up an African fiefdom for a back-street conjure shop in Harlem? Why indeed, unless the city is the kingdom and the man who can master it truly the figure able to escape the determinations of cause and effect.

The Conjure Man Dies stands as the most engagingly humorous and yet perceptively critical of Fisher's urban narratives. As he explores the nature of African American urbanity, he discovers the multiple and dissonant voices that make up the spirited conversation about African American urbanism in the 1920s. That these voices are often outlandish and exotic does not render Fisher's novel 'primitivist' in any straightforward way. Nor does his exploration of so-called white philosophical debates mark the novel as compromised by white influence, nor his embrace of the blues make it a folk text. Rather, Fisher understands that the 'Bang Clash' modernism of Harlem is made up by the cacophony of these voices as they seek to define the nature of urbanism and racial being for African Americans. In taking up the role as Harlem's populist interpreter, Fisher delineates a city of refuge that often fails as a material reality but is maintained as the future (space) of the race.[25]

CHAPTER 3

Passing and the Spectacle of Harlem

The previous two chapters have allowed us to map out some of the major concerns about the urban experience of modernity for African Americans. This should in some degree shift debate away from an exclusively racial criterion of assessment of Harlem Renaissance literary production, toward one which judges the Renaissance as part of an ongoing debate about the conditions of urban citizenship, aspirations toward urbanity, and the limitations imposed on these ambitions by the racial organisation of city life in this period. The three chapters following take up these concerns in a slightly different way by examining the writings of a number of African American women whose work suggests a still more complex engagement with the conditions of urban life for African Americans in the first half of the twentieth century. The work of Nella Larsen, explored in this chapter, and Angelina Weld Grimké, Marita Bonner, Ann Petry and Gwendolyn Brooks, addressed in subsequent chapters, focus our attention on the peculiar problems experienced by women in the rapidly expanding urban centres. These women take up issues we have seen discussed in major male writers – particularly the problem of colour-consciousness, the ambiguous lure of the city of refuge, the pursuit of a racial urbanity – but they complicate the picture we have already drawn through examination of the ways in which the experience of the race capital – its racism as well as its freedoms – is conditioned also by the mores and restrictions organising gender roles in the period. In particular, we are asked to consider the reproductive roles of African American women and the impact this has on their experience of poverty. We should also note the peculiar position in which middle-class women are placed in terms of the (near eugenic) stress on the cultural desirability of light skin. This, as we shall see in Larsen's work, becomes an even more difficult problem when the mores of the middle-class African American community conflict with the developing styles of urban living cultivated by the bohemian elites commonly associated with Harlem and the Harlem Renaissance. Furthermore, we see across a very broad range of female-authored African American texts an insistence on the impossibility of separating the experience of racism in the city with the experience of gendered modes of oppression and restriction. The following chapters will respond to this complex rendering of gendered African American modernity. As we move through we will see the development of a clearly recognisable feminised debate over the striving toward urbanity, and a women-centred mode of social protest rather different from conventional understandings of African American protest literature.

The first chapter of Paul Gilroy's *The Black Atlantic* poses questions central to this study when he asks us to consider the importance of Black Atlantic experience to the cultures of modernity one sees developing in the West in the early twentieth century. He focuses particularly on histories of the many migrant artists and authors – the restless carriers of disaporic consciousness – and asks what differences would become apparent if the travelling or exile experiences of the many African American, Caribbean and African scholars were seen as crucial facets of their cultural productions and consciousness. He asks, to stress the connection between his mapping of Black Atlantic consciousness and this chapter: 'What of Nella Larsen's relationship to Denmark, where George Padmore was held in jail during the early 1930s and which was also the home base of his banned newspaper the *Negro Worker*?' (p. 18). Larsen's European ancestry has been explored in biographical terms by Thadious Davis and it appears her relationship to Denmark is likely to have been rather more distant than she claimed.[1] This chapter takes up Gilroy's suggestive questioning to explore in broader terms the significance of the gendered experience of Black Atlantic modernity for those New Negro writers who were also new women, presenting a reading of Larsen's two novels, *Quicksand* (1928) and *Passing* (1929), which sees them as a feminine response to the changing conditions of African American modernity.[2] In pursuing an interest in modernist forms of literary experimentation, her work engages directly with the rapidly changing urban scene and the possibilities this offers for representation of African American women.

This is a reading contrary to views of Larsen, held until recently, which places her work at the rearguard of the Harlem Renaissance movement.[3] It also further diversifies conceptions of the Renaissance Larsen was a part of, as with the works examined in the previous two chapters. My focus in this chapter will be on the importance of spectacle for thinking about Larsen's writing, which develops a non-absolutist attitude to identity, particularly racial identity. This attitude to identity is formulated through attention to the points of intersection between trajectories of racial, sexual, gender, and class identifications. Exploration of the relationship between urban space and African American writing, and between race (both whiteness and blackness), gender, sexuality and class raises uncomfortable questions about current theoretical models of what has become known as 'intersectionality'.[4] This chapter suggests that we think anew about the implications of critical (and modernist) fetishisation of the fragmented, the contingent or the performative self. By focusing on representations of light-skinned or passing women in the novels of Nella Larsen we shall see that these 'impossible' subjects lead us to consider the conservative as well as the radical meanings of the shifting or mutable racial self. Reading the array of spectacles (spectacles of gender, racial and sexual display) the texts present, one can develop a feminist reading of Larsen's novels which integrates attention to the problematics of racial identity with analysis of gender roles during this period. Before we turn to the novels, however, it is useful to map out some of the cultural dynamics shaping perceptions of African American femininity during the Renaissance period. In particular, the ways in which debates about racial uplift cross over and conflict with wider cultural interest in eugenics have a very significant impact upon perceptions of black womanhood in general: an impact we see reflected in the middle-class mulatto or passing novel produced in the period.

New Women, New Negroes

The cultural situation for educated African American women in the 1920s city is highly complex, as the dilemmas facing Nella Larsen's heroines amply demonstrate. On the one hand, as the crudest stereotypes of the Jazz Age remind us, this was the age of (supposed) female emancipation in personal and political terms, with the figure of the flapper providing the most potent image of the age.[5] At the same time this figure is the subject of intense cultural anxiety, as the asexual image of the new woman challenges gendered mores and suggests that the primary role of woman might be something other than childbearing.[6] The increasing availability of contraception and the eugenic stress on a Darwinian procreative virility mean that managing reproduction becomes an issue for middle-class women in this period and not simply the concern of the working-class woman or the prostitute, although the considerable fear around woman's liberation can be seen in popular terms in the representation of new women as prostitutes.[7] This medicalisation of reproductive relationships is, as Robyn Wiegman argues, part of new definitions of the body of the citizen that follow on from advances in science and medicine as well as through the massive popularity of the new psychological discourses of the mind and body presented in the work of Freud.[8] In a period concerned with managing the body as a means of controlling the body politic the position of women is profoundly ambivalent: they achieve a liberation from the body only to find themselves pressed into directing that management toward the health of the nation at large.[9] This is especially the case for African American women, for whom the rhetoric of racial uplift demands that they should transcend the body, but that they should also be the veritable embodiment of Negro improvement: the good mother of the race.[10]

The 1920s is also the period, as Levering Lewis demonstrates, when ideas about racial uplift have a profound impact across a wide range of discursive fields and Harlemites are urged to become citizens fit for their burgeoning race capital. In the literary field there is an ongoing debate about how the race should best be represented: an acrimonious discussion which is often figured as a tension between genteel women writers (like Jessie Fauset) and the coarse sensationalists (like Claude McKay) who are associated with Carl Van Vechten and his reviled primitivism.[11] The writings by women examined in this book provide compelling counter-arguments to this rather too simplistic division: a necessary complexity given that African American literary history has tended to devalue the genteel, feminine side of this pairing. Du Bois was perhaps the most forceful spokesperson on the responsibilities of writers to represent the race well, as his editorials and reviews in *The Crisis* amongst other places make abundantly clear. Perhaps the most famous example of this – one with some relevance to this study – is Du Bois's dual review of Nella Larsen's *Quicksand*, 'in general the best piece of fiction to come out of Negro America since Chesnutt', and Claude McKay's *Home To Harlem*, 'for the most part [it] nauseates me, and after the dirtier parts of its filth I feel distinctly like taking a bath ... He has used every art and emphasis to paint drunkenness, fighting, lascivious sexual promiscuity and utter absence of restraint in as bold and as bright colors as he can.'[12] In fact, Du Bois's comparison does both novels a disservice. McKay's text is a complex analysis of the alienation of working-class and educated African American characters in a Harlem characterised more by its low-brow authenticity (in music and dancing) than by its complicity with bohemian white culture, and Larsen's Helga, as I will demonstrate, shows herself to be quite familiar with the 'bold and bright colors' of low-down Harlem life.

Alain Locke, though opposing what he saw as Du Bois's propa-gandist intentions, is actually of the same mind when he suggests in *The New Negro* that achievement in the arts will most signifi-cantly change the lot of the Negro at large. Langston Hughes's famous 'The Negro Artist and the Racial Mountain' seems to take the opposing view, but in fact his description of an authentic cultural nationalism is still bound within the terms of a debate that saw art as an integral part of a triumphant racial improvement, truly a 'refuge' narrative.[13] As the long-running debate in the pages of *The Crisis*, 'The Negro In Art: A Symposium. How Shall He Be Represented',[14] shows, despite different agendas and affiliations most cultural producers and commentators fell in with the belief articulated by Nella Larsen in 1928 that 'the artistic type has a definite role to play in solving the race problem'.[15] This is impossibly naive in the light of historical events but an important reflection of the links made at the time between literary representation and civic improvement, as cultural vanguardism prevailed as the primary mode of Negro self-improvement.

The literary concern with 'uplift' is matched by a significant if thoroughly contradictory attitude toward racial improvement in Harlem culture at large. The advertisements for skin-lightening creams and hair-straightening products one sees in *The Crisis* and *Opportunity*, and the vast fortune made by Madame C.J. Walker who owned the most popular range of skin-lightening cosmetics, demonstrate that beauty ideals were definitely light-skinned.[16] The advertisements which provided the revenue for magazines like *The Crisis* and *Opportunity* are a telling mix, featuring sales pitches for Howard, Tuskegee and other Negro universities and teaching colleges next to testimonials for Madame C.J. Walker's range of products. These strange pairings are embodied in the figure of A'Leila Walker, who used the vast fortune left to her by her mother's business in part to finance the Negro Renaissance events. One delightful advertisement on the back cover of *The Crisis* (March 1924) features a nineteenth-century picture of a (white) fairy princess with a text that ran: 'FAIRY LIKE – is she whose luxuriant, well-kept tresses frame a beauty-kissed complexion. To aid you use Madame C.J. Walker's Superfine Preparations for the Hand and Skin.' The number of popular stories which feature the admonition to light-skinned women to marry well (more bluntly to marry another light-skinned man) suggests that often, particularly among middle-class Negroes, the stress on uplift had rather more disturbing eugenic overtones – something pursued to its satiric limit by George Schuyler's *Black No More* (1932).[17]

Schuyler's story takes to its logical conclusion the connection between fetishisation of light skin and eugenic science. His novel presents a quite literal 'black is white' world where African Americans, courtesy of a machine that could easily grace the pages of an H.G.Wells novel, become whiter than the white folks. In a preface which lends a spurious scientific authenticity to the satire we are told: 'With America's constant reiteration of the superiority of whiteness, the avid search on the part of the black masses for some key to chromatic perfection is easily understood. Now it would seem that science is on the verge of satisfying them' (p. i). The novel follows the adventures of the young blade Max Disher as he undergoes Dr Junius Crookman's *Black-No-More* treatment and passes into white society to become a leading light of a white supremacist clan, The Knights of Nordica. The plot pursues the consequences of this reversal of the chromatic order across the social spectrum: the Harlemite Disher marries the haughty daughter of the clan leader Reverend Givens (after she had spurned him as a black man in a Harlem club) becoming part of upper-class Atlanta society, while the dickty race leaders of Harlem find it rather more difficulty to replicate their social standing once they pass into the white world. The white supremacists attempt to make the *Black-No-More* business the burning issue of a presidential campaign – parodying the extent to which US politics always already turns on the race question. This backfires on the Knights and their associates as the whitest of the white – Mr Arthur Snobbcraft and Dr Samuel Buggerie – are discovered to have African American ancestors and, after falling into the hands of a militant redneck community (while wearing blackface, just to add to the absurdity), they are lynched. Eventually, scientific research indicates that those who have undergone the *Black-No-More* treatment are, in fact, whiter than their former oppressors and the novel closes with the proliferation of beauty salons offering skin-darkening techniques (*Poudre Negre*, *Poudre Le Egyptienne* and the like) and calls for the segregation of the palest.

Much of Schuyler's satire turns on the extent to which the race problem in the US cloaks economic oppression, and the uproar at the turning of blacks into whites is depicted as the wailing of a master race for the loss of the riches they derive from their minions. He goes further, however, to suggest that the celebration of African American culture in Harlem during the 1920s stems from similarly dubious capitalistic motives. A thinly disguised skit on Madame C.J. Walker's empire depicts the collapse the beauty business, the premier indigenous business of Harlem, as no one any longer needs skin-lightening creams. Similarly, the night-clubs of Harlem and the so-called authentic forms of African American creativity, the blues and jazz and the spirituals, disappear in the stampede to flee the economic ghettoisation of blackness. Schuyler calls into question the race loyalties of the New Negro movement as he satirises its major figures (from Garvey to Du Bois to Locke); revealing them as craven cowards or pretentious buffoons who are as keen as the next man or woman to take the path to chromatic indistinction. In this respect Schuyler's novel is of a piece with that other satire of 1932, Wallace Thurman's *Infants of the Spring* (often cited as the death knell of the New Negro movement), in that both texts seek to puncture the pretensions of New Negro Africanism and each questions the assumptions about black authenticity that underpin claims to a uniquely African American art.[18] Schuyler's novel moves beyond mere spleen at New Negro leaders, however, in that he seeks to question the idea that there might be any such thing as an essence of blackness that can be claimed as uniquely and unequivocally African American: something he also takes up in his essay called 'Negro Art Hokum'.[19] His suggestion is that any such desire leads ultimately to a form of eugenicism that he sees at work in the Harlem world around him. His astute assessment is that much of the cultural anxiety surrounding racial mixing – and the extent to which this is projected onto women – represents eugenic tendencies that differ from his satirical vision only in terms of degree. Appropriately, the *Black-No-More* enterprise runs into trouble when it transpires that there is no guarantee of the genetic conference of whiteness: making reproduction a risky game of chance for any former African American – a neat parallel of concerns among well-to-do African Americans about the risks of having a 'dark' baby.

If one turns from fiction to look at magazines of the period, from the premier African American journals like *Opportunity* or *The Crisis*, to those radical white journals with substantial Negro interests, one finds that race science and eugenics are part of the common language for the discussion of the role and meaning of 'the Negro': whether this is angry refutation as in Charles S. Johnson's editorial salvoes against spurious anthropological suggestions of Negro inferiority and those who would assert that Negroes and women had smaller brains, or the serious attention given to the work of Melville Herskovits on the genealogies of the American Negro.[20] Herskovits's work draws on race science and eugenics but he frames his analyses within an anthropological approach that avoids racial prescriptivism, or outright racism. Other commentators were more straightforward in their support of the eugenic possibilities for African Americans. Albert Sidney, in a 1924 article for *The Crisis* called 'Applied Eugenics', stated:

> The future problems of the Negro will be the elimination of the unfit and the perpetuation of the fit. Eugenics applied to the Negro will be a successful experiment. If the Negro is to come into his full capacity he must not be afraid to experiment. He must see how the facts of modern science can contribute to his progress.[21]

The extent to which the notion of progress that underpins such comments coincides with Schuyler's cynical vision in *Black No More* is made disturbingly clear by James Weldon Johnson, who comments approvingly in *American Mercury* that upper-class Negroes were becoming lighter in complexion with each successive generation.[22]

Much of the stress on uplift when it is applied to African American women is, of course, bound up with the desire to refute the stereotypes of African American femininity promulgated during and after slavery, and the stress on gentility amongst women as a mark of civility is inextricably linked with the need to escape the definition of African American femininity as sexuality.[23] In this light the lady-like behaviour one finds in New Negro writing (Fauset or Larsen in particular) is less a class-bound parochialism than an understandable attempt to circumvent pernicious racial stereotyping and a model which is adopted at much personal cost, as black feminist critics have pointed out.[24] This genteel mode of African American femininity steers well clear of the models of new woman femininity largely because a primitivism which might be actively sought out and prized by white bohemians veers far too close to the savage, primitive and promiscuous stereotypes which gave a spurious moral justification to the slave-holding system. What conceptions of the new woman and the race woman do share at points is an eugenicist insistence on femininity and reproduction as intrinsically linked to racial being (and the purity of the racial line).

The issue becomes even more complex when one considers the light-skinned ideal fostered as the desired representative of the race woman. The middle-class denizens of Striver's Row (in well-to-do Harlem) occupied their privileged position largely because of their birth into a very small elite of rich Negro families, whose influence in debates over racial representation goes beyond their numbers and whose conservative ideas about matters sexual is legendary.[25] The unspoken contradiction in all of this is that the fetishisation of light skin speaks to a family history of inter-racial relationships during slavery; a legacy that the cult of gentility is at pains to disavow. The race woman is therefore the key to racial uplift, both in terms of her socially improving behaviour and her reproductive capacities. Yet, the valued light skin speaks to a history of inter-racial relationships (including rape) during slavery which explicitly contradicts any idea of pure race lines and undermines the terms of the eugenic debate on which the logic of uplift draws. In fact, as recent work on inter-racial identity (including mulatto and passing characters) points out, the light-skinned Negro calls into question the very idea of race, something which is acknowledged implicitly in the cultural anxieties in both black and white communities about the phenomenon of passing.[26]

The obsession with family lines is one way in which the middle-class Negro community guarantees the purity of the race, another is the construction of fairly rigid class hierarchies; and fiction of the time, from Jessie Fauset to Rudolph Fisher to Nella Larsen, repeatedly dramatises and critiques just this kind of social organisation. The extent to which the protection of these Negro aristocracies proves impossible in the rapidly expanding urban scene of Harlem is demonstrated with notable panache in Fisher's *The Walls of Jericho*. At the Negro Improvement Association Ball (a telling name in itself and undoubtedly a skit on the NAACP) Miss Agatha Cramp (a thinly disguised version of the famous white patron Mrs R. Osgood Mason) assumes Fred Merritt, the light-skinned, blonde man she engages in conversation, is white because he is moving into her well-to-do (white) street. Her racist benevolence is exposed in cringemaking fashion as she talks to Fred, and culminates in her horrified comeuppance as she issues him an invitation to call on her only to find out too late that he is 'really' black. The parody turns on the fact that Fred is well aware his 'appearance' does not coincide with his 'being', a set piece that is common to many passing texts.[27] What is more interesting here is that Fisher connects the failure of racial classification with African American urban expansion. In fact much of the anxiety about racial passing, as well as much of the policing of African American femininity which characterises the period, has to be read as part of wider anxieties about the potentially chaotic nature of city life, and the threat that racial undifferentiation will become the norm in the new city context.[28] What is interesting about these anxieties is that they are at points shared by race-conscious African Americans and by advocates of the most extreme racism.

Spectacle, Race and Gender

Nella Larsen's two novels provide us with rich textual examples of the cultural anxieties that come to be focused in this period around racial admixture, and the ways these generalised debates take on a particular urban cast by the late 1920s. Her novels link the debates about the New Negro with the nascent (feminist) debate about the new women: she engages, then, with the position of middle-class women in the modernising city context. *Quicksand* is concerned with the rise and ultimate demise of Helga Crane, a light-skinned woman of Danish and African American parentage. The story is ostensibly one of the mixed-race woman's inability to discover any viable sense of racial community, but Helga has perhaps as much in common with the alienation of the itinerant artist or outcast figure of classic modernism.[29] The similarities between Larsen's heroines and female modernist protagonists can be seen if one compares Helga Crane with Melanctha from Gertrude Stein's *Three Lives* (1909), a book Larsen had great admiration for, or with the errant Robin from Djuna Barnes's *Nightwood* (1936).[30] Larsen's second novel *Passing* is the story of two light-skinned women, Irene Redfield and Clare Kendry. Clare, a childhood friend of Irene, has passed into white society, only to be prompted to return to her race after accidentally meeting Irene in a hotel in Chicago; a return which proves to have disastrous consequences. Irene (who narrates much of the novel) becomes increasingly obsessed by Clare but this fascination is displaced onto a plot of heterosexual jealousy and discussion of the dangers of passing, both of which are unconvincing narrative ploys. The highly ambiguous ending where Clare fatally tumbles out of an open window does not resolve these conflicting narrative trajectories, but it does suggest that Irene (for whatever reason) is dangerously implicated in Clare's mysterious death.

Larsen's texts focus almost exclusively on the cultured members of the 'talented tenth' and this, combined with their persistent attention to women who pass out of the race, has ensured that they have often not quite qualified as 'race writing'. Yet she deals with the complex dynamics of modern life for urban educated African American women – particularly in her trenchant critique of the gendered and sexual double standards of the well-to-do black middle-classes of which she was a part. Larsen's novels have persistently been read as exhibiting the wrong kind of racial identification (that is white orientated, conservative, middle class) and she is seen as operating within an urban scene which offers nothing more than the commodification and compromise of African Americans by white society. What this fails to address is the extent to which the novels, particularly *Quicksand*, present Harlem as an *image* to be interrogated.

After decades of being seen as too retrograde to be significant in the African American canon, there has been since the mid-1980s a veritable Larsen renaissance. Mary Helen Washington, writing in 1981 'Nella Larsen: Mystery Woman of the Harlem Renaissance', could hardly have imagined the extent to which Larsen's work would be taken up by black feminists, queer theorists, critical theorists and literary scholars.[31] The significance of sexuality in her work has been examined at length, first and most provocatively by Deborah E. McDowell in her role as editor of the Serpent's Tail reissue of Larsen's novel, who suggests that one can see in *Passing* a nascent or 'unspoken' lesbian relationship between the central female characters Irene Redfield and Clare Kendry.[32] This suggestion has been taken up and contested in many and various ways: notably by Judith Butler, who sees in Larsen a challenge to the psychoanalytic privileging of sexual difference itself as the foundational point of identity formation and confirms the suggestion of powerful lesbian identification in Larsen's texts; by Ann DuCille, who contests the lesbian identification but confirms the complex exploration of sexual as well as racial identity in the novels; to recent pieces by Claudia Tate, Mary Esteve, and Beverley Haviland, all of whom confirm the complexity of Larsen's examination of race and sexuality. Ultimately these essays confirm her as a writer definitively engaged with the terms and issues of New Negro modernism as well as the urban contexts of modernity. As her biographer Thadious Davis argues, 'She came of age in a city propelling itself into an unparalleled acceptance of urban modernity as progress ... Her behaviour expressed resentment of confinement into race without ethnicity, into feminine roles without substance.'[33]

Larsen's fascination with the primitive, the oriental and the sexually exotic should be considered an appropriation and a critical reworking of the motifs of the primitive and exotic which are part and parcel of the modernist movement. This locates Larsen in context with both her African American modernistic peers, Thurman, Fisher and Nugent and McKay, whom she knew and admired, and with modernist writers such as Gertrude Stein and James Joyce who are cited by these authors as models and influences.[34] For example, Davis's biography of Larsen recounts her request of a friend who was travelling to Europe to bring her back a copy of Joyce's *Ulysses* and Larsen was familiar with Stein's work and knew her socially through Carl Van Vechten. She wrote to Stein: 'I never cease to wonder how you came to write [*Three Lives*] and why you and not someone of us should so accurately have caught the spirit of this race of mine.'[35] Nugent's work, Wallace Thurman's writing and the New Negro material presented in *Fire!!* analysed in the previous chapters should be borne in mind as one turns to Larsen's novels because it gives a context for her preoccupation with spectacle, sexuality and the mutability of identity. As with the example of *Fire!!*, we should read Larsen's texts as an attempt to respond to the changing conditions of urban life.

That these modern debates should be intrinsic to Larsen's works is unsurprising if one considers the contexts of Harlem Renaissance literary experimentation outlined in this book, but Larsen's particular interest in modern life and its more decadent trappings is revealed in her (self-penned) flyleaf to the first edition of *Quicksand*. As a young author seeking to place herself on the map Larsen's description is delicious in its wannabe bohemianism: 'Nella Larsen is a modern woman, for she smokes, wears her dresses short, does not believe in religion, churches and the like, and feels that people of the artistic type have a definite chance to help solve the race problem.'[36] In fact, as Davis's biography makes clear, Larsen's class position and upbringing mark her as anything but bohemian and the elaborate masks she adopted throughout her writing life suggest considerable anxiety about being judged a bona fide modern. The confidence in the power of art and cigarettes perhaps goes some way to explain why more overtly politicised African American writers have had little time for Larsen's kind of fiction, but to disparage this for its superficiality is to seriously underestimate the complexity of Larsen's work and its formal sophistication, as well as to miss the powerful challenge of passing, as a literal and theoretical phenomenon, to discourses of identity and ideas of racial authenticity.[37] How one might reconcile this radical analysis of the passing nature of identity with a racial politics often reactionary in the extreme has, however, remained a puzzle, one I shall attempt to tease out here.

Quicksand presents us with a woman, Helga Crane, caught in a classic tragic mulatto dilemma, unable to find any viable sense of self or community as she is caught between the role of desexualised lady prescribed for women of the black middle classes, typified in the novel by the society matron Anne Grey, and alternative white (modernist-bohemian) definitions of her body as exotic, hyper-sexualised object, exemplified by the painter Axel Olsen's opinion of Helga in the Denmark section of the novel. In fact, Larsen goes some way further than simply rejecting the polarised alternatives of black middle-class respectability or bohemian licentiousness and *Quicksand* presents us with a scenario where femininity and heterosexuality are each suggested as a problem. Helga tests a whole variety of female roles in the novel; she successively tries professional woman, whore, desexualised middle-class lady, exotic other, mistress and finally wife and mother, which becomes her deathly nemesis. At no stage does heterosexual femininity (at least in its middle-class, African American form) seem a viable option, and is instead represented persistently as a form of pathology. One does, though, see a narcissistic fascination with the self as loved object and this narcissism develops into an exploration of the possibilities of spectacle, the self as spectacle and with a fascination for the bodies of other women as objects of erotic attention. I would not go so far as to call *Quicksand* a lesbian novel, but in line with much modernist and bohemian discourse of the period an exoticising fascination with and between the bodies of women is an unmistakable presence in the novel, and the drama of sexual and racial identity continually exceeds the limits of either of these narratives of identity.

I see a connection in Larsen's writing, as in the earlier example of Nugent's story, between a fascination with the visual field, an avant-gardist attitude toward sexual and gendered mores, and African American modernist tendencies within a broadened conception of the Harlem Renaissance. This analysis is presented in her work through attention to the construction of the self as spectacle and through the repeated use of the motif of the exchanged glance between women in a public space. In *Quicksand* and *Passing* we see women (first Helga Crane, then Irene Redfield and Clare Kendry) move through and encounter one another in prototypical modernist urban spaces, the street, the bedroom, the hotel, the night-club and the theatre: spaces which are characterised by their semi-anonymous, and graphically performative, status.[38] These semi-anonymous spaces, as Rachel Bowlby suggests, are places where one pays for the experience of inhabiting a realm that is both public and private. This payment is exacted in the form of a performance of an appropriate identity for these spaces. It is not necessarily enough to have the financial ability to inhabit these places; one must also look as if one has the money. The spaces allow that one pays (in money and in symbolic terms) for the privacy (in the hotel room, at a cafe table or in a shop) to enable the production of a public identity which may or may not have any relation to the subject's 'real' location in social or economic or racial structures (this is, of course, the essence of the shopping fantasy presented in a film like *Pretty Woman*). While this identity drama usually crystallises around class anxieties about city spaces, it is even more interesting to consider how semi-anonymous self-authoring takes place when the subject is racially passing: something I shall return to later in the chapter when I consider the rooftop cafe scene in *Quicksand*. These encounters direct attention towards appearances, glances and surfaces and they ultimately work to emphasise the transitory and performative nature of urban identity for these women despite the apparent fixity of racial identity. For example, in confronting the teeming masses of the city crowd we witness Helga Crane's extraordinary disavowal of racial kinship: 'Why, she demanded in fierce rebellion, should she be yoked to these despised black folk?': an expression of wretched individualism which serves her only as long as she chooses to maintain the fantasy of urban self-sufficiency, and notably is dropped as soon as those racial bonds she so fiercely repudiates are challenged in the Denmark section of the novel.[39]

In *Quicksand* Harlem is represented as the exotic scene of desire for a leisured white (or near-white) elite, but rather than this being the central failure of the novel Larsen's understanding of subjectivity is peculiarly enabled by the textual focus on an urban scene of commodified social relations. Larsen's texts show self-consciousness about the spectacle of the urban and the negotiations that are possible within this scene. *Quicksand* and *Passing* are structured around a series of overdetermined moments of racial and sexual spectacle. The looks exchanged between characters and between the woman and her own image carry the burden of complex constructions and disarticulations of racial, sexual and gender identifications. Larsen's texts suggest this intersection is where one sees the pulling away, rather than the confluence, of different identity formations; this is the site of danger, of incompatible demands, of conservative as well as radical impulses, indeed even of violence. Here one sees the substitution of one form of understanding of the self with another. This suggests the inter-section obscures, or covers over difference, as a series of disjunctive moments, rather than being the site where incompatible forms of difference are seen simultaneously as a kind of heightened awareness of the subject's complex location within ideological formations. *Quicksand* gives us a central character as self-consciously decadent as Nugent's outrageous Alex and shows Helga as a subject, like Alex, who presents and experiences herself primarily as visual spectacle.[40] In doing this Larsen goes beyond tracing attempts on the part of the dominant white culture to objectify African American women as the object of exotic and erotic attention, toward speculation about the (limited) freedoms these narratives might offer through their focus on black female sexuality.[41] *Quicksand* is a complex study of the difference in political terms between *being* a particular kind of subject and *looking* like one.

The construction of this kind of visual economy and the conse-quences this has for grasping the meanings of race in Larsen's work can be charted quite precisely at the very beginning of the novel. *Quicksand* opens with Helga sitting in her bedroom in the 'soft gloom' (p. 1) of evening. This scene, narrated in the third person, is described in intense detail:

> Helga Crane sat alone in her room, which at that hour, eight in the evening, was in soft gloom. Only a single reading lamp, dimmed by a great black and red shade, made a pool of light on the blue Chinese carpet, on the bright covers of the books which she had taken down from their long shelves, on the white pages of the opened one selected, on the shining brass bowl crowded with many-colored nasturtiums beside her on the low table, and on the oriental silk which covered the stool at her slim feet. (p. 1)

The bedroom is, from the first, represented as an exotic space, one that has been furnished by Helga's 'rare and intensely personal taste' (p. 1). Colours, objects and arrangements are of the utmost importance, both to the construction of Helga as a beautiful object amongst a panoply of beautiful things, and for the construction of the narrative style itself, which builds by the progressive addition of rare and precious items. This is a domestic interior where icons of Western culture jostle with icons of orientalism. It is worth noting, in terms of Larsen's engagement in the novel with myths and narratives of primitivism and the exotic, that the objects which fill Helga's room are precisely those that might be taken to represent those myths. The icons represent the myth of the Orient as constructed by Europe, which is then shown as an ironic commentary on the construction of the myth of the African American woman as exotic object. The room also functions as a bohemian space, where the collectable signs of oriental exoticism are carefully arranged to define the Western subject as decadent, artistic and modern: this space seems paradigmatically white.

This description, then, could be taken to suggest that Helga is defined by her position in commodity culture, and signifies a fairly elitist class positioning which allows her to disavow her blackness. Indeed, this is what Hazel Carby's reading of the novel suggests: 'Quicksand is the first text by a black woman to be a conscious narrative of a woman embedded within capitalist social relations.'[42] I concur with this and suggest that what Carby identifies contributes substantially to Larsen's response to modernity. The next paragraph complicates the scene in a way that suggests a self-conscious manipulation of the objectification that appears to be taking place. In this paragraph the object of aesthetic attention is Helga herself. She becomes an object in this room that is fitted to, but also by, her need(s):

> An observer would have thought her well fitted to that framing of light and shade. A slight girl of twenty-two years, with sloping shoulders and delicate but well-turned arms and legs, she had, nonetheless, an air of radiant, careless health. In vivid green and gold negligee and glistening brocaded mules, against whose dark tapestry her sharply cut face, with skin like yellow satin, was distinctly outlined, she was – to use a hackneyed word – attractive. (p. 2)

The opening phrase, 'an observer would have thought', significantly alters interpretation of the description that follows it. It suggests that the voyeuristic perspective provided by the third-person narrator, which one would expect in conventional narrative objectification of the female form, is here insufficient. Larsen builds a further and excessive level of mediation into this structure of looking. It is 'an observer', not the narrator or the reader, but someone else, someone who is defined by their special interest in looking, who would have thought about Helga and her environment in this apparently objectified manner. The description of Helga as object is presented as a scene where the act of looking itself is foregrounded. What seems to be at first a conventional delineation of the woman as aesthetic object is destabilised by the overdetermined presence of the mediating gaze of this imagined external observer.

There is a beautifully ironic acknowledgement of this structural doubling in the middle of the second paragraph. The narrator, not the observer, provides the comment that Helga is 'to use a hackneyed word – attractive'. The irony lies, of course, in the fact that the whole description is hackneyed in the extreme; in fact, the designation 'attractive' is the least hackneyed aspect of it. But this displaced acknowledgement propels attention back to the act of looking. It confirms the fact that Helga is actively constructing this scene for a particular kind of gaze she knows only too well. Helga manages to circumvent her objectification, at least temporarily, because the narrator colludes with her in identifying very explicitly the gaze that would perform this objectification and positing a position beyond it. Neither Helga nor the narrator is wholly encapsulated within this economy of objectification. Some part of each of them is elsewhere, observing, critiquing and parodying this schema of looking.

This disjunction between being looked at and knowing the mechanics of the look leaves at least some room for manoeuvre. Larsen has an investment in looking – objectification and voyeurism – at the same time as she mounts a critique on looking. This contradictory position is further emphasised as one progresses through the first chapter. Helga is about to leave this gloriously constructed boudoir; indeed, she is about to flee Naxos itself, the college in which she has worked as a teacher for the past two years. Naxos, an African American college (constructed by Larsen as something of an amalgamation of Fisk, Tuskegee and Atlanta), is governed by a desire for bourgeois respectability and racial uplift. Helga's principal, Dr Robert Anderson, makes this very clear (and inadvertently ensures Helga's flight) when he comments: 'You have something that we need very badly here in Naxos ... You're a lady. You have dignity and breeding.' Of course, as Helga angrily perceives, what Anderson means is that she is light-skinned. This complicity with oppressive (white) cultural values disgusts Helga, for though she has little or no race consciousness elsewhere in the novel she holds to a kind of modernist 'terrible honesty' and despises hypocrisy in all its forms, while allowing that she may herself practise it. As a symbol of her rejection, she seizes a 'paraphernalia' of papers and text books and throws them in the bin:

> Frantically, Helga Crane clutched at the lot and flung them violently, scornfully toward the wastepaper basket. It received a part, allowing the rest to spill untidily over the floor. The girl smiled ironically, seeing in the mess a simile of her own earnest endeavour to inculcate knowledge into her indifferent classes.
> (p. 4)

Here one can see another form of narrative doubling, which again works to add a further, excessive level of mediation to the spectacle presented. Whereas in the second paragraph the narrator split and doubled, here the character does. Helga throws her papers away knowing how 'the girl' will look when she does it. The scene is therefore a spectacle of rejection presented by a subject who knows very well how it will be read. The ironic smile of the girl as she views the symbolic content of her act is a sign of Helga slipping the yoke of objectification. At no point does Helga make a total identification with the performance she enacts and thus is able to circumvent subjection to it.

Whenever Helga is compelled into any singular identification, when she finds herself straying into a place of authenticity, she evades the attempt to contain her by asserting herself as spectacle, and by moving decisively from one performance of identity to another. For example, when she is categorised as exotic, sensual object by the painter Olsen in the Denmark section of the novel: 'You have the warm impulsive nature of the women of Africa, but, my lovely, you have, I fear, the soul of a prostitute' (p. 87), she refutes his definition of her identity by asserting an alternative race based one: 'Herr Olsen, in my country the men, of my race, at least, don't make such suggestion to decent girls' (p. 87). The hypocrisy of this statement is rapidly revealed as Helga returns to Harlem after turning down Olsen's proposal and is presented with a drunken Dr Anderson, a man of her race, making just such a proposal, which in this situation she is more than willing to accept.

I want to describe this as a passing structure whereby the narrative style is marked by indeterminacy at least as significant as the racial indeterminacy of the central figures of Larsen's novels. From the opening of the novel Helga is defined through her embeddedness in a consumer culture marked quite clearly as white and bourgeois, and yet the textual self-consciousness about this commodification drives a wedge between subject and subjection to the object. It also suggests that the 'real' Helga is elsewhere, not entirely caught by what appears to be the truth. But this in itself is deceptive because as with so many incidents of passing we lack any evidence of this other 'real' self, and the text simply circles around the question of who is the true Helga Crane. This is dramatised in the text when Helga encounters her modernist-primitivist other as depicted in the portrait painted by Axel Olsen. After Helga rejects his advances he comments: 'I think my picture of you is, after all, the true Helga Crane' (p. 88). Helga responds: 'It wasn't, she contended, herself at all, but some disgusting sensual creature with her features ... Anyone with half an eye could see it wasn't she' (p. 89).

While we may not be able to perceive a supposed true self, we can see that Helga defines herself through her fetishisation of commodities. This allows her to perform a white bohemian identity despite the so-called truth of her racial identity being otherwise. She does this in order to claim the status of bohemian artist (that most revered of figures for Larsen as for many of the Harlem

Renaissance writers), which undermines the middle-class pieties of Naxos, and also avoids subjection to the sexualised image of the exotic black woman. What is most clear, however, is the potential for slippage between these identities. This goes beyond being a strategy employed to extricate Helga from limiting racial or gender definitions of herself and evolves into a structural passing where we are made aware of the instability of the racial and gendered assignations we presume. It is this fundamental questioning of the bases of racial and gendered typification that stands as the most provocative element in Larsen's work.

Danse Sauvage

As I suggested earlier, Harlem of the late 1920s raises complex issues of racial agency, appropriation and commodification. But the experiences offered in Harlem's legendary exotic spaces should not be wholly dismissed as interesting political configurations do emerge out of the conscious understanding in the period of Harlem as visual spectacle. Andrea Barnwell emphasises this in her discussion of the extraordinary fascination in the USA and Europe with the dancer Josephine Baker, who becomes a veritable primitivist-modernist icon.[43] Accounts from the period, which feature in Baker's biography, describe her pulling scornful faces while performing her trademark 'Danse Sauvage', undermining the 'primitive' identity she supposedly performs. In Chapter 2 we saw how Rudolph Fisher's concern with African American urbanity draws him to attend to the spectacle of Harlem. In Larsen, we see less concentration on the mass spectacle – the large scale performance of urbanity – and more attention to the subjective immersion in a spectacular scene, as she explores the compulsion toward being urbane. We see a particularly interesting example of this in Chapter 11 of *Quicksand*, which takes place in a Harlem night-club. One night, after a dinner party, Helga reluctantly follows her friends to the night-club. She knows, and is disgusted by, the kind of spectacle she is supposed to form a part of,

> the reek of flesh, smoke, alcohol, oblivious of other gyrating pairs, oblivious of the color, the noise, and the grand distorted childishness of it all. She [Helga] was drugged, lifted, sustained by the joyous, wild, murky orchestra. The essence of life seemed bodily motion. And when suddenly the music died, she dragged herself back to the present with a conscious effort; and a shameful certainty that not only had she been in the jungle, but that she had enjoyed it, began to taunt her. She hardened herself in her determination to get away. She wasn't, she told herself, a jungle creature. (p. 59)

Whilst she dances Helga finds herself experiencing an authentic
sense of racial belonging, described as narcotic and ecstatic – a
kind of primitivist regression. It is an intense bodily experience in
which Helga has lost control of the economy of spectatorship that
she was negotiating at the beginning of the novel. She is 'oblivious'
to everything except her own sensuous enjoyment. The experience
of dancing is hyperbolised in such a way as to suggest this is a
primitivist fantasy of authentic blackness. We might note, for
example, the use of some key primitivist terms – 'childishness',
'jungle' and 'wild'.

Helga ultimately refuses the seductions of a dangerously 'real'
racial understanding of herself, preferring instead in the second
half of the scene a strongly sexual identification with a passing
woman, Audrey Denney, whom she sees dancing in the night-club
with Robert Anderson, her former principal and object of some
apparent desire on Helga's part. This is a reversal of the situation
with Olsen in Denmark. There she refuses a sexual definition of
herself, insisting instead on her race and class credentials to escape
Olsen's objectification as prostitute. Here she refuses a racial identification overwhelming in its realness, preferring instead a sexual
identification with another woman. Audrey has repeatedly
scandalised Helga's friends by passing as white and by associating
with white visitors to Harlem's night-clubs, but also by openly
flaunting her passing status, a unique parading of the passing
woman's customary veiled ambivalence:

> Helga Crane studied her. She was pale, with a peculiar, almost
> deathly pallor. The brilliantly red, softly curving mouth was
> somehow sorrowful. Her pitch-black eyes, a little aslant, were
> veiled by long drooping lashes and surmounted by broad brows,
> which seemed like black smears. The short dark hair was brushed
> severely back from the wide forehead. The extreme décolletage
> of her simple apricot dress, showed skin of an unusual color, a
> delicate creamy hue, with golden tones. 'Almost like alabaster,'
> thought Helga. (p. 60)

In the context of plot development this scene signals the beginning
of Helga's attraction to Anderson, but the content of the look
militates against and exceeds this narrative of heterosexual desire.
Helga's look dwells with romantic intensity not upon Anderson
but Audrey and the conventions of hetero-romance are troped
upon and critically destabilised. Again, we see a kind of passing
structure to the narrative and the conventions of normative sexual
as well as racial identifications are thrown into crisis. As Helga
watches Audrey dancing with Anderson, the 'envious admiration'
(p. 62) she had felt of Audrey's passing status is 'augmented by
another more primitive emotion' (p. 62). The ostensible meaning

is that she feels jealous of Audrey's relationship with Anderson, but meaning slides as the content of her desiring gaze raises the ghost of what psychoanalysis during and after the 1920s saw as the primitive, archaic sexual desire of women for each other. In making a sexual identification with Audrey, Helga also makes an identification with a passing woman, a fascinating prospect since this depends on a recognition of that which within the usual conventions of passing needs to remain hidden in order to succeed (one can not logically see a successful pass). What is important here is that the envy associated with passing – the desire to refuse racial belonging – and the adoption of a decidedly conservative attitude to racial matters, are inextricably linked with the possibility of making a sexual identification that is both transgressive and radical. This possibility, seen through examination of these moments of commodified urban desire, explores the way in which every performative negotiation is at least partly an attempt to solve problems located at another level of identification.

Passing Encounters, City Scenes

Both of Larsen's texts can be seen as negotiations of visual economies, economies that are bound up with the representation of very specific forms of difference. The novels are concerned with how difference manifests itself, and particularly how it can be seen and recognised (or in many cases misrecognised). The visual scene is crucial to understanding the relationship between gender, sexuality and race with the city that forms the canvas on which these identity formations are marked and played out. The significance of desire and urban spectacle and the peculiar indeterminacy of the visual field are if anything even more central to Larsen's second novel, *Passing*. Visual indeterminacy is, of course, the provenance of the passing subject. Judith Butler's discussion of *Passing* in *Bodies That Matter* suggests that racial passing cloaks, or covers over, a passing of a sexual kind. I'd argue that it may not be possible to make a choice between one form of passing and another, because of the ambivalence of the visual field self-consciously presented in the text. Butler's reading suggests that the novel challenges psychoanalytic assumptions of the primacy of sexual difference, that it 'articulates the convergent modalities of power by which sexual difference is articulated and assumed' (p. 168). However, her emphasis on the convergence of different identity formations elides the way in which race, gender, sexuality and class work against one another in Larsen's work. These categories are presented in Larsen's novels as disarticulated and divergent trajectories, which carry contents, possibilities and dangers different from each other. It is this pulling apart, the non-compatibility of narratives of gender, race or sexual identity, which not only characterises Larsen's writing but also constitutes a major part of her attempt to respond to the changing conditions of urban modernity. We can see this in any number of scenes in the novel, but it receives its fullest treatment in a paradigmatic city context, a hotel rooftop cafe.

This is the first scene in which we meet Clare Kendry, the passing woman, as Irene Redfield unwillingly recalls the meeting that sets the novel's events in motion. After losing contact for many years when Clare opts to pass for white, Irene bumps into her accidentally in the rooftop cafe of the Drayton Hotel. The scene initiates a necessary doubleness of looking relations, which persists through the novel, and allows the elaboration of desire (between women). The scene begins: 'This is what Irene Redfield remembered' (p. 146). Irene's memories are presented as a series of visual tableaux and she figures as observer and observed in the scene. We are presented with a female voyeur scrutinising the city and the people in it. Irene has been shopping on a blisteringly hot summer's day and after almost fainting on the street she is rescued by a 'Samaritan' (p. 147) of a taxi driver. He reads Irene – wealthy, laden with bags, in a glamorous shopping street, hailing a cab – as white and immediately takes her to the Drayton where there is a cool rooftop cafe. So, Irene's presence in the Drayton is dependent on a prior recognition as white, and her tacit acceptance of that position.

The deceptions of vision, and the disjunction between appearance and identity, are foregrounded. The possibility of this misrecognition depends on the urban scene that Irene moves through and carefully recreates as she remembers. There is a stylistic fascination with the visual spectacle of the city – buildings, car-tracks, automobiles, shop windows. Later in the passage Irene adopts a camera's-eye view, surveying the panorama of the city from the roof of the hotel. As she gazes down 'at the specks of the cars and people creeping about in streets, thinking how silly they look' (p. 148), her view seems to penetrate further than the eye can see, reaching the 'undetected' (p. 148) horizon. Her gaze is filmic as it pans across the urban panorama, and she plays the role of leisured lady in a characteristic semi-anonymous urban space with consummate grace. The distinctive troubling of the public/private division seen in the semi-anonymous urban locale is here heightened to extremes by Irene and Clare's passing status, adding urban complexity to the conventional passing narrative. The usual trauma of the passing narrative is a melodramatic scene of recognition where the passing character is exposed or risks exposure by one of their kin. Many features of passing are conflated here since it is usually a (dark) member of their own family who may reveal their 'true' identity; yet at the same time we see here the basis for the claims that an in-group member will always recognise another passing. There are also obvious analogies to be drawn between this primal moment and the account provided by psycho-analysis of the traumatic recognition of sexual difference in the context of the family romance. This gives us fresh and provocative ways of thinking about the conjunctions of racial and sexual identity formation, particularly in authors like Larsen who were conversant with Freudian psychoanalysis.[44]

Larsen's text is unusual in that she embraces the city as a means to avoid the conventional passing narrative inevitability. All of Larsen's heroines have conveniently dead relatives. What this disguises is the extent to which it is the city's anonymity that makes passing possible, though characters still suffer the difficulties of their gendered positioning.[45] Irene's adoption (temporarily) of a white subject position seems to produce a celebration of the city laid out before her and an ability to see but not be seen, a structure which obviously echoes her passing status as it also mimics a camera's way of seeing. The pose Irene adopts once she is in the cafe recalls Alex from Bruce Nugent's story:

> The tea, when it came, was all that she had desired and expected ... so much so that after the first deep cooling drink she was able to forget it, only now and then sipping, a little absently, from the tall green glass, while she surveyed the room about her. (pp. 147–8)

The role of the urban dilettante is here appropriated, as in Nugent, to suggest an adoption of decadence that seems at once inappro-priate but is also the condition for the elaboration of desire and a suggestion of the instability of identity.

If Irene's experience of cafe society is pleasurable her encounter with Clare suggests the traumas of 'misrecognition'. They encounter each other through the exchange of intensely prolonged glances. Irene has been staring at Clare, she looks again only to find Clare staring back and Irene begins to blush. What we see here is a slowed down version of the shot/reverse shot structure of classical Hollywood cinema, the classic visual cliché 'eyes meet across the room'.[46]

> Very slowly she looked around, and into the eyes of the woman in the green frock at the next table. But, she evidently failed to see that such intense interest as she was showing might be embarrassing, and continued to stare. Her demeanour was that of one who with the utmost singleness of mind and purpose was determined to impress firmly and accurately each of Irene's

features on her memory for all time, nor showed the slightest trace of disconcertment at having been detected in her steady scrutiny. (p. 149)

Clare refuses to look appropriately, but continues to gaze in a manner more readily associated with the male gaze of classical Hollywood cinema, and her lawless looking initiates the motif of the prolonged and portentous look that runs through the novel.[47] The observer Irene becomes the observed, but the content of this look is radically ambivalent as Clare's passing status makes it difficult to decide whether her stare is aggressive or inviting. We also find ourselves in the peculiar situation of looking with peculiar intensity at a subject who in a sense cannot be seen (in her passing state).[48] This confusion is felt by Irene as a threat, and yet is immediately dismissed as such: 'Did that woman, could that woman, somehow know that here before her very eyes on the roof of the Drayton sat a Negro? Absurd! Impossible! White people were so stupid about such things for all that they usually asserted they were able to tell; and by the most ridiculous means, finger-nails, palms of hands' (p. 150). Absurd indeed, since Irene has failed to detect that the person looking at her is also a passing Negro. Identity here is not a matter of ontological distinction, what one can see, but a more difficult epistemological question of what one knows, or thinks one knows. There is no truth hidden behind Clare's 'strange, languorous eyes' (p. 150), instead a defamiliari-sation of vision and identity. In this scene this is activated by troping on the visual clichés of (white) heterosexual romance, racialised and sexualised differently through the indeterminacy of the visual field.

To look for a moment at another scene, one central to Judith Butler's reading of *Passing*, we see a similar focus on the look as we witness Irene and Brian Redfield competing for possession of the spectacle that is Clare Kendry:

> She remembered her own little choked exclamation of admiration, when, on coming downstairs a few minutes later than she had intended, she had rushed into the living room where Brian was waiting and had found Clare there too. Clare, exquisite, golden, fragrant, flaunting, in a stately gown of shining black taffeta, whose long, full skirt lay in graceful folds about her slim golden feet; her glistening hair drawn smoothly back into a small twist at the nape of her neck; her eyes sparkling like dark jewels. (p. 203)

Irene descends from her bedroom to find Clare waiting in her living room with her husband. As Irene finds Clare, Brian seems also to have found her. So, the reader finds Irene and Brian both finding each other finding Clare. Awareness of this is registered on Irene's part only, partly because it is she who controls the narrative and partly because the reader is never given access to Brian's thoughts in the novel, reinforcing the feeling that his presence is always in some way superfluous to the drama which unfolds. Through Irene we have an almost obsessive interest in the body of Clare Kendry, with the visual codes through which she is apprehended, and with how the visual scene is seen and read. Noting the convergence of Irene and Brian looking, Judith Butler asks, 'what is it that they find in her, such that they no longer find each other, but mirror each other's desire as each turns toward Clare?'[49] Her answer to this is, somewhat reductively, the love (that is, lesbian desire) that dare not speak its name. Butler notes that as Irene's eyes light upon Clare her exclamation of admiration catches in her throat. The narrator then goes on to say what Irene apparently never can and for Butler 'this suggests that Larsen's narrator serves the function of exposing more than Irene herself can risk'.[50]

This view of the narrator as quite traditionally omniscient, helpfully informing the reader of the significance of the actions of the rather more limited characters, does not seem to do justice to the structural complexity of the narration. The dynamics of the narrative exhibit shifting relations of power between narrator, character and reader. That Irene is an unreliable narrator has long been noted in criticism of the novel and at certain points the narrator does indeed fill in interpretations that Irene does not supply, or corrects a self-deception that Irene has perpetrated.[51] It is not the case, however, that the narrator consistently tells us the truth of the story despite Irene's protestations to the contrary. At certain points Irene reveals through visual description more than can be said by either herself or the narrator. This is not entirely because this is a story (of lesbian desire) which cannot be spoken at this point historically, though this does have an impact. The evidence of works by Bruce Nugent or Wallace Thurman examined elsewhere in this text should counter this suggestion somewhat, as does the counter-history outlined in Isaac Julien's *Looking For Langston*. Rather, Irene and Clare's story is one which is inextricably linked to an inquiry into questions of representation and difference in the field of vision, something I would identify as a modernist response to the problems of writing and representation for African American women during the Harlem Renaissance. Further, the model of the narrator filling in the words when Irene chokes on them does not explain the failure of both Irene and the narrator to say anything at all when Clare falls to her death at the end of the novel; something one would imagine the narrator would have plenty to say about. For Butler, this textual silence reinforces her reading that lesbian desire must remain unspoken in order to

exert a destabilising force on the trajectories of normative heterosexual and racial identities. As I see it Butler's reading usefully
affirms the dynamic centrality of sexuality to the novel, but it
renders the drama of seeing and reading racial identity invisible
(even as she asserts the interconnectedness of race and sexuality).

The scene quoted above has to be read as, at least in part, an
ironic parody of the melodramatic spectacle of the beautiful woman
taking her watchers' breath away. Further, in terms of the heavily
overdetermined conventions of passing which the novel plays on
and exploits, one expects that nothing will ever quite be as it
seems.[52] In reading this scene it is less important to note what is
'unspoken' than to pay attention to what is seen and flaunted; that
is, the visual spectacle presented. The whole scene is artificial in
the extreme, and the detail with which Clare's clothing, body and
hair are described explicitly recalls the opening scene of *Quicksand*.
The scene is an intensely visual encounter and as the three
characters enter the room, they do not make bodily contact, but
instead initiate visual contact: this is a scene of looks, not bodies,
colliding. What is debated in *Passing* are forms of difference that
cannot be seen, or rather, markers of difference that can only be
seen by viewers who know what they are looking for. The passing
woman, whether that passing is taken to be racial or sexual, poses
an epistemological challenge because she refuses to occupy the
identity designated for her, precisely because she does not have to.

Acknowledging the crucial dependence on a visual economy of
spectacle in this and the earlier scene allows us to understand the
textual dynamics of *Passing*. These scenes are extremely artificial
and appear as visual clichés that parody stereotypes of heterosexual romance. The complex troping on both heterosexual romance
(with strongly cinematic resonances) and modernist preoccupations with urbanity, with semi-anonymous encounters and with
the instability of the visual field, would give us further examples of
inter-cultural modernistic innovation in Larsen's writing. We see
in Larsen's work a fascination with the urban scene, with cultural
discourses on primitivism, fashionably bohemian sexual identities,
new technologies such as cinema, and the expansion of commodity
culture: avoiding total subjection to these structures in an ongoing
engagement with the changing conditions of modernity. In
presenting a contested visual field in her novels Larsen quite self-
consciously exploits a series of conventions that are perhaps more
readily associated with film. I would argue that if one sees the scene
above as something akin to a cinematic encounter then the fact
that Irene's words are choked back recedes in significance, it is
rather a case of 'a look can say a thousand words'.

In an illuminating discussion of early film's representation of
the body, as a response to and compensation for the perceived

technological threat of modernity, Mary Ann Doane makes the following observation:

> Modern urban space presents itself to the subject as a dilemma of reading, of recognition, of identification. In the context of fears about loss of identity, various technologies for stabilising identity – including photography and cinema – are invoked.[53]

Of course, as Doane makes clear, the body which technology and modernity is deemed to threaten is a racially and sexually unspecific one, so the scenario of 'trauma' which Doane is tracing is a white male heterosexual one. Nevertheless, the threat which modern urban space presents to the subject is extremely suggestive in thinking about Larsen's novel since it parallels the problem embodied in the passing woman. I would suggest that a potentially threatening technological modernity is acknowledged in Larsen's narrative. However, instead of threatening to destroy the subject, in the case of the sexually and racially ambiguous woman the modernising city scene represents certain conditions of possibility. It is precisely because the rapidly changing urban scene threatens the stability of the subject that a writer like Larsen can find the space for the exploration of dissident, contingent identities. As Doane points out in her discussion, the stability of the male body is potentially secured during this period with an appeal to the superiority of the male body over the primitive, particularly the racial other. In Freud (as Doane argues in *Femmes Fatales*) there is also a metonymic chain constructed which links infantile sexuality, female sexuality and racial otherness.[54] She goes on to say: 'Similarly, movements in arts in modernism define themselves in terms of a complex and ambivalent relation to the "primitive."'[55] This would give a further explanation of Helga's refusal of primitive authenticity in the night-club scene in *Quicksand* and it affirms that what one should look for in *Passing* is not the *meaning* of Irene and Clare's encounters, but their refusal and circumvention of an authentic, stable identity that would position them as absolutely other. Larsen's novels, in this reading, constitute a racialised response to the impact of technologies of modernity on the body, and to discourses of primitivism which helped to shape modernist aesthetics, in a process which continues inquiry into Black Atlantic modernity.

A Vital, Glowing Thing

This utilisation of visual clichés might well be a useful way to read the problematic ending of *Passing*. Even in positive accounts of the novel the ending has largely been regarded as a failure. Larsen, it is suggested, could not find a satisfactory means of concluding the story so she disposes of the troublesome Clare out of the window. This is read as a disappointing turning away from the issues of race and sexuality that are raised throughout the novel. If, on the other hand, we see the final scene as a logical development of the problematics of difference in the visual field, and the distinction between knowing and seeing difference, then the ending may make more sense.

The novel ends when Clare is discovered by her racist husband, John Bellew, at a party with the Redfields. Bellew, who has persistently denied Clare's racial heritage (whilst perversely reiterating it by calling her 'Nig') reads her as black now because the context dictates that this must be the case. This revelation is denied, however, by Irene's visual perception of the scene, which paradoxically encodes Clare as white most strongly at precisely the moment she is exposed as black. The trauma of this contradiction seems to incapacitate Irene as narrator and results in the brutal erasure of Clare from the narrative; an angst ridden expulsion of the threat her ambivalence embodies: 'What happened next, Irene Redfield never afterwards allowed herself to remember. Never clearly. One moment Clare had been there, a vital, glowing thing, like a flame of red and gold. The next she was gone' (p. 239). Clare is there, a glowing, flaunting image – coded as white in contradiction to the howl of her husband – in a flash she is gone. The narrative cuts to 'the rush of feet down long flights of stairs' (p. 239) then back to Irene who is left alone and frozen to the spot in the room. There is a strong sense that it is the threatening nature of Clare's image that has been erased. As this image is Irene's construction of Clare this affirms her complicity with Clare's death as it secures the priority of the visual field:

> Gone! The soft white face, the bright hair, the disturbing scarlet mouth, the dreaming eyes, the whole torturing loveliness that had been Clare Kendry. The beauty that had torn at Irene's placid life. Gone! The mocking daring, the gallantry of her pose, the ringing bells of her laughter. (p. 239)

The image of Clare persists in spite of Irene's apparent incapacity as narrator, indeed one might say that visual perception entirely structures the narrative at this point, and conditions our perception of the dramatic closing moments of the novel. But at the same time the visual delineation of Clare marks what cannot be seen – her blackness – marking the limits of the 'truth' of vision and reiterating the impossible status of the passing subject. This allows, finally, appreciation of the complexity and motivation for the obsession with looking, how to look, and visual spectacle in the novel. It is the means by which the text negotiates the terrain of racial, sexual and gender identity. *Passing* is the articulation of the conflictual

nature of identity an
power of the image. It
and the conflict betwe
and what it, and othe
a testing of the limits
of these categories an
within the expanding

CHAPTER 4

Women in th

This ch
Harl
B

The City of Refuge

This chapter deals with the short story writing of two lesser-known Harlem Renaissance figures, Angelina Weld Grimké and Marita Bonner. Despite high literary profiles during the 1920s, works by these and many other women of the Renaissance period are now difficult to get hold of and still more difficult to judge as integral to Negro Renaissancism. Gloria T. Hull's important study of Grimké, Alice Dunbar Nelson and Georgia Douglas Johnson, the sole book-length study of Grimké's work, reminds one of the importance of women writers when thinking about the Harlem Renaissance.[1] Likewise, Cheryl Wall's more recent *Women of the Harlem Renaissance* presents a wide-ranging and challenging reading of the literary production by women during the Harlem Renaissance, one which places Grimké and Bonner as part of Harlem history alongside their better-known compatriots Nella Larsen, Jessie Fauset and Zora Neale Hurston.[2] Yet analysis of the fascinating short stories produced by these two women is surprisingly thin even in these recent reconstructionist texts. Marita Bonner has been particularly ill-served by histories of Harlem writing, many of which do not acknowledge her work at all.[3] As we shall see her early stories of the struggles of working-class African American women to come to terms with city life are unique for the period and her later 'Frye Street' stories constitute a city panorama which begs to be read alongside the Rudolph Fisher stories examined earlier, as well as presenting a vital precursor to the writing of Gwendolyn Brooks and Ann Petry which is the focus of Chapter 5.[4]

Grimké and Bonner were seen by contemporary observers as important and influential writers. Grimké's first play *Rachel* (1916) was written for the NAACP and performed by the well-known Krigwa Players, and its publication four years later drew favourable comments from Jessie Fauset as literary editor of *The Crisis* and from Walter White at *The Nation*.[5] Later in the 1920s estimation of her significance as a writer can be seen by the numbers of her poems published in *Opportunity* magazine, in *The New Negro* and Countee Cullen's anthology *Caroling Dusk* (1927).[6] Bonner received prizes during the 1920s in both *The Crisis* and *Opportunity* literary competitions and continued to publish in *Opportunity* throughout the 1930s and into the 1940s; she also produced a number of plays in the late 1920s.[7] Both were also regular attendees at Georgia Douglas Johnson's S Street Salon in Washington, an important meeting place for many Harlem Renaissance writers. Johnson's salon was a focal point for an interconnected group of women writers whose writing has been neglected since the 1920s despite its contemporary success. These women included Grimké and Bonner, Clarissa Scott Delany, Jessie Fauset, Mary Burill and Alice Dunbar Nelson.[8] The salon was also a meeting place for a number of the most famous male writers from the period, including Langston Hughes, Bruce Nugent, Alain Locke, Eric Walrond, Jean Toomer, Countee Cullen and even on occasion W.E.B. Du Bois, as well as a host of white writers and European visitors who came to meet Harlem's rising stars.[9] The informality of these meetings means that our subsequent knowledge of them comes from letters and autobiographical accounts and is inevitably sketchy and speculative, but it is clear that as well as fostering literary exchange this space functioned as a meeting place for writers whose homosexuality was as certain as the closeted nature of it.

What is interesting about this is not so much the potential liaisons fostered at these literary meetings, but that in terms of the subsequent writing of Harlem's histories the pivotal importance of a literary forum run by and, in large part, for women is, outside the pages of recent feminist scholarship, rarely acknowledged. Most notably, the established classics on Harlem by Nathan Huggins, Jervis Anderson and David Levering Lewis substantially minimise the significance of female contributions to the Harlem Renaissance, something which the wealth of material presented in Wall's *Women of the Harlem Renaissance*, particularly on Jessie Fauset's incredibly diverse career, reveals in an almost embarrassing fashion.[10] Recent studies like Hutchinson's *The Harlem Renaissance in Black and White* do surprisingly little to alter these texts' assessment of male centrality and female secondariness to the whole Harlem phenomenon. This is combined with the absence of discussion of the (homo)sexual preferences of many of the leading Harlem writers I observed earlier on. Although Bruce Nugent was the only 'out' writer of the Renaissance, and it is a dubious project at best to extrapolate the significance of sexual preference from the evidence of textual tendencies or from gossip, when one looks at the well-documented relationships between figures such as Countee Cullen and Harold Jackman and Langston Hughes and Alain Locke, or examines the significance of attendance at certain parties, or looks to Bruce Nugent's fairly frank recollections of his and others' sexual exploits (including Wallace Thurman, Langston Hughes, Locke and Cullen) the significance to the writers then of a sexual as well as literary camaraderie is undeniable in its importance.[11] Given the wealth of research undertaken by Harlem's best-known historians one is led to the conclusion that the absence of homosexuality in their studies is less a 1920s phenomenon than it is a problem of their own time and the particular construction of African American history and culture that they operate within and reinforce – something this study works against.

One needs to view the S Street salon as part of the wide-ranging activities fostered by women during and after the 1920s in and importantly outside Harlem. For as Cheryl Wall makes clear, focusing on the activities of women during the Harlem Renaissance years forces one to think outside the geographical boundaries of Harlem to see Washington, Chicago and even Boston and Philadelphia as part of Harlem Renaissancism.[12] These activities would include the literary soirées hosted by A'Leila Walker in Harlem as well as Jessie Fauset's role as literary editor at *The Crisis* in its most influential years.[13] We might also consider Gwendolyn Bennett's modernist-inspired art work that graced the covers of *Opportunity* magazine – alternating with those of the subsequently more famous Aaron Douglas – and her long-running literary gossip column 'The Ebony Flute' in the same magazine, which provided a witty and illuminating commentary on the Renaissance as it happened. Bennett spent time studying painting in Paris where she came into contact with some of the foremost modern painters and writers including Henri Matisse and Ernest Hemingway. Her cosmopolitan modernism is reflected less in her art, which remains largely conventional in tone, than in her gossip column which presents a racy and modern Harlem.[14] The S Street salon and the women who worked and talked there should be regarded as important as those more famous Harlem proselytisers like Alain Locke or Carl Van Vechten.[15] A telling illustration would be the Civic Club dinner discussed earlier, which it is easy to forget was in celebration of the publication of Jessie Fauset's *There Is Confusion* and was organised in part by the members of the S Street group.

This critical exclusion of Grimké and Marita Bonner, along with many other women writers from the Harlem Renaissance period (some of whom are collected in Marcy Knopf's useful collection *The Sleeper Wakes*) would perhaps be reason enough to analyse their work here but this is not my primary motivation.[16] Grimké and Bonner provide an alternative vision to the one commonly associated with women of the Harlem Renaissance even in the work of feminist scholars like Gloria Hull or Cheryl Wall. Far from being genteel – a common charge against Harlem's female authors – these writers present a city scene characterised by bitterness, misery and lack of opportunity for women even as they hold on to the city as *the* place for the exploration of the lives and experiences of African Americans. Examining Grimké's and Bonner's writings – as early and late contributors to Harlem Renaissancism – allows us to see a much more complex tradition of female social protest writing, which would run from Grimké's early 1920s propagandist efforts about the continued ramifications of slavery and white supremacy for African American women, through to the 1940s and 1950s writings of Ann Petry and Gwendolyn Brooks on the subtle racial and gender implications of US urbanism and the development of consumer culture. This tradition of female social protest, working through various genres and dealing with a wide range of subjects, stands outside modes of racial social protest associated with writers such as Richard Wright, and in its persistent attention to the gendered dynamics of African American urbanism these works call us to re-examine many of our preconceptions about the contribution of women artists to African American urban literature and culture. Bonner and Grimké examine the nature of racial and sexual identity for African American women in the early twentieth-century city, foregrounding gendered issues of reproduction, inter-racial relationships and family, which are configured through the violent collision of black and white communities in the field of sexuality.

'The Closing Door'

The work of African American playwright, poet and prose writer Angelina Weld Grimké is little known and rarely studied. Despite her success during the years of the Harlem Renaissance and her illustrious family background she only infrequently crops up in discussions of the period. Grimké came from a famous family of anti-slavery and anti-lynching campaigners. Her father Archibald Grimké was a well-known journalist, lawyer and campaigner for African American rights and her great-aunt Angelina Grimké Weld (for whom she was named) was a well-known white abolitionist-feminist. Angelina Weld and her sister publicly declared that Archibald was their brother's illegitimate child, a highly unusual and politically charged act in their period.[17] In recent years her poetry has enjoyed something of a resurgence, particularly as it receives attention from black feminist critics like Gloria T. Hull, but her prose work is still overlooked. Her short story 'The Closing Door' (1919) focuses explicitly on the difficulty for African American women in reconciling the changing conditions of urban life with the memory of slavery and the South.[18] This is associated in Grimké's work with problems around reproduction and maternity, when that reproduction is conflated with racial and sexual violence, during and after slavery.[19] The story recounts a disturbing narrative of the impact of racial violence, in the form of lynching, on a woman and her family living in the North.

'The Closing Door' was published in 1919 in *The Birth Control Review*, a rather odd place of publication given the magazine's distinctly eugenicist editorial policy, but which nicely illustrates my point about the importance of eugenic ideas to discussions of race and reproduction.[20] The story concerns the fate of Agnes Milton and her husband Jim, and is narrated by their ward Lucy. Lucy lives with them after being passed from relative to relative when her mother returns to domestic service, her father having died from taking, as Lucy puts it, 'one cup too many' (p. 124). Agnes, a very distant relative, takes Lucy in and becomes a surrogate mother to her. From the start the role of the mother is problematised by the impact of material conditions, but in the first few pages the tiny flat into which Agnes welcomes Lucy is constructed as idyll and retreat from the exigencies of life. After many years of trying Agnes becomes pregnant, which introduces an intimation of terror as she begins to fear that it might be possible to be '*too* happy' (p. 130) and indeed her happiness is destroyed when her adored brother is lynched. She goes on to have a baby boy, but concludes that God is not merciful, since he continues to allow African American boys to be born for the 'sport' of white racists, and she murders her long-wished-for child.

The lynching changes the shape of the story remarkably, shifting it from sentimental romance to racial propaganda. These two forms are held in an uneasy compromise through the remainder of the story, as the narrative asserts that lynching is both an individual crisis and an ideological disciplining of the race. The story is riven by the tension between attempting to teach a lesson as a piece of propaganda and the contrary desire to show the profound psychic disintegration of a woman in the face of a violent and fundamentally irrational system of racial oppression. This is also a tension between wishing to document the pernicious effect of slavery on the institutional role of the mother for African American woman, and the contrary demands of the developing discourse of racial uplift which requires the African American woman to be mother to the (progressively modernising) race in Harlem and other Northern cities. At the beginning of the story the urban locale has strong resonances with the 'City of Refuge' myth examined in previous chapters, as a space of escape from Southern violence and the memory of slavery. The refuge is notably reconfigured in gendered terms as a protected domestic and clearly feminine space: Jim returns from the world of work to a highly idealised interior idyll. Attention to the micro-politics of domestic space and its relation to public space and to public discourse on race and gender is one of the more notable features in the women's writing examined in this book, revealing a complex dialogue on the conditions of city life for African American women – as Grimké's story clearly shows. As Agnes's pregnancy progresses this domestic refuge is progressively exposed as a romantic dream that cannot be maintained in the face of white violence against African American peoples, suggesting the instability of the Northern 'refuge' Grimké initially constructs.

When Agnes's older brother Joe comes to visit he informs Lucy and Jim that her brother Bob was lynched after getting into a fight with a white man:

> 'An orderly mob, in an orderly manner, on a Sunday morning – I am quoting the newspapers – broke into the jail, took him out, slung him up to the limb of a tree, riddled his body with bullets, saturated it with coal oil, lighted a fire underneath him, gouged out his eyes with red hot irons, burnt him to a crisp and then sold souvenirs of him, ears, fingers, toes. His teeth brought five dollars each.' He ceased for a moment.
>
> 'He is still hanging on that tree. We are not allowed to have even what is left.' (p. 139)

The recounting of the lynching takes the form of what Grimké calls in a letter 'the teaching of a lesson', hence the passage is deliberately horrific and unflinching in its detail.[21] The horror is focused on the oxymoron 'orderly mobs' and the almost unbearable sense that this was an organised spectacle. The reproduction of this spectacle in the text presents the reader with the inhumanity of the practice of lynching. As David Hedrich Hirsch makes clear, Grimké bitterly recognises that lynching is not only violence enacted against an individual body, but a lesson to the Negro about his place in the world.[22] Grimké's extremely 'orderly' re-presentation of this lesson in 'The Closing Door' effects the reversal of the lesson described above in order to present the reader with the violent dis-order of lynching. Agnes, who was to be protected from this lesson because of her 'condition', overhears Joe's words and reacts with 'a little choking, strangling sound' (p. 139), the articulation of a horror which is beyond discursive representation. This results in Agnes's withdrawal into silence, figured by her retreat behind the 'imperceptibly closing, slowly closing, opposite door' (p. 141) that gives the piece its title. But if Agnes can find no words to express her pain, she does commit an act that speaks of the violence and horror. After refusing absolutely to mother her child, Agnes eventually murders her baby in its sleep rather than allow it to grow up in a society where she imagines herself to be an instrument, literally a reproductive machine, for producing victims for the racist 'sport' of lynching:

> Yes! – Yes! – I! – I! – An instrument of reproduction! – another of the many! a colored woman – doomed! cursed! – put here! – willing or unwilling! For what? – to bring children here – men children – for the sport – the lust – of possible orderly mobs – who go about things – in an orderly manner – on Sunday mornings! (p. 140)

Agnes's speech draws its language from contemporary debates around eugenics with its (frequently racist) suggestions of 'managing' reproductive processes, promulgated amongst other places in the pages of *The Birth Control Review*. This links also to the discourses of racial responsibility and uplift discussed earlier. Agnes's words can be read as a bitter commentary on (and potential abdication of) the responsibilities for the race which African American women are required, ideologically, to carry at this particular historical conjuncture.

Grimké was in part motivated to write this lesson by an actual incident in Georgia of which she was informed. In a letter to the editors of *Atlantic Monthly* she wrote:

> I am sending enclosed a story. It is not a pleasant one but is based on fact. Several years ago, in Georgia, a colored woman quite naturally it would seem became wrought up because her husband had been lynched. She threatened to bring some of the leaders to justice. The mob made up of 'chivalrous' and brave white men determined to teach her a lesson. She was dragged out of town to a desolate part of the woods and the lesson began. First she was strung up by her feet to the limbs of a tree ... and then she was set afire. While the woman shrieked and writhed in agony, one man ... ripped her abdomen wide open. Her unborn child fell to the ground at her feet. It emitted one or two little cries but was soon silenced by brutal heels that crushed out its head. Death came at last to the poor woman. The lesson ended.[23]

Grimké's particular angle on this lesson is the connection she makes between lynching, as a form of sexualised racial violence, and reproduction, shown here through the murder of the child the lynched woman was carrying. For Agnes in 'The Closing Door' God has revealed himself to be without mercy and the idealised domestic space of her Northern home is shown as no more than a naive and child-like fantasy. In the context of Agnes's radically changed world view her act of murder, which is a refusal to reproduce another child of her race, seems a logical response to a manifestly unjust, illogical system which perpetrates horrifying acts of racial violence. At the same time her act is outrageous in its specifically gendered dimensions: it is an outrage because a mother murders. Agnes does not make any attempt to exact vengeance from the white mob that committed the lynching; instead she murders that which is closest and most precious to her. One is prompted to ask why it is that Grimké chooses to direct her heroine's violence against the body of her child, rather than against the 'vengeful' white society which has committed this atrocity?

I would suggest that the answer lies in Grimké's attempt to grasp the difficulties of protesting against lynching at her particular historical juncture. These difficulties hinge on detailing the continuing legacy of slavery for the modern urban situation, and the ways in which this perpetuates sexualised forms of racial violence even in the new city context. Motherhood, then, has a very particular and highly problematic involvement in the system of slavery and its post-emancipation repercussions. Slavery, as Valerie Smith points out, pathologises sexuality and reproduction for the African American woman, through the practices of inter-racial rape, the forcible removal of children and the complicated history of miscegenation.[24] Grimké's story addresses the consequences of ascribing value to the bodies of female slaves – precisely as commodities who (re)produced commodities in the form of more slaves – and relates this to the situation of post-emancipation African American women. Her concentration on the possibilities of silence as a refusal or protest about lynching is an attempt to restage the confrontation between those who would speak (the dominant) and those who are spoken for or silenced.[25] Silence is a refusal to make the spectacle of lynching fully meaningful, as part of a critique of the systems of meaning and rationality which engender such acts.

The Silent Story

The brutal exigencies of motherhood and the issue of inter-racial relationships are taken up in a rather different way in a 1927 short story by Marita Bonner, entitled 'One Boy's Story'.[26] In this story the refusal of a white father either to acknowledge his mixed-race child or relinquish his claim to paternity results in his murder by his son and the conclusion, 'a paradigm of literary silencing' as Joyce Flynn observes, makes it a useful foil to Grimké's narrative. The story is told in the first person by the young son, Donald, and is a reworking of the Oedipus legend, the biblical story of David and Goliath, and Greek myths of Orestes and the Furies. Bonner's provocative redrawing of these foundational Western myths racialises Freud's interpretation of the Oedipus legend, suggesting the inter-relation of racial and sexual identity particularly in the context of coercive inter-racial sex. Donald is the son of a hard-working black woman Louise Gage, who has had a baby by a rich white man, Dr Swyburne. Donald reads the legends of Oedipus, Orestes and David and understands his life in terms of these universalist narratives, an ironic indictment of their exclusion of race which precipitates the ending of the story. When his mother determines that she will break free from the influence of her son's white father, Donald follows her and plays David to his father's Goliath, unaware of course that he is also playing out the role of Oedipus in murdering his own father. The finale of the Oedipus legend is reprised as his mother gathers him to her breast and his tongue is pierced by her breast-pin rendering him mute.

The stump of his tongue becomes the marker of the silence surrounding the racial inequalities and sexual exploitativeness of inter-racial sex: a fascinating reversal of the priority given to speech and vision in the Oedipus story. Donald is a visible reminder of his true parentage in terms of his light skin, yet as black he simply cannot be seen to be the son of the affluent white patriarch, something which Bonner plays on when she has him kill a man who (in his own racial terms) cannot be his father. She then has Donald silenced (rather than blinded) as an indictment of the silence about a history of racial intermixture that is visibly embodied in the light-skinned person, a contradiction Bonner returns to repeatedly throughout her short stories and which is a crucial element in understanding the cultural potency of stories of inter-racial sex:

> So I got a black stump in my mouth. It's shaped like a forked whip.
> Some days I pretend I am Orestes with the Furies' whip in my mouth for killing a man.
> Some days I pretend I am Oedipus and that I cut it out for killing my own father.
> That's what makes me sick all over sometimes.
> I killed my own father. But I didn't know it was my father. I was freeing Ma ...
> ... I am bearing my Furies and my clipped tongue like a Swyburne and a Gage – 'cause I am both of them. (p. 106)

The curious weaving together of myth with the childish naiveté of the first-person narrative suggests that Bonner believes this to be a racial primal scene – or at least a truth at the silent heart of American national identity. What it most poignantly speaks to are the racialised structures organising reproduction and gender roles for African American women and, as we see in the jubilant response of Donald's mother to his being rendered mute, the cultural reluctance to speak openly about this legacy of white supremacy.

We could see these strategic uses of silence as of a piece with the silent protest marches against lynching on the streets of Harlem, the most famous of which took place in 1917.[27] Agnes withdraws into silence, closing the door always behind her, and her silences have to be appropriated and represented by Lucy as narrator, but represented in their incompleteness. David Hirsch sees the murder as an attempt to 'effect closure upon a generationally repetitive history of birth and lynching which is the white-written narrative of her people'. He judges that Lucy's repossession of the words of Agnes's story refuses the closure that Agnes tries to accomplish.[28] Bonner's story fills out the less immediately violent, but nonetheless tragic, consequences of the racially inflected history of reproduction in post-slavery America. In 'The Closing Door' we see bitter critique as Grimké's 'lesson' must be re-told because the City of Refuge myth disguises the extent to which brutal violence against African Americans continues, a potent issue for the Northern Negro communities as the protest marches in 1917 and after demonstrate. The text also insists on the implication of the North in Southern racist violence: '"Agnes! Your child will be born in the North. He need never go South." ... "The North permits it too," she cried, "The North is silent as well as the South"' (p. 140). To be sure, this 'silent' social critique is a vital component of a story written in 1919, a year infamous for its 'Red Summer' of lynching violence, riots and for the concerted protest on the part of black activists and intellectuals against the practice. Yet to focus exclusively on this loses sight of the mother, the *agent* in the story, and the act of murder she commits. Most problematic in Grimké's (and Bonner's) story is the relationship of the mother (and the responsibilities that go with this) to the race.

The figuring of silence has strong resonances with Paul Gilroy's comments in *The Black Atlantic* about forms of racial terror that surpass understanding, producing actions which appear to supersede 'rational, moral calculation' (p. 66) as he suggests occurs in the story of Margaret Garner's infanticide. He argues that artistic reproductions of these encounters (for example Toni Morrison's *Beloved*) contribute to 'the aporetic status of post-emancipation black art' (p. 218). It is possible to read Grimké's and Bonner's stories as just such aporetic statements if one considers the mode of rational, moral calculation that informs each mother's actions as one which emphasises the association of reproduction and capital accumulation so central to the Margaret Garner story. Furthermore, the stories suggest that this association is one that has ramifications that continue from the slave era into and beyond the 1920s. Garner's act can be read as a specific crime against property (unlike Frederic Douglass's encounter with his master which Gilroy compares to Garner's story), and less a refusal of assent to the authority of the master – she does not 'turn toward death' (p. 63) herself – than a strike against the (capitalist) system of property accumulation which supports the master's position: something which is reprised in a different cultural context in 'The Closing Door'. If Garner's action is a refusal to offer the body of her daughter to a system that will consolidate and literally reproduce slavery, then Agnes's assertion that she is an 'instrument' should be read in a similar light. What both acts suggest is an agonised refusal of the maternal role when the society into which the child is born refuses to accord full citizenship to that child. This is as true for Agnes's Northern post-emancipation situation, though with obviously different dimensions, as it is for Garner's position as a slave in the South.

If one takes into account the gendered dimensions of the murders central to Garner's, Grimké's and Bonner's stories then the notion of death as a form of agency formulated by Gilroy comes to seem less celebratory.[29] In these female accounts the turn toward death is an ambivalent, agonistic act. In the sense that Garner's act is a strike against the system of property accumulation that underpins slavery, then her action may be seen as an assertion of agency. What it also speaks of is a suggestion of the inappropriateness of the idea of maternity for female slaves, when the injunction to mother is bound up with the all-too-frequent possibility of forced, coercive motherhood. In Grimké's story Agnes refuses to mother, because of the threat of lynching, and thus directly refuses twentieth-century narratives of maternity as racial responsibility, asserting instead she has the responsibility to arrest generational progression. This is understood in the story in terms of the histories of slavery and racial violence, which Grimké presents as continuing after the experience of slavery and far beyond the South. Though Bonner's story seems less immediately concerned with the failure of motherhood, the shadow of miscegenation fatally taints the relationship between race, reproduction and mothering – as powerfully in the 1920s as it did during slavery.

Grimké's and Bonner's short stories invite a fresh interpretation of Morrison's famous phrase from *Beloved*, used by Gilroy to conclude his book: 'this is not a story to pass on'. While Garner's, Grimké's and Bonner's narratives pose in related ways the problem of historical memory for the African American woman, this is not fully resolved through the notion (Morrison's) that this is bound up 'with the impossible desire to forget the unforgettable'.[30] The stories re-present the memory of slavery and racial violence in chilling ways and force consideration of issues of responsibility and complicity (with that history) that are not easy to resolve. However, central to each story is a refusal to pass the story on in that they murder (or otherwise silence) the next generation to which that story would be passed. This constitutes an assertion of will that is a brutal erasure of the future (embodied in the child) which would carry that story forwards. Grimké and Bonner each expose the North's complicity with legacy of slavery; they also suggest the fragile and illusory nature of the city as refuge narrative. One might now reconceive this as what Gilroy calls a 'discourse on the nature of freedom itself' (p. 68), a complex commentary on the narratives of modernity, rationality and progress that the spectacle of lynching and the fact of miscegenation brutally tears apart, a situation Grimké and Bonner assert as an agonised fact of life for African American women in the post-emancipation North.

'On Being Young – A Woman – and Colored'

Commencing writing eight years after Grimké during the headiest moments of the Harlem Renaissance, and continuing through the Great Depression years until 1941, Marita Bonner's work serves as a discomforting reminder of the lives of those ordinary Negroes who, Langston Hughes asserted in retrospect: 'Never heard of the New Negro, and if they had he hadn't changed their wages any.'[31] More than this she provides the fullest engagement with the new conditions of city life by any African American woman writer before Petry, and perhaps the only Renaissance example of writing about urban working-class women. Her writing style differs remarkably from Grimké, as she produces a fractured modernist style in order to do justice to the city scenes and peoples she takes as her subject. Indeed, she characterised herself as a modernist writer and develops in her Frye Street cycle an unusual combination of stream-of-consciousness perspectives, brutal socio-logical detailing and stern allegorical patterning. Her Frye Street stories present a series of jeremiads on the impact of poverty, low educational achievement, bad parenting, female-headed households, drugs and violence on an inner-city scene which holds none of the promise of Harlem we saw in previous chapters, despite remaining the aspirational locus for migrants from the South as well as for immigrant populations. Furthermore, in Bonner's Frye Street universe the black middle classes exacerbate the cycle of misery for the underclass as they are portrayed as viciously snobbish and 'color-struck': upholders of a bankrupt moral authority rather than an uplifting cultural vanguard.

Bonner's writing first came to notice with a 1925 essay 'On Being Young – A Woman – and Colored', one of the bitterest attacks on the prevailing sexism as well as racism of the times and a spirited assault on the gendered assumptions of many of her New Negro compatriots.[32] The piece is characteristic of Bonner's early works, being framed as a personal meditation and employing the second person pronoun 'You' to describe both a personal complaint and a generalised condition of African American femininity:

> For you know that – being a woman – you cannot twice a month or twice a year, for that matter, break away to see or hear anything in a city that is supposed to see and hear too much. That's being a woman. A woman of any color. (p. 5)

The piece presents Bonner as a member of the 'talented tenth' even as she points out the contradictory dimensions of 'race pride'. More critically than any of her New Negro contemporaries Bonner demonstrates the anomalies of the logic of uplift: that the education and refinement deemed requisite for the New Negro are precisely the qualities likely to alienate them from the masses whose lot they are supposed to improve: 'There are all the earmarks of a group within a group. Cut off all around from ingress from or egress to other groups. A sameness of type. The smug self-satisfaction of an inner measurement' (p. 4). The powerful centre of her argument is her elaboration of the conflicting demands of femininity and racial identity as it is formulated within and without the African American community. As she points out, educated to be a race leader because of her class background she is simultaneously prevented from participation in the developing city life around her because of the gendered mores of her well-to-do community on the one hand and the racist assumptions of white culture on the other. Analysis of the vicious cruelty and class snobbishness of elite African Americans is the focus of a number of Bonner's stories including the horrific 'On the Altar' (1937–40, unpublished), where a colour-conscious matriarch arranges for the annulment of her granddaughter's marriage to a darker-skinned classmate and then has a doctor poison the child her granddaughter is carrying for fear it may be born dark. The violence of class hierarchies is also the focus of 'Black Fronts' (*Opportunity*, 1938), 'Hate Is Nothing' (*Opportunity*, 1938) and 'Stones For Bread' (1940, unpublished). Her critique of the restrictive racism of white attitudes toward African Americans in stories such as 'Drab Rambles' (*The Crisis*, 1927) and more fully in 'Nothing New' (*The Crisis*, 1926) is, as we shall see in a moment, just as scathing. In a uniquely perceptive way she cuts to the quick of the pressures restricting African American women's possibilities, and in her detailing of impossible contradictions of racial and gender discourses of the period she manages quite remarkably to hollow out some space within the genteel or primitive alternatives which typically demarcate African American women's choices:

Why do they see a colored woman only as a gross collection of desires, all uncontrolled, reaching out for their Apollos and the Quasimodos with avid indiscrimination?

Why unless you talk in staccato squawks – brittle as seashells – unless you 'champ' gum – unless you cover two yards square when you laugh – unless your taste runs to violent colors – impossible perfumes and more impossible clothes – are you a feminine Caliban craving to pass for Ariel? (p. 5)

In refusing a primitive authenticity and also insisting that gentility must be more than hollow white impersonation, Bonner catches perfectly the double-bind of the race woman, who is both embodiment of the race and its transcendence.

This focus on the restriction of choices for women is something that preoccupied Bonner throughout her writing life in stories such as 'Drab Rambles', 'The Whipping' (*Opportunity*, 1939) and 'Black Fronts', which all deal with the impossible limitations imposed upon the protagonists by a city prejudiced against them in social and economic terms for being black and for being female. This theme finds its fullest treatment in Bonner's last published story 'One True Love' (*Opportunity*, 1941).[33] This presents the story of Nora, 'just a butter-colored maid with the hair on the "riney" side' (p. 219), who determines to be a lawyer after encountering a female attorney at her white employers' home. Nora eventually dies from overwork as she attempts to put herself through law school and work as a domestic, but Bonner manages to present effectively a sense of Nora's ambition and desires – 'the sense of wonder in her' (p. 224) – as well as the larger structures of institutionalised racism that effectively proscribe her dreams. It is a combination of aspiration and limitation that we will see again in Ann Petry's *The Street*.

The acuity of Bonner's analysis of the limitations of gender roles, the class-based snobbery that organises elite African American communities hierarchically: 'Those at the bottom crushed into a sort of stupid apathy by the weight of those on top' (p. 4), and the boldness of her critique of the potential narrowness of the notion of uplift by example make her essay one of the most significant female contributions to what Henry Louis Gates calls the debate over the 'trope of the New Negro'.[34] In fact, her intuitive understanding of the problematic consequences of representation as 'the best of all of us' rather than 'the most typical of all of us' prefigures Richard Wright's rejection of his predecessors on just these grounds, whilst at the same time managing to catch the complex counter-energies structuring the New Negro philosophy.[35] Bonner renders more complexly than Wright the tension between black working-class authenticity and black middle-class complicity with

white culture, partly through her analysis of gender but also
through her understanding of the 'talented tenth' as part of a black
community which ought to be appreciated in its diversity rather
than as an undifferentiated black essence. This exploration of what
actually constitutes black solidarity apart from 'the race' – an essentialism Bonner works against throughout her stories – is the most
characteristic feature of her work and one which draws her toward
analysis of the racial organisation of urban space, and in her Frye
Street cycle to embrace a deep sociological pessimism about the
future of black communities in the American city. Given the
complexity of this early piece and her continued attempts to tease
out the meanings of urban life for African American women (and
to a lesser degree men and boys) it is all the more disheartening to
know that contemporary awareness of Bonner is largely limited to
this one short essay: a situation which leads her to be seen solely
as a recorder of black middle-class female experience – when this
is least characteristic of her subject matter – and as a writer likely
to be of interest only to feminist scholars of African American
literature and culture, as if these issues have no bearing on debates
about African American writing as a whole.

Frye Street: All the World is There

Far from being of marginal interest, I would suggest that Bonner's
work is of crucial importance to the study of African American
literature, particularly as one moves away from the heady years of
the Harlem Renaissance and through the Depression period when,
as many observers have commented, the Negro was no longer in
vogue.[36] It is during these years that the majority of Bonner's Frye
Street stories are written. Consisting of some fifteen stories and
reflecting in part Bonner's own life in the urban centres of
Washington and then Chicago the stories as a group go far beyond
autobiographical experience. Frye Street is the most fully realised
expression of underclass life by any African American woman
writer and one of the most ethnically diverse by a non-white writer
in her period:

> Now, walking along Frye Street, you sniff first the rusty tangy
> odor that comes from a river too near a city; walk aside so that
> Jewish babies will not trip you up; you pause to flatten your nose
> against discreet windows of Chinese merchants; marvel at the
> beauty and tragic old age in the faces of the young Italian
> women; puzzle whether the muscular blond people are Swedes
> or Danes or both; pronounce odd consonant names in Greek
> characters on shops; wonder whether Russians are Jews, or Jews,
> Russians – and finally you wonder how the Negroes have

managed to look like all men of every other race and then have
something left over for their own distinctive black-browns.
There is only one Frye Street. It runs from the river to Grand
Avenue where the El is. All the World is there.

('A Possible Triad on Black Notes', p. 102)

This story begins, as do many of the Frye Street portraits, with
the elaboration of a fictional multi-ethnic universe that clearly
references an actual city – Chicago – in terms of its location and
its migrant and immigrant populations, but at the same time strives
toward representation of a generalised racial space through an
unflinching depiction of the bleak life of the ghetto. In fact, Bonner
is one of the first African American writers to use the term ghetto
as an appellation for black urban space and she reminds one of the
Jewish derivation of the term:

Not a Ghetto placid like the Strasse that flows, outwardly
unperturbed and calm in a stream of religious belief, but a
peculiar group. Cut off, flung together, shoved aside in a bundle
because of color and with no more in common.
Unless color is, after all, the real bond.

('On Being Young', p. 4)

At the same time she displays a sense of the range of immigrant
communities – Jewish, German, Italian, Russian, Greek,
Scandinavian, Chinese, Afro-Caribbean as well as city-born African
Americans and huge numbers of Southern migrants – who make
up the ghetto citizens. The interaction between these different
groups, in terms of conflict and correspondence, forms a primary
dynamic of the Frye Street stories and is reflected in her concern
with the differential fates of the white ethnic and non-white
communities, and in her extremely pessimistic predictions for the
future of racial interaction, particularly in the field of sexual
relations.

If Grimké's 'The Closing Door' demonstrates that the
experience of black city life is complicated by the legacy of slavery
and its impact on women's roles as mothers, then Bonner's analysis
of the sexual and gendered dimensions of urban black life goes
much further. Her writing stands as direct refutation of the
optimistic predictions of the future of racial interaction in the cities
contained in *The Negro in Chicago* which had such an important
impact on the urban attitudes of the New Negro writing discussed
in earlier chapters. The expansion of black urban communities
and the diversity of their racial, ethnic and class make-up are
presented in Rudolph Fisher's work as a critical cosmopolitanism.
In Bonner, the racialised city is the site of conflict between and

within the races and the diversity of ethnic and racial groups merely adds to the larger problems of structural racism and economic disenfranchisement. As we shall see, this attitude is apparent from Bonner's earliest work but becomes in her later material a fully articulated belief that relationships between the races will not move past the stage of conflict unless there is a monumental shift in the social organisation of the cities which are, for Bonner, the primary location of African American life. To quote from her last unpublished Chicago story, 'Light in Dark Places' (1941):

> Too many young people: too few houses: too many things to long for and too little money to spend freely: too many women: too few men: too many men weak enough to make profit of the fact they happen to be men: too few women with something in them to make them strong enough to walk over weak men: too much liquor: too many dives: too much street life: too few lovely homes: life from the start – too many people – too few houses. (p. 282)

That this relentlessly negative analysis of urban life should take Chicago as its primary inspiration is testament to the unfulfilled nature of the bright city futures promised in the Chicago Commission's report, and Bonner's writing is a bleak commentary on the works of Robert Park and his associates. Nonetheless, it would be too simplistic to discard the vision of the 'City as Refuge' that was so central to the writers discussed earlier. For despite the nihilism of much of the Frye Street cycle it is still the city, in its awfulness and in its glamour, which is the site and source of African American life and culture in the decades after the Renaissance. There are a number of stories which deal with the South in terms which suggest reasons why so many African Americans migrated to the Northern urban centres; in particular 'The Whipping' (1939) and 'Patch Quilt' (1940) outline dreadful conditions, particularly for women, in the Southern towns. 'One Boy's Story', discussed above, points to one reason for Bonner's negative portrayal of the South; that it may permit inter-racial contact where black women are at the mercy of white sexual advances – a recurrent theme and fear in Bonner's work. In the end it is the multi-ethnic urban world which joins the river to the city that remains her subject to the end of her writing life.

'Nothing New'

Two early stories, 'Nothing New' and 'Drab Rambles', published in *The Crisis* in November 1926 and 1927, neatly illustrate the departure her fiction makes from the dominant 1920s creed of aspiration and uplift. The stories give a different model than the earlier example of *Fire!!* magazine of how aesthetic innovation goes hand-in-hand with the attempt to represent the conditions of black urban life. 'Drab Rambles' in particular employs a multiple perspective prefaced with an allegorical interpretation of a generalised condition of blackness – a technique used across a number of Bonner's stories – to produce a fractured and profoundly nihilistic literary style. This emphasises the extent to which Bonner's writing stands at odds with that of her better-known contemporaries; especially those writers like Fauset, for whom gentility and restraint as a formal principle, as well as at the level of content, were such important aesthetic criteria. In terms of her working-class characters the writer with whom Bonner shares greatest similarity is Zora Neale Hurston. In fact, one could see Bonner as an urban Hurston. The crucial difference between them is that there is no trace in Bonner's writing of the romanticisation of 'the folk' that is such a key element in Hurston's work. What she shares with the other women writers discussed in this text is an insistence on the implication of sexual politics in the racial politics and social organisation of the black urban centres.

'Nothing New', published in one of the premier New Negro magazines at the height of promotion of Harlem and Harlem writing, sounds a dissonant note in its presentation of the invisibly marked limits to inter-racial contact within a racially and ethnically diverse urban scene. The story is the earliest of Bonner's Frye Street narratives and examines the lives of Reuben and Bessie Jackson, migrants from Georgia, and focusing principally on their son, Denny. The story appears at the outset to position itself as a tale of migrant aspirations for their new city home. Reuben and Bessie see good luck where others see bad, affirm the virtue of hard work and ultimately see their son go to an integrated art school. Furthermore, the framing preface to the story holds out the possibility of contact and cooperation, rather than contact and conflict, within the migrant quarter of this fictional Chicago. In a metaphor which orchestrates the story as well as marking its unspoken relation to the events that sparked off the 1919 Chicago riots (as we shall see in a moment) Bonner imagines this urban space as a brook where diverse waters muddy together, pool and clear and finally move on:

> You have been down on Frye Street. You know how it runs from Grand Avenue and the L to a river; from freckle-faced tow heads to yellow Orientals; from broad Italy to broad Georgia, from hooked nose to square black noses. How it lisps in French, how it babbles in Italian, how it gurgles in German, how it drawls and crawls through the Black Belt dialects. Frye Street flows

nicely together. It is like muddy water. Like muddy water in a brook. (p. 69)

The story affirms difference as the key marker of the social organisation of urban space and the muddy waters of Frye Street may gesture towards a utopian understanding of underclass urban life. It is a utopian element ultimately undermined: the story concluding with affirmation of the fluidity of ethnic identity but insistence on the immutability of racial boundaries. The division between ethnicity (particularly white ethnicity) and race – a feature across Bonner's writing – interestingly prefigures contemporary theoretical debates about the distinction between race and ethnicity. The stress on racial containment in Bonner's stories and the repeated focus on the perils of inter-racial relationships, particularly sexual ones, as well as Bonner's observation of ethnic progress and racial impoverishment, suggest some problems with seeing ethnicity and race as self-authored identity formations that share a common process of cultural construction. In many ways Bonner refutes the crux of the argument put forward by scholars like Werner Sollors.[37] His contention that that one should see both ethnicity and race as essentially similar discursive constructions, formed through cultural practice and historically contingent, is denied in Bonner's Frye Street world. Although she asserts shared cultural definitions of race and ethnicity (through the practices of everyday life) she also notes the differential trajectories for those defined racially and those labelled as ethnics. In the world that her protagonists inhabit, race is always associated with blood – with absolute difference – as opposed to the cultural definitions of ethnic identity; something which is then used to justify racial containment and ethnic progress.

In 'Nothing New' the absolute separateness of black and white communities, despite their ethnic variousness, founds a structure of narrative repetition whereby Denny discovers, first as a child and then as an adult, the violently policed lines of conflict between races. In the first incident Denny is at a picnic playing with his Frye Street companions and the hillsides and fields present the fantasy of freedom of movement despite racial and ethnic difference and division, 'mixed as usual ...Young Frye Street could soar through all twelve heavens of enjoyment' (pp. 70–1). As Denny pauses to collect a flower for a little girl he crosses an invisible line which divides up this apparently free play space: 'This is a white picnic over here! Stay away from our side' (p. 71). As fighting breaks out childish rivalry is amplified into a mirror for the wider social and economic structures which divide black from white, as the battle is fought not for the thing Denny wants (a milkweed for a little girl) but over the racialised dimensions of urban space. It is likely, as Joyce Flynn observes, that this episode is inspired in part by the famous event that triggered the Chicago race riots seven years previously.[38] Eugene Williams was drowned after swimming out from the unofficially black Twenty-Seventh Street beach and being stoned when he tried to swim in at the unofficially white Twenty-Ninth Street beach. The forcefulness of Bonner's story comes in part from its echoing of this historical incident but also because of the horror with which we observe children enforcing systems of racial containment ordinarily deemed to be the provenance of the adult world.

The 'Nothing New' of the title underlines the inevitably tragic repetition of this scenario as Denny moves into adulthood. Bonner's sense of the inevitability of racial conflict is based on her understanding of the psychological dimensions of geographical containment. Denny does not know what precisely is at issue in his conflict with the white children, but already his sense of exclusion is psychic as well as physical and is enough to impel him violently to refuse to stay on his side. This psychological dimension echoes Bonner's usage of the Oedipus legend in 'One Boy's Story' analysed earlier. The structural inevitability she draws from the Oedipus myth is stronger in that story, but both develop a mode of repetition that in psychoanalytic terms registers the psychic implications of a racist social order. This is a feature of a number of Bonner's stories, mapping a psychogeography of racial containment. In a move which is also typical of Bonner's concern, when the childhood incident is replayed in Denny's adult life it is a battle over sexual as well as spatial relations, emphasising the intimate experience of larger (racialised) social structures.

Denny goes to an art school, against his father's wishes and against the (unsolicited) advice of the ethnic opinions of Frye Street, whom Bonner stereotypes as she presents their preconceptions of appropriate African American aspirations: '"He should earn money! Money!" protested one portion of Frye Street through its hooked noses. "Let him marry a wife," chuckled the Italians' (p. 73). Despite the progressive aspirations of the integrated school Denny becomes embroiled in a battle over territory, this time marked on the body of a woman, and this culminates in a battle that has fatal consequences. When Denny and Pauline Hammond, a white girl, fall in love an adult version of the kid Denny battled with over a flower comes to rescue Pauline from Denny's clutches: 'Let that white woman alone, nigger! Stay on your own side!' (p. 75). In a reversal of the real-life incident which stands behind Bonner's story the white boy dies and Denny is sentenced to death. The progressive school bans black students and Frye Street also segregates itself. The muddy stream of multi-ethnicity allows itself to be channelled back along the deep divisions of racial separation which have invisibly structured ethnic interactions all along: 'Frye

Street unmixed itself. Flowed apart' (p. 76). For Bonner, the limits of New Negro aspirations are marked on the surface of the racialised city and on the psyches of its inhabitants.

'Drab Rambles', published in *The Crisis* the following year, takes up Bonner's interest in the sexualised dimensions of racial deprivation, as it also extends the nascent formal experimentation of 'Nothing New'. The story is divided into two separate sketches prefaced by a strange allegorical rendering of the existential horror of being black in a racist world. The preface is written in the first person, but its projected 'I' is clearly not intended to be the voice of one person but instead a generalised 'I' that stands for African Americans within a social order which dramatically proscribes their existential and actual freedom:

> I am all men. I am tinged and touched. I am colored. All men tinged and touched; colored in a brown body.
> Close all men in a small space, tinge and touch the space with one blood – you get a check-mated Hell.
> A check-mated Hell seething in a brown body.

What is most noticeable about this driving passage is the way a quasi-religious language of 'a check-mated Hell' is infused with a language of blood that develops an almost eugenic insistence on racial intermingling as the characteristic condition of racial confinement and American identity: 'I am all men tinged in brown … I am you and I am myself.' This is riven with contradiction as Bonner claims racial interaction as the inevitable product of the urban scene at the same time as she presents the horror of inter-breeding which is the raison d'être of racial segregation. This veers dangerously close to affirming the racism which has 'check-mated' relationships between the races, particularly across the gender divide. At times Bonner's pessimism boils over in a manner analogous to her nihilistic predictions for urban racial interaction, 'how long can Hell seethe before it boils over?' (p. 93). As the story develops she draws on social observation to provide evidence for what is nevertheless clearly a tortured psychosexual reality and one is left at the end of the preface feeling that this is a scathing indictment of the position of an 'everyman' who has no place in the world. This belief comes very close to the existential angst of those other more famous men with no place in the world, Wright's Bigger Thomas or Ellison's Invisible Man, and there is a distinctly modernist strain to the condition of alienation and dislocation which Bonner outlines in this preface. What is added to this in Bonner's story is the reliance on a language of blood that marks a gendered understanding of the perils of interbreeding and the check-mated social world. As so many of Bonner's protagonists mother, or fail to mother, children one must concede that the everyman whose fate she draws here in such uncompromising terms is likely to be a woman, and that for Bonner the fact of racial segregation is marked as clearly on the intimate relations between mother and child as it is on the geography of a racialised underclass environment.

After this opening it is surprising to go on to the sketches which are much more conventional in style and content. The first concerns Peter Jackson, who has worked himself nearly to death and is subject to the racism of a hospital system that expects his broken health to be the result of a bad life rather than a hard one. The second story develops Bonner's sense of the vulnerability of African American women who work in the white world and fall prey to sexual advances by white employers (a scenario that is also a feature of Ann Petry's *The Street*). Madie Frye, who worked as a domestic for the white Nolan family, loses her job when light-skinned Madie-the-second is born and her subsequent life is a battle to hold down jobs with a baby, and avoid contact with men who would have her repeat the experience that resulted in the birth of her daughter: 'Madie second had cost her jobs and jobs. She came by Madie keeping that first job. Madie was black brown. The baby was yellow. Was she now going to go job hunting or have a sister or brother to keep with Madie second?' (p. 101). The putative freedoms of urban space are noticeable here only in their absence. Daily life is dictated by her position as the lowest cog in the well-oiled, white-run machine that is the laundry she works in. This is a dehumanising routine of tubs and heat and washing that Bonner parallels with a prose style of short, repetitive sentences and truncated, brutal observations. She labours to provide for her child while Madie second is progressively poisoned by a neighbour who feeds her paregoric to keep her quiet. At the level of content and at the level of style the story hems Madie and any aspirations she might have into a limited and grinding reality, and even in this immiserated black workspace Madie is open to the sexual preda-toriness of the white managers and bosses who see her as freely available flesh.

It is flesh, blood and space that are finally revealed as the key points of connection between the fractured philosophy of the preface and the prosaic social observation of the sketches. Women are the ones who have to bear the weight of blood and it is women who find their position most untenable in a city that both forbids racial interaction and places women at the mercy of it. In Bonner's critical assessment at least, it is the women who are punished for the contained and containing space of the ghetto. They are left to bear and raise children who are the commonest sign of the breaking of the taboo against racial interaction. In Chapter 5 we will see the rearticulation of this belief, tempered by a more positive belief in the value of black community and, more ambivalently, by the belief in the opportunities proffered by consumer culture. In Bonner's work there is little to celebrate as her awareness of the multi-ethnic make-up of the city is held against a despairing understanding of the intransigence of racial exclusion based on the power of blood.

Black Notes/City Notes

Bonner's later stories have an even more pessimistic focus than the stories examined thus far. Her concern with tracing the sexual politics of black urban life never wanes but in her later Frye Street work she looks less at black and white relations than she does at the internal struggles of the Frye Street African American community. In fact, in contrast with Grimké, and with her own earlier work, the later pieces show violence and oppression to be internal to the workings of the ghetto community, with white influence held at one remove figuring in the larger social and economic structuring of the city and the ghetto. As we read through the stories Frye Street becomes increasingly detailed, in ethnic, sexual and individual terms, at the same time as Bonner maps on to this the institutional patterns of black failure in the city. In the tripartite 'A Possible Triad on Black Notes' we see a young African American who aspires to be a bell-hop and earn like a man, who dies (in dubious circumstances) after encountering his light-skinned prostitute mother in bed with a man at the white hotel in which he works ('There Were Three'). We learn of the Jewish shopkeeper who is having an affair with an African American woman, while his Jewish wife longs to return to Poland ('Corner-Store'), and we see the slick manoeuvrings of a snobbish African American woman who makes a play for the doctor who comes to tend her dying husband ('Jimmy Harris'). In 'A Sealed Pod' we hear about the African American woman whose jealous Italian American lover murders her. We witness across many of the stories migrant aspirations for urban life, and the deadly crushing of those hopes and dreams. Finally there is a pattern repeated again and again across stories whereby women and children find themselves victim of the racialised socio-economic structures they are mired within. Children die, or kill themselves, get put in reform school or prison, aspire to become numbers runners as their mothers turn to drugs, or find themselves unable to find a way out of the ghetto except through violence.

This overbearing sense of pessimism is connected to Bonner's sense of the draining away of African American economic hopes as the Depression years bit deep and the government programmes set up to ameliorate the extremes of poverty for the urban poor were revealed to be as racist as they were inadequate.[39] The increased pessimism is also bound up with Bonner's developing style which takes a greater interest in sociological exploration of African American urbanism, something which clearly links her to those urban writers who followed her – Petry and Wright. This is combined with experimentation in documenting the inner reality of women's lives, often through use of a stream-of-consciousness perspective, in serial sketches that give us an intensely subjective appreciation of the inner experience of urban poverty. This is taken to its most successful conclusion in another of Bonner's tripartite narratives 'Black Fronts', where she juxtaposes the inner consciousness of a thieving but fully self-justified maid with the wearied counter-thoughts of her harassed (but equally self-assured) employer. What continues to mark her work until the very end of her writing life is her focus on racialised sexuality, both in terms of the social realities she chooses to document and in her attempt to convey how it is subjectively experienced. In ways that appear peculiarly contemporary (indeed her concerns would not seem out of place in fiction from the 1960s and 1970s) she isolates key issues for urban African Americans: the dysfunctional family (particularly in terms of bad parenting and poor schooling), the role of the mother, and the relationship between familial experience and the social world.

The end of 'On Being Young – A Woman – and Colored' provides us with an appropriate conclusion for this chapter. In it she imagines a woman (herself?) in a curiously powerful but still yet-to-be realised image of feminine potentiality:

> Like Buddha – who brown like I am – sat entirely at ease, entirely sure of himself; motionless and knowing, a thousand years before the white man knew there was so very much difference between feet and hands ... Still, 'Perhaps Buddha is a woman.'... And then you can, when Time is ripe, swoop to your feet – at your full height – at a single gesture. (p. 8)

It is hard to square this image of a woman waiting patiently for the 'ripe' time with distraught Ma at the end of 'Tin Can' or broken down Lizabeth from 'The Whipping', who both see their children die despite their best efforts to raise them. Yet, the very negativity of Bonner's analysis of urban life still holds in place this image of the potential power of ordinary African American women. Her attempts to write the diversity of Frye Street life catch the complex psychosexual reality of African American urban experience, especially for women, in a more disturbing, comprehensive and contradictory fashion than any other writer of her period and almost any other since. This 'motionless and knowing' protest is a potent image for these (and other) women writers of the 1920s and 1930s whose writing is so often passed over as they 'silently' present powerful counter-narratives of urban existence. As she holds out with Buddha-like composure, she waits for the conditions of urban civility, for the possibility of urbanity, which was the promise of the New Negro Renaissance. That these hopes are not realised in the lives of the ordinary denizens of Frye Street is perhaps no surprise to any but the most naive analysts of African American history and culture. That Bonner manages to develop a mode of writing that can do justice to the complexity of those lives she is one of the few to attempt to portray is a fact which ought to be better known by those who study the twentieth-century development of African American urban writing.

CHAPTER 5

Consumer Desire and Domestic Urbanism

This chapter discusses the work of Gwendolyn Brooks and Ann Petry, looking specifically at Brooks's *A Street in Bronzeville* and Petry's *The Street*.[1] While this moves us on to the 1940s, my focus remains literary exploration of the meanings of racial and gender identity within the confines of racialised city spaces. Brooks and Petry both had long literary careers and neither has received the critical attention their work deserves: something that this chapter seeks to redress. I confine my discussion to the texts produced by these women in the mid-1940s as these writings continue debates over the relationship between urban life, gender and maternity for African Americans, which characterised the writing of so many women during the Harlem Renaissance. This is not to see these authors as historical leftovers from the Renaissance period (indeed the style, focus and content of Petry's and Brooks's writings are very different from someone like Larsen) but rather to suggest the continuity of forms of social protest writing by African American women from the 1920s to the end of the 1940s and into the 1950s. In fact, one might suggest that the usual division made in black literary histories between the decadent 1920s and the protest 1940s is an inadequate and limiting one for understanding black urban writing, and more particularly African American women's writing. The writing career of Marita Bonner, as we saw in the last chapter, spans these usually opposed periods and gives us the best example of a continuity of interest across the decades. We shall now see how Petry and Brooks take up her focus on urban working-class (female) communities. The authors explored thus far in the book provide a vital context for understanding the writing of both Brooks and Petry.[2] Despite the obvious and significant differences between Larsen, Bonner, Petry and Brooks they are linked through their exploration of the embeddedness of African American women in consumer culture and in the city. Furthermore, we see in Petry and Brooks the persistence of anxieties about reproduction and motherhood and their effect on racial and gender identity.

Petry published eight books, *The Street* being the first. Prior to this she published short stories in *The Crisis* and *Phylon*, the success of which resulted in a Houghton Mifflin fellowship in 1945 that allowed her to complete her first novel. Inspiration for *The Street* came from time Petry spent living and working in Harlem. She was a journalist on *People's Voice* in Harlem, and also worked for nine months on an experimental teaching project in one of Harlem's elementary schools. She was an important figure in the literary scene of the 1940s and 1950s, associating with better-known figures such as Du Bois, Hughes, Weldon Johnson and Richard Wright. Petry went on to publish two more novels, *The Country Place* (1947) and *The Narrows* (1955), four books for children, including a history of Harriet Tubman's life, and a collection of short stories, *Miss Muriel and Other Stories* (1971).

Gwendolyn Brooks has one of the longest careers in African American writing stretching from the years just after the Second World War, through Civil Rights, then Black Power in the late 1960s and early 1970s (where she was radicalised through her admiration for younger African American poets like Don Lee, Sonia Sanchez and Amiri Baraka) to her last collection in the mid-1980s.[3] She is a revered figure in her home city of Chicago, though her international reputation suffers from the common fate accorded to poets (especially African American poets) – of being too frequently out of print. Her first collection of poetry *A Street in Bronzeville* was published in 1945, followed by *Annie Allen* in 1946 which won the Pulitzer Prize and made her the first African American to be thus honoured. She has published ten collections of poetry, three books for children, and a novel, *Maud Martha* (1953). Despite this prolific career recent critical attention to Brooks's work has been sparse to say the least; all of her poetry is currently out of print in Britain and the only major survey of her work is the collection of critical essays edited by Maria K. Mootry and Gary Smith, *A Life Distilled*.[4] Her poetry has received some attention from theoretically oriented black critics such as Barbara Johnson and Hortense Spillers, unsurprising given the acute questions about issues of race, gender, identity and writing raised throughout her poetry.[5] She is, however, often sidelined in surveys of African American writing, which points to the construction of African American literature as primarily a novelistic tradition (which, of course, this book repeats in many ways). Even black feminist critics such as Barbara Christian, Deborah McDowell, Cheryl Wall or Mary Helen Washington who have done such important work in raising the profile of African American women's writing in the early twentieth century pass over Brooks, commenting, if at all, on her novel *Maud Martha* (the text which has received by far the most attention).[6]

I shall read the writing of Brooks and Petry against undoubtedly the most famous African American novel of the 1940s, Richard

Wright's *Native Son* (1940).[7] Although this text avoids for the most part such canonical figures as Wright, it is impossible to ignore *Native Son*. Wright's novel is not merely the best known and most influential literary representation of black urban alienation, but also initiates a mode of 'protest' writing (as I argued in my introduction) which has had a profound influence on the construction of African American literary history. Wright's idiom and approach to the 'race problem' in this novel in many ways dictates the key terms for the evaluation and construction of African American literature at least until the shifts in literary form and critical approaches associated with the renaissance of black women's writing in the 1980s. More specifically the reception of *Native Son* has had significant effects (and rarely positive ones) on the reception of Petry's writing.

We can see this if we look at two of the more provocative and influential surveys of African American literature, Robert Bone's *The Negro Novel in America* published at the end of the 1950s, and Addison Gayle's 1973 text *The Way of the New World: The Black Novel in America*, the definitive Black Aesthetic judgement on African American literary history.[8] Both discuss Petry's novel at some length and allow that it is worthy of consideration, but it seems overshadowed by the presence of Wright's novel. They both criticise its overt didacticism and deterministic tone (judgements my reading of the novel will contest) and the novel never seems able to achieve the racial radicalism or authenticity which both critics insist on, to use Wright's phrase, as the 'Blueprint for Negro Writing'.[9] Bone, although allowing that the novel is worthy of comment, calls it 'a *roman a these* ... which offers a superficial analysis of life in a northern ghetto'.[10] Gayle asserts that although the novel is 'provocative and powerful' it fails to present a satisfactory resolution of the problems Lutie encounters, and is effectively a carbon copy of Wright's *Native Son*. The problem with both these judgements is that they work with an oversimplified notion of what constitutes oppositionality in African American writing (which is bound up with their regard for Wright's novel) and with a belief that racial protest is *the* criterion for valuable African American texts. This exclusive focus on the racial politics of the text elides the important analysis of gender and sexuality (a major feature of Petry's text) because these factors fall outside this racially absolutist model of African American literature.

Petry's *The Street* and Gwendolyn Brooks's urban poetry offer substantially different responses to the city, and to the conditions of modernity for African Americans, than *Native Son*. My reading of these differences takes us some way beyond Addison Gayle's dismissive judgement that *The Street* is a less successful carbon copy of *Native Son*, and accords with Maria Lauret's suggestion that *The Street* is more usefully regarded as a counter to, rather than a copy of, Wright's novel.[11] My reading of *Native Son* asserts it remains substantially contained within a binarism of white presence and black absence mapped across the surface of the urban scene and refuses to acknowledge the implicatedness of these opposed positions. The novel depends on a conception of racial being which is inextricably linked to forms of aggressive masculinity, and which actively requires the suppression of gender and sexuality as significant dimensions in the formation of racial identity.[12] At the same time it is the sexualised nature of white conceptions of racial being which entrap Bigger and seal his fate. I would suggest the sense of absolute difference between black and white worlds the novel apparently asserts is continually disrupted by the gender and sexual differences which the novel seeks (but does not succeed) to suppress. This stands in contrast to Petry's exploration of racial and gender ambivalence as a fundamental aspect of urban experience.

In the following reading I shall be arguing that comparison between the novelistic and poetic representations of space by Brooks and Petry highlights a tracing of alternative life practices.[13] These practices are mapped across the city, inscribed in and between the official story of racism and oppression, struggling to retain the possibility of black female agency within the constraints of a segregated city space. Brooks's and Petry's writing continues the debates we have seen in women writers from the Harlem Renaissance and after about the meaning of racial and gender identity, within an urban scene which poses unusual problems but also manifest opportunities for the African American female subject. The significance of the urban settings of Brooks's and Petry's work has only rarely been explored, and where it has the centrality of the urban scene to the delineation of subjectivity and (potential) agency in the writing has not been noted. It seems to me impossible to separate the trajectories of individual characters in these works from their placement within and reaction to an urban scene marked as peculiarly modern and modernising. Both writers make extensive reference to the technologies of the urban, in terms of cars, commodities, fashion and advertising: the whole gamut of characteristic features of a rapidly developing consumer culture. Fashion and the cultures of consumption (in places such as bars, hairdressers, speakeasies) are particularly important in Brooks's *A Street in Bronzeville* as characters step out around their Bronzeville locale. Indeed, the delineation of the city scene through engagement with the material objects and spaces of urban consumption is a primary aesthetic and political motivation for the collection. In Petry's work characteristic features of mass commodity culture – from broadcasting and advertising to subways, night-clubs and brothels – are marked out clearly as Lutie moves through the city, as part of the interior landscape of her experience rather than simply the bleak backdrop to her life. Moving forward from the 1920s to the 1940s gives us a more developed sense of the importance of commodity culture and systems of capital in shaping the experience of African Americans within the city. The scenarios in Harlem and Bronzeville, described by Petry and Brooks, present us with a situation which demands consideration of the impact of racism, racial difference and physical, economic and cultural segregation on the rapidly modernising city, as David Goldberg's analysis of the racialised topographies of cities suggests.[14] The memory and influence of the South fades into the background to be replaced by an urban aesthetic that has no use for the nostalgic imaginings of some other (better) place than the city. Brooks's and Petry's works explore how race is systematically encoded as absence or negativity in discursive conceptualisation of the city, but also how the demands of a consumer society on both black and white, male and female subjects within the city space undermine this. Their work contends that the daily practices of African American urban life will repeatedly exceed the structural containment or erasure of racial presence within the city, whilst at the same time protesting against this geographical, economic and cultural containment.[15] Their writing attends to the racial and gendered boundaries drawn up within the city space; boundaries that shape profoundly the experience of space, time and social being. Their attention to African Americans as workers, consumers, as travellers within the city, gives us a racialised account of the conditions of mid-century modernity; in particular, their attention to domestic, or interior space, and the interface between this and the supposedly public arena of the city. Although the narratives I shall examine are far from celebratory about the possibilities offered within the city they stay within its boundaries, asserting that debates over racial and gendered subjectivity are bound up with understanding the experience of the city for African American women.

Reading the Urban Domestic

The writings of Ann Petry and Gwendolyn Brooks elaborate the city as interior, domestic environment as well as exterior or public sphere, and it is the domestic life of the city that is the particular focus of this chapter. Interior space, especially that associated with domestic settings, or women's everyday work space, plays a muted role in many forms of urban analysis including the work of the

Chicago School sociologists discussed earlier, despite their concern
with the practice of everyday urbanity. Likewise, the relationship
between what we might call the inside and the outside of the
material city has never played a primary role in those paradigmatic
accounts of the experience of the city – works by George Simmel
or Walter Benjamin or, more recently, Michel de Certeau – which
have had such a major effect on theorising about modernity and
urban space; again, despite the attention these writers pay to the
subjective apprehension of urban experience.[16] Petry and Brooks
explore the shaping effects of race and gender on the experience
of city life, and speculate about the conditions of domestic urbanity.
Their writing, in Gilroy's terms, is an immanent critique of an
Enlightenment project that sees its apotheosis in the spaces of
modernity. This antinomian (racialised) modernity is not, as Gilroy
insists throughout *The Black Atlantic*, an expression of an
'alternative' racial experience but an insistent questioning of the
terms and conditions of modernity from within its material, cultural
and philosophical formations. In Brooks's and Petry's work this
questioning most often takes place through exploration of the racial
and gender politics of domestic space. This interior realm is
repeatedly projected outward onto the public realm of the city in
a manner which genders racial experience, and disrupts accounts
of the public realm of the city.[17]

Gwendolyn Brooks's 1945 collection of poems, *A Street in
Bronzeville*, is a suggestive illustration of this process. The collection
consists of a series of meditations on life on and within the street
of the title. It seems appropriate to consider Brooks's response to
the post-war situation for African Americans alongside Petry's
despite the fact that poetry has mostly been beyond the scope of
this study. Her attention to the geographical and psychological
dimensions of race within the urban milieu, and the determination to examine the public and private dimensions of urban life for
African American women places these two writers in productive
dialogue. The geographies of their writing differ, in the obvious
sense that Brooks writes of Chicago's Southside and Petry of New
York's Harlem, but also in the sense that Petry's Harlem is
presented as far more constraining and violently segregated than
Southside Chicago. These differences are important to note, and
undoubtedly have some relation to the material conditions shaping
these respective communities during the 1940s. The apparent
nihilism and gothic horror of Petry's Harlem bears some relation
to the despondency felt amongst writers, intellectuals and social
commentators at the failure to convert the vibrant excitement about
rapid expansion of Harlem during the 1920s into concrete or
sustainable gains for the African American community. This was,
of course, also the case in Chicago but the sense of Harlem as a

'race capital' makes that disappointment over 'the dream deferred' particularly acute.[18]

The point of greatest similarity between these two writers is in their common focus on the effect of living and moving through the city as consumers and workers. In Brooks's *A Street in Bronzeville* these experiences are considerably more positive than in Petry's novel, particularly in terms of the possibilities offered by places and practices which are characterised as feminine. Poems such as 'Southeast corner' 'Hunchback girl: she thinks of heaven', 'Sadie and Maud', 'When you have forgotten Sunday: the love story' and the sequence of poems which make up 'Hattie Scott', fill out a city landscape with the everyday practices of women's lives. These prosaic, but meaningful, activities mark African American women as agents within the urban landscape at the same time as (and often because of) the economic, racial and gendered constraints which mark the limits of black female agency. The poems hold this representation of daily rituals and practices against long-held stereotypes of women's possible roles in the city, consistently seeking to undermine these stereotypes (which limit Lutie Johnson's options so profoundly in Petry's novel). Poems like 'Sadie and Maud' reverse the still-forceful perception that the city (or more precisely the ghetto) will offer no possibility for its African American inhabitants and that the only alternative (in a variant of the uplift narrative) is to educate yourself out of the trap (of the city). In this poem it is Sadie who stays at home, rather than Maud who escapes the ghetto by going to college, who triumphs. Sadie 'scrapes life/With a fine tooth-comb' (p. 16). This potent image, a feminised conception of a life organised in terms of need and pleasure, sees Sadie as an everyday detective capable of deducing and sustaining her own vision of meaningful existence within circumscribed circumstances. Sadie is, then, a resourceful creator of the terms of her own subjective existence. This is made clear at the end of the poem when the admiring narrator of the poem is revealed as 'Maud' sitting alone in 'this old house'. As reader of her sister's experience Maud manages to contest the deterministic force of material location for both women, and in doing so calls for a more nuanced reading of black women's experience in the city in a powerfully feminine racial voice.

I want now to look in some detail at one poem from *A Street in Bronzeville*, though the features noted in this analysis apply across the collection. The poem 'Kitchenette Building' is particularly appropriate for my purposes here in that it explores the dynamics of domestic space but projects this as exterior public space, or at least exposed to the surveillance of the public realm, through its utilisation of a recognisably modernist language of city planning, rationalisation, and organisation. The poem makes explicit the dimensions of urban poverty and the ways in which the domestic refuge is perpetually disrupted by the demands (material, racial, gendered) of the public realm of work because of this poverty. Nevertheless, the poem also pulls in an opposite direction by mediating the demands of this outside realm through a transforming language of interior experience. By the end of the poem the material and discursive constraints on African American life are contested, and the squeezed up, 'limited' home is substantially expanded in a witty refusal of the confining space of the ghetto.

> We are things of dry hours and the involuntary plan,
> Grayed in, and gray. "Dream" makes a giddy sound, not strong
> Like "rent," "feeding a wife," "satisfying a man."
>
> But could a dream send up through onion fumes
> Its white and violet, fight with fried potatoes
> And yesterday's garbage ripening in the hall,
> Flutter, or sing an aria down these rooms
>
> Even if we were willing to let it in,
> Had time to warm it, keep it very clean,
> Anticipate a message, let it begin?
>
> We wonder. But not well! not for a minute!
> Since Number Five is out of the bathroom now,
> We think of lukewarm water, hope to get in it.
>
> 'Kitchenette Building' (p. 4)

The poem begins with containment within a circumscribed urban space: 'We are things of dry hours and the involuntary plan,/ Grayed in, and gray'. The 'plan' signals an organisation of geographical, economic, political and temporal realities from without, which the poem's delineation of interior domestic space eventually attempts to destabilise. The geographical location of the poem in a 'Kitchenette Building' presents a limited space and offers the first of several available meanings of the word 'plan' in the poem's opening line. This interior space is arranged and delimited by planners, the official organisers of urban space; it is an economically circumscribed and racially segregated location. This has strong correspondences with the descriptions which open Petry's novel of 'the street' as periphractic space.[19] The economic dimensions of this domestic location are confirmed in line three with the presentation of the word 'rent' in scare quotes, which is followed by 'feeding a wife' and 'satisfying a man', the quotation marks effectively securing their connection to one another. The geographic, economic and subjective implications of this involuntary plan are inter-related through the necessity for financial planning in order to live up to the strength of these loaded phrases. The particular gender responsibilities of this economic necessity are, one must note, also detailed precisely.

The economic necessity to produce these plans is attested to by the poem's juxtaposition of the giddy 'dream' in the second line with the pressure of 'rent' in the third. The quotation marks isolate these phrases from the descriptive progression of the rest of the poem, and suggest these words are a form of daily law/lore that is learned as communal, or territorial, knowledge. It also emphasises their potency as defining (planning) concepts against which the rest of the poem is measured. By this point the political resonances of this urban plan make themselves clearly felt (pinpointed by the use of the descriptive term 'involuntary') demonstrating the lack of choice, or plan in lifestyle for the inhabitants of the 'Kitchenette Building'. These are clearly places of containment, where (black) people are put. On the other hand, 'involuntary' also signifies an unwillingness to implement the plan, so the poem very precisely locates blame for the limited nature of kitchenette existence outside the building, as the fault of the planners of this urban location. The location of blame outside the domestic realm is suggestive in that it leaves open the possibility that some other order or organisation of experience may be constructed within the space. The notion of the 'involuntary plan' also helpfully suggests the precariousness of this apparently constrained existence. The life plan within 'Kitchenette Building' is an on-the-hoof one, responsive on a day-to-day basis to the needs and demands of those inhabiting the space.

The multiple meanings of the oxymoron 'involuntary plan' engage with clearly designated orders of reality in the poem, an order imposed from without and a subjective counter-order of life experiences within the building. This interior counter-order spirals outwards as a reconstructive possibility in the second stanza of the poem. The discarded, giddy dream of the first stanza is picked up to speculate on its movement through the building. Echoing the doubled positive and negative valences of 'involuntary' noted above, the stanza juxtaposes the dream with the 'onion fumes' and 'yesterday's garbage'. In terms of the ability to maintain a fluttering dream, the capacity to 'sing an aria down these rooms', the poem seems to lapse into negativity in the last stanza: 'We wonder. But not well! not for a minute!' Indeed, there is speculation as to whether the giddy 'dream' with its utopian aria would have a positive meaning even if it were a possibility: 'Even if we were willing to let it in ... Anticipate a message, let it begin?' The third stanza seems to militate against the possibility of maintaining the nascent counter-order of the first stanza and indeed seems to question the usefulness of such alternative imaginings.

There is, however, a counter-movement that contradicts the peremptory withdrawal from the dream. Although the dream itself is discarded, its exploration through the poem and the tracing of its movement interestingly transforms the subjective (temporal) experience of living in that space. The tracing of the dream redefines the meanings of the limited environment, at the same time as rightly protesting those conditions. The second stanza starts with the projected 'But could' which, by the end of stanza three, seems to stand for this could not ever come to be. However, in progressing through the poem one sees the 'grayed in, and gray' hours transformed into a 'white and violet' dream that fights and struggles for space and meaning within the enclosed kitchenette space. The dream floats up, and the returning aria drifts back down producing a vertical spatialisation which exceeds that of the official planners, whilst at the same time contesting the horizontal containment of this planned space.

This procedure is supported by the progress of time in the poem. As I observed, the 'involuntary plan' refers in one sense to temporal considerations – at the most obvious level there are not enough hours in the day to plan for the economic, emotional and political demands of this space: 'Even if we were willing to let it in, /Had time to warm it, keep it very clean'. The last stanza of the poem makes it clear that these musings have taken place whilst the narrator is standing in the queue for the bathroom. There is a peculiar closing construction. Our narrator has not, it appears, been wondering about the possibility of dream and arias: 'We wonder. But not well! not for a minute!', but instead has been thinking 'of lukewarm water, hope to get in it'. However, by now the bathroom queue in which this narrator stands has been transformed by these thoughts, and whilst there may not be a minute, it is clear that the 'dry hours' of the beginning of the poem have been transformed into the wet hour of bath time. The multi-layered involuntary plan of the first stanza therefore also refers to the prosaic organisation of this queue for the bath. The kitchenette building is shown to be delimited by the planners but also constructed through the individual's apprehension of that space, and we see the space's official story destabilised by the inscription of their everyday life practices; a suggestion which asserts a counter-order of everyday organisation. The poem is concerned with a 'dream deferred', but a deferral that is nevertheless transformative of both the kitchenette space and the waiting time for the bathroom!

In this poem domestic life is used to counter the repressive external organisation of space and time. The use in this poem of a language of planning is characteristic of the whole collection. Against this order is not the dis-order of ghetto life, but the suggestion that the life practices of the urban poor will always 'mean' in excess of the planned possibilities of the contained environment. What this does is consistently maintain the possibilities and potential of subjective agency within the city: simultaneously non-utopian but also positive.

The Street

Ann Petry's novel *The Street* offers in many ways a much more pessimistic account of urban life in the 1940s for African Americans and in particular for African American women. The novel makes explicit the containment of the black urban poor within the ghetto. However, as in Brooks's work this containment is balanced by a sense of subcultural solidarity and (limited) subjective agency within this marginal space. To summarise briefly the novel, Lutie Johnson, the protagonist, and her son Bub move into the Street of the novel's title, after the breakdown of Lutie's marriage. This breakdown has been precipitated through Lutie's absence from home working as a domestic in a white home while her husband cannot find a job. The novel documents in uncompromising fashion Lutie's attempts to extricate herself, through self-reliance and self-confidence, from an urban scene characterised by poverty, decay and lack of opportunities for black people. Her mantra: 'I'm young and strong, there isn't anything I can't do' (p. 49), is ultimately revealed to be a mocking illusion of the American Dream. The Street Lutie works to escape from is represented through repeated spatial metaphors of walls closing in around her, trapping her within the economically and racially segregated city margins:

> It was any city where they set up a line and say black folks stay on this side and white folks on this side, so that the black folks were crammed on top of each other – jammed and packed and forced into the smallest possible space until they were completely cut off from light or air. (p. 149)

Lutie travels in and out of Harlem to work and to try to remove herself from (following my analysis of 'Kitchenette Building') the planned containment of the Street and of Harlem. The deleterious effect of the urban environment on the people who live in the Street is made emphatically clear in the opening paragraphs of the novel, where the cold November wind blowing down a street seems to substitute the detritus of urban squalor for human presence:

> [The wind] did everything it could to discourage people walking along the street. It found all the dirt and dust and grime on the pavement and lifted it up so that the dirt got into their noses,

making it difficult to breathe; the dust got into their eyes and blinded them; and the grit stung their skin. (p. 7)

Petry presents a ghetto that simultaneously repels its inhabitants, alienating them from the place they nevertheless have to recognise as home, and draws them in and traps them within its decaying environment. The extent to which the urban scene Petry describes effectively closes off alternatives to this geographical, financial and social entrapment is emphasised as Lutie moves from the enclosing Street to the shrinking rooms of her flat, which by the end of the novel become the walls that close in around her. As Lutie realises near the novel's close, this entrapment is a consequence of the racialised dimensions of urban topography:

Junto [a white property owner] has a brick in his hand. Just one brick. The final one needed to complete the wall that had been building up around her for years, and when that final brick was shoved in place, she would be completely walled in. (p. 303)

This deterministic and deeply pessimistic attitude is at odds with the dreams and aspirations (to be a singer, a secretary) which Lutie holds almost until the end of the novel. In order to take these aspirations seriously, and not simply see them as a rather crude representation of Lutie's ideological duping by a racist society, we need again to examine the life practices of the characters, which work to construct this marginal space as well as respond to it. This manifests itself as a tension in the novel between documenting an oppressive regime of ghettoisation, and tracing individual and communal relation to the spaces the inhabitants (are essentially forced to) inhabit. In doing this, the novel suggests the ambivalent status of its heroine Lutie. She is not so much a victim of her environment but rather subject to the demands of racial, class and gender location, a series of ideological contradictions that enmesh her and are refused resolution within the novel. As I argued in the analysis of Brooks's 'Kitchenette Building' these contradictions are seen most clearly in the disjunction between the planned space of the ghetto, and the everyday practices of those who inhabit the Street. Again, these contradictions point to the precariousness of the racist system of geographical and social containment which the novel so starkly documents. The novel presents us with a series of material, economic practices, and systems of travel, media and technology in the city which trouble the aggressively maintained borders between black and white communities. The relationships examined by Petry between African American women and white employers within the domestic sphere relate in a dialectical way the inscription of life practices in the city space.[20] They also suggest the precariousness of a segregating periphractic order of city organisation. This order, which is inscribed within, and imposed by, the official organisation of city space (as David Goldberg argues), also requires (and always has required) black insiders to that space as workers.[21] This contradictory ideological placement, both insider and outsider, is most insistently the case for African American women given the large numbers working as domestics during the period. Further, these women also inhabit the city space as consumers within a commodity culture that, as we shall see, is rather more indiscriminate in its appeal than might at first be imagined.

Reading the Signs Inside

Reading *The Street* as a relatively crude, deterministic account of the effect of urban poverty (as many commentators do) fails to acknowledge the complicating effect of Lutie's relationship to her present urban scene as she inhabits it as both a worker, a traveller and a consumer. These subject positions call her in a direction that directly contradicts the (oppressed) racial subject position she is assigned to. This antagonistic calling into being is represented in the novel through Lutie's apparent embrace of the classic American Dream, 'I'm young. I'm strong. There isn't anything I can't do', which is persistently juxtaposed with Lutie's downward spiral toward the murder that concludes the novel. On the surface, then, Lutie wants one thing (a white dream of social mobility and financial security), but the Street pulls her in the other direction and exposes the unavailability of this escape for African Americans (particularly for African American women with children). This does not account for the complexity of Petry's analysis of black women's experience in the city. As with the writing by women during the Harlem Renaissance it is difficult to maintain this sense of the deterministic binarism of racial difference if one takes seriously the implications of potentially conflicting discourses of gender, sexuality and class identity. Changing cultural conditions from the 1920s to the 1940s seem to heighten the felt polarisation of black and white communities which shows in far more pessimistic literary accounts of black life in the city, as we saw in the stories by Marita Bonner. However, this should not suggest that Petry's or Brooks's writing does not see the exploration of gender and sexuality as coterminous with their understanding of racial identity. On the contrary, as we shall see it is the representation of Lutie as both (racially) despised and (sexually) desired subject that forms the crux of the novel. I would suggest an important connection between Petry's novel and Larsen's accounts of African American women as participants in a capitalist consumer culture. The horrifying and despairing repudiation of motherhood at the end of the novel also asserts connections with both Grimké's writing and the short stories of Marita Bonner. It seems essential, then, to view the novel as engaging with the ongoing pressures of both urban life and maternity for African American women. Examining Lutie's experience on the street and moving around the city, one can see particular moments of identification which help to inculcate the version of the American Dream she seems to adhere to. Attention to these moments reduces the temptation to regard Lutie as simply deluded in her quest for self-determination and success in a racially divided America. Her desire to escape from the Street and, crucially, the forms in which she represents these desires to herself, do not float down from the ether, nor are they purely a product of her existence in the Street. This kind of 'environmental' explanation of Lutie's experience seems particularly unsatisfactory when we note the very different visions of escape produced by the three women – Lutie, Min and Mrs Hedges – we encounter living on the Street. Min places her faith in a conjure man (pointing again to the damaging adherence to superstition that Fisher writes of) while Mrs Hedges takes entrepreneurial advantage of the black sex industry: only Lutie imagines herself in thoroughly white aspirational terms. Her simultaneous positioning as black outsider and insider in the worlds she inhabits produces Lutie's dreams, and the forms these aspirations take.

Lutie undoubtedly wishes to escape from the Street; but what she wants to escape to, her fantasies and her aspirations, are produced by her experiences working outside this space as a domestic for the Chandler family. The novel is a damning condemnation of white attitudes to the black female workers who sustain their leisured lifestyle. In terms of economic and cultural conditions in the 1940s (particularly employment opportunities for African Americans) it is an unsurprising topic for Petry to pick up. As Gloria Wade-Gayles discusses, domestic labour was one of the main sources of employment for black women during this period.[22] It is also the basis of a particularly pernicious racist stereotype: the black Mammy. Based on a racist interpretation of black experience, and on a fundamentally sexist view of the relationship between women and motherhood, the legend is created (through sociological, historical, literary and film and television texts) of the fundamental predilection of black women for motherhood and domestic service, something which Petry's examination of Lutie's material and emotional aspirations explicitly critiques.[23]

Some time after Lutie leaves the Chandlers' home she receives a note from her employer:

'*Lutie dear: We haven't had a decent thing to eat since you left. And Little Henry misses you so much he's almost sick –* ' She didn't answer it. She had more problems than Mrs. Chandler and Little Henry had and they could always find someone to solve theirs if they paid enough. (p. 44)

As Lutie's response to the letter bitterly notes, the myth of the black Mammy hides the economic and social reasons for the large numbers of black women who worked as domestics, a fact which *The Street* foregrounds consistently. The novel makes clear that Lutie works as a result of a progressive feminisation of the labour force as jobs for African American men become less and less available:

The men stood around and the women worked. The men left the women and the women went on working and the kids were left alone ... The women work because the white folks give them jobs ... the white folks haven't liked to give black men jobs that paid enough to support their families. (p. 278)

Lutie's experience as a domestic supports, at least in part, Wade-Gayles's contention that: 'Because of the exigencies of black life in white America, black women have been forced to function heroically in the role [of mother/domestic], and their heroic functioning is often perceived as fulfilment.'[24] This heroic functioning is, however, only part of Lutie's experience working inside the white household. As well as critiquing the stereotype of the eternally capable black mother figure, Petry also presents us with the flipside of this racial stereotype, the black Sapphire.[25] Mrs Chandler's mother voices this sentiment directly to her daughter, in Lutie's earshot: 'Now I wonder if you are being wise, dear. That girl is unusually attractive and men are weak. Besides, she's colored and you know how they are' (p. 37).

What is interesting here is not just the condemnation of white racism, although that is undeniably significant, but rather the fact that Lutie can simultaneously be the cement that holds the family together (mother to the white family as well as to her own) and a potential threat that would blow that family apart. It seems that Lutie is a *desired* employee, a desired subject, in two very different ways: as economic underpinning for exclusive white leisure and, as sexual temptress and racial threat, a potential destroyer of that lifestyle. This contradiction between definitions of Lutie's maternal and sexual identities is elaborated through the novel as the starting point for the dialectical reading of black and white relations. There is a tension between desire and revulsion, between inclusion and exclusion, which Petry analyses but cannot resolve. What has been systematically underestimated in readings of the novel (even those like Barbara Christian's and Gayle Wurst's that recognise Lutie's contradictory ideological placement) is Lutie's position as a worker and a consumer.[26] Her participation in the ideology of the American Dream not only demonstrates how she is excluded from this mythology because of her race, but also deconstructs this racially exclusive American myth by showing how she is invited to participate in commodity culture. This antagonistic situation hinges on the fact that Petry presents us with a domestic scene where Lutie's presence is essential, but is represented through racist popular mythology as a threat. So even though she has an economically sanctioned position – one confirmed through racist stereotyping – she must remain silent, out of the way. However, the ambivalence of being inside this white household, where she is inside but made to feel most strongly her outsider status (through pernicious sexual as well as racial stereotyping) is explored by Petry in a way which exposes how Lutie is also a *desiring*, as well as desired subject.

Exploration of this tension between segregated space and the daily practices of work and leisure that undermine this planned segregation begins early in the novel, with Lutie's experience of travelling through the city. As she moves through New York Lutie notes with evident bitterness the segregation of areas of the city along racial lines. She also presents, as we saw in the description of the assaulting wind on the street quoted above, an almost gothic perception of what it means to be ghettoised. Nevertheless, as she traverses the planned segregation of the city she is aware of a subjective transformation that takes place as she returns to Harlem, ostensibly the place she wishes to escape from:

> She got the train, thinking that she never really felt human until she reached Harlem and thus got away from the hostility in the eyes of the white women who stared at her on the down-town streets and in the subway ... These other folks feel the same way, she thought – that once they are freed from the contempt in the eyes of the downtown world, they instantly become individuals ... suddenly grew so large they could hardly get up the stairs to the street together. (p. 46)

This would seem to testify to the capacity of the ghetto dweller to refuse the disciplinary gaze of the white women downtown, and to refuse the de-individuation that that periphractic location supposedly entails. The experience of being rendered invisible by the gaze of the white city is held in the novel against an insistent construction of black presence expanding within the ghetto: 'She [Lutie] reached the street at the very end of the crowd and stood watching them as they scattered in all directions, laughing and talking to each other' (p. 46).

In Petry's novel (and Brooks's poetry) this presence does not remain contained but impacts upon and disrupts the official segregation of the city. There is a positive subjective transformation once back within black space which undermines some of the novel's more nihilistic conclusions about the detrimental effects of the ghetto environment. There is, it seems, at least the possibility of community and forms of racial solidarity. This subcultural resistance maintains a sense of the intractability of the racialised boundaries of the urban landscape. But looking more closely at the thoughts which are prompted by Lutie's experience of travelling across the city one can begin to see ways in which the organisation of racial space is contested, albeit in tentative and ambiguous ways.

On the crowded train travelling back towards Harlem, Lutie stares ahead of her at an advertisement which sparks memories of her time at the Chandlers' house, and we are informed of the background to Lutie's arrival on the Street:

> For the advertisement she was looking at pictured a girl with incredible blonde hair. The girl leaned close to a dark-haired, smiling man in a navy uniform. They were standing in front of a kitchen sink – a sink whose white porcelain surface gleamed under the train lights. The taps looked like silver. The linoleum floor of the kitchen was a crisp black-and-white pattern that pointed up the sparkle of the room. Casement windows. Red geraniums in yellow pots. It was, she thought, a miracle of a kitchen. Completely different from the kitchen of 116th Street flat she had moved into just two weeks ago. But almost exactly like the one she had worked in Connecticut. (p. 25)

This is an obvious image of the America Lutie is debarred from because of her racial and class location. Lutie recognises her alienation from this advertising fantasy, because of the racist ideologies that this image represents and perpetuates, and so recognises her place as marginalised outsider from a (white-orientated) consumer culture. On the other hand one might argue that here, drawing on her experience of working for the Chandlers, Lutie effectively falls for the ideological message of the American Dream manifest in this advertisement. Lutie's acceptance of the advertising fantasy would go some way to explain her professed belief (absorbed from the Chandlers): 'Anybody could be rich if he wanted to and worked hard enough and worked it out carefully enough' (p. 36).

These two interpretations of Lutie's responses to the image contradict one another, and in large part determine how one views the novel as a whole. Lutie is apparently offered a choice between alienation from the image presented, and alienation from her racial identity. She cannot, it seems, be black and have any kind of identification with this image. However, this does not fully explain the complexity of Lutie's response to the image, nor her contradictory memories of working with the Chandlers. The advertising image instead calls Lutie in two directions at once. She considers her alienation from the scene of domestic affluence, and the pernicious effect just such a scene has had on her life. Nevertheless, she still has a strong identification with the scene, one that is not simply self-delusion. This contradictory calling is testament to the gendered complexity of Lutie's racial location.

Lutie's thoughts while staring at the advertisement lead her to consider her gender and racial interpellation. She recalls how this image of (white) domestic bliss has effectively destroyed her marriage. Working in the Chandler household Lutie becomes drawn into their 'work hard and you'll make it' philosophy. She stops going home to see her husband Jim and son Bub in order to save money and eventually Jim installs a new woman in her place. Lutie recognises the damage done by her adoption of the Chandlers' values, and that the position she has been forced into is a form of economic racism. The juxtaposition of a black woman looking at the gleaming white fantasy of domestic affluence seems then at one level a heavily symbolic representation of black alienation (of which there are many others in the novel). This has strong resonances with the early sections of Wright's *Native Son*. In the first section of the novel ('Fear') Wright shows Bigger, his central character, moving around a racially segregated Chicago. The novel shows Bigger encountering images of whiteness which progressively underline his alienation, oppression and segregation. These overdetermined moments of alienation in *Native Son* are an instructive counterpoint to Lutie's encounter with the kitchen image, and provide a way of highlighting the complexity of Petry's representation of the city in gender and racial terms.

The first, and perhaps most notorious, image of whiteness which Bigger encounters is the huge poster of State Attorney Buckley he sees on a billboard. Bigger has just left his house and is wandering around the streets. This scene precedes Bigger's journey to the white part of town when he is forced to take a job as a live-in chauffeur with the white Dalton family. The extent to which he is always already excluded from the Dalton's (white) space is presented as incontrovertible (and has its most heavily symbolic representation in Bigger's much noted flight, in the middle section of the novel, across the white snow-covered city after he has killed Mary Dalton). The poster of Buckley, which is pasted up as Bigger watches by two men in white overalls, is a Big Brother-like invocation of the controlling and dominating white presence and gaze. This is a more extreme version of Lutie's experience of de-individuation by the threatening gaze of the white women downtown. Wherever Bigger goes he is always already disciplined by a gaze which labels him as criminal:

> He looked at the poster: the white face was flesh but stern; one hand was uplifted and its index finger pointed straight out into the street at each passer-by. The poster showed one of those faces that looked straight at you when you looked at it and all the while you were walking and turning your head to look at it it kept looking unblinkingly back at you until you got so far from it you had to take your eyes away, and then it stopped like a movie blackout. Above the top of the poster were tall red letters: IF YOU BREAK THE LAW YOU CAN'T WIN! (p. 16)

Bigger's sense of what happens as he finally passes out of the range of Buckley's surveillance is described as a movie blackout. His experience of alienation is thus from an *image* of whiteness: this is developed in the novel through persistent attention to the visual and discursive construction of the racial geographies of the city spaces which Bigger and his friends inhabit. This can be seen best through the events following Bigger's observance of (and by) Buckley as he and Jack decide to go to the cinema.

This scene functions as a further example of Bigger's racial alienation and exclusion from the discursive construction of the city. The racial language of mainstream Hollywood cinema offers no place for him except as degenerate, and exoticised, primitive. Furthermore, the gender and sexual aspects of this crude exclusion of racial difference are as significant as the heavily emphasised demonisation of racial others. Bigger and Jack see two films. The first, *The Gay Woman,* is a melodrama featuring images of white American affluence, which are under threat from the twin evil of Communism and assertive women. The second, *Trader Horn,* is a colonial adventure film with barbaric Africans and exotic jungle locations. *The Gay Woman* presents a racial scenario from which Bigger feels excluded and alienated: '"I bet their mattresses is stuffed with paper dollars," Bigger said' (p. 34). Bigger and Jack's understanding of their alienation from the scene is expressed not so much through anger as bitter and ironic laughter. Further, they engage with the images of white affluence through a reversal of the image of black women as sexual predator explored in Petry's novel: 'Ah, man, them rich white women'll go to bed with anybody, from a poodle on up' (p. 33). This sexualised reading of the cinematic images is complicated by their comments on the film's Communist villain, whose status as a Red – 'Reds must don't like rich folks' (p. 35) – adds a further dimension to the two boys' interpretation of the film.

However, class and gender location are disallowed as significant interpretative factors in this section of the text, the focus instead being the overwhelming importance of racial identity as a hermeneutic model. Bigger's reading of the films, shaped by his absolutist understanding of his (racial) identity, is formulated even before he actually enters the cinema. Outside the cinema there are two posters advertising the film. The poster for *The Gay Woman* shows images of white men and women lolling on beaches and dancing in night-clubs, and the image for *Trader Horn* shows black men and women dancing against a backdrop of barbaric jungle. These are representations of the polarised and stereotypical constructions of black and white culture produced within mainstream Hollywood.[27] Bigger makes almost no comment on the racist images of black Africans presented in the *Trader Horn* film. His attention is focused instead on the images of white affluence that the films feed him. He desires the scenarios of wealth and leisure presented to him, but these images are racially exclusive (and exclusionary). The only means by which he can connect with these images is in terms of a sexual fantasy (sleeping with white women) which is, in terms of the novel's deterministic framework, a (racist) script already written for him. Bigger's misogyny in this scene is understandable in terms of a response to the racism which is the implicit background to the images of white women dancing and lolling on beaches. However, this inadvertently confirms the myth that black men automatically desire, and will rape, white women and that this desire is uncontrollable and animalistic: a racial myth disturbingly close to the presentation of Africans in *Trader Horn*. This is, of course, also the script which Bigger immediately recognises when he is caught in Mary Dalton's bedroom, and which precipitates his destruction. Bigger's destruction seems to crush the possibility of black subjectivity in the face of a white city that legislates and disciplines him through its construction of racial place as identity. This is a monolithic representation of a racialised city space – which Petry's novel and Brooks's poetry do not endorse – achieved through the suppression of the complicating effect of gender and class identity on racial subjectivity, in the service of a polemical protest that depends on absolutist notions of racial being. In contrast to the presentation of Lutie in *The Street*, Bigger reads the cinematic and advertising images in a non-dialectical way, which elides the patterns of identification and disidentification which shape his response.

Like many other instances in the novel (such as when Bigger and his friends see a plane writing 'white words' in the sky, or when Bigger chauffeurs Jan and Mary around the city) this representation of Bigger's position in the city is crudely totalising. Its placement before Bigger's experience of the inside (the domestic space) of the white city he sees so clearly emblematised in the plane scene, effectively robs him of any means of interpreting his situation except as utterly alienated. The polarised black and white realities presented in the opening sections of the novel oversimplify the experience of African Americans as urban workers and consumers – an experience which makes racial boundaries in the city highly mobile and intermittently policed, as is apparent in Petry's novel. It also does not even begin to speculate on the ambivalence of being a consumer of both products and images which give pleasure (and Bigger does experience pleasure – predominantly of a sexual nature – from his cinematic watching) at the same time as they enforce racial oppression and alienation. In Wright's text we are left feeling there is virtually no sense that Bigger could be inscribed upon this city scene except as an ideological absence or threat.

Small Victories

Lutie's identification with the advertisement on the train in *The Street* suggests, on the contrary, something other than total alienation from this 'gleaming white kitchen'. The manner in which she represents her experience of working in a kitchen like this one does not suggest the kind of total exclusion from the perceived white world that characterises the racial polemic of *Native Son*. As we saw, Lutie gazes at an advertisement which emphasises white affluence, rather as Bigger looks at the cinema poster, but Lutie's gaze takes her back into a reverie which explores her own ambivalent relationship to the advertisement she looks at. After thinking about her time with the Chandlers Lutie comments:

> That kitchen in Connecticut had changed her whole life – that kitchen all tricks and white enamel like the one in the adver- tisement. The train roared into 125th Street and she began pushing her way to the doors, turning to take one last look at the advertisement as she left the carriage. (p. 45)

It is significant here that although Lutie recognises the tricks this image presents she still says the kitchen changed her life. Given what we have already learnt about Lutie's position it would seem more appropriate to say that this kitchen ruined her life. This makes her interpretation of the image, and its associations, much more uncertain. The novel as a whole does not support a straight- forwardly positive view of the impact of consumer culture upon African Americans, indeed it repeatedly asserts the opposite. But, what it does admit is Lutie's involvement in the ideology that underpins this advertising image. This is not necessarily a positive thing in itself, but it does represent the possibility of Lutie making identifications (through her readings of images like the advertise-

ment) which mark her on the face of the city as something other
than absence. This admits the possibility of what the novel calls
'a small victory' (p. 45):

> She didn't have any illusions about 116th Street as a place to
> live, but at the moment it represented a small victory – one of a
> series that were the result of her careful planning. First, the white
> collar job, then a flat of her own where she and Bub would be
> by themselves ... Even after living on 116th Street for two weeks,
> the very fact of being there was still a victory. (p. 45)

In terms of my earlier analysis of Brooks's 'Kitchenette Building'
this suggests the possibility of Lutie being a planner of her own
existence in a way that exceeds the racist organisation of space. In
this sense the advertisements, which form part of the fabric of the
urban scene described in the novel, have a dangerously random
appeal. Their address to consumers is indiscriminate in that there
is no way of legislating against who looks at them and there is no
way of controlling absolutely the identifications that are produced
by this looking. Obviously, these identifications are delimited in
that the image is one that appeals to a particular (white) racial
audience and in this way the image is similar to the posters we saw
Bigger looking at outside the cinema. However, the crucial
difference in Lutie's case is that the possibility is allowed that she
will still make identifications with this image despite its racial
content, because of her experiences as a female worker in a scene
which corresponds to the image itself. Lutie becomes a viewer who
effectively racialises that exclusionary image of white domestic
affluence. So, Lutie is shown as part of a narrative of capitalist
accumulation which is officially that of the white inhabitants of the
city (we might recall here the inaccessibility of this narrative in
Native Son). Her institutionally recognised place as domestic
worker within this narrative also tentatively allows that she will
participate in that narrative as consumer and as desiring subject
in a way which contravenes its racial regulation.

So what is it then that allows Lutie's connection with these
images, when as we have seen they were unavailable to Bigger?
Explanation forces consideration of those gendered dimensions of
racial experience that are suppressed in Wright's narrative. It is
undoubtedly significant that we see Bigger moving around the city,
observing and reading signs (of whiteness) before he goes to work
for the Daltons, whereas Lutie reads the images surrounding her
after working in the world she sees represented in the image. Lutie's
journey downtown provokes a recognition of her invisibility in the
white sectors of the city, but the observation of her erasure from
the white urban scene comes after her protracted gaze upon and
interaction with the image of whiteness presented in the adver-

tisement. So, Lutie's description of her exclusion from the city is given as she marks her presence in it (particularly within domestic, female space). This contradictory position can be best understood by examining the relationship between Lutie and her employer, Mrs Chandler.

Mrs Chandler is presented as a relatively generous, but unthinking and patronising employer. When she and Lutie travel on the train to New York – Mrs Chandler for a weekend break and Lutie returning home to Harlem – she talks to Lutie as an equal, about newspaper stories, clothes or films. However, as Lutie notes, when they leave the train Mrs Chandler never fails to resume her position as Mistress: 'the wall suddenly loomed up. It was Mrs. Chandler's voice that erected it. Her voice high, clipped, carrying, as she said: "I'll see you on Monday, Lutie"' (p. 41). What is most interesting is the suggestion that this wall, unlike the one that encloses Lutie by the novel's end, is not an absolute barrier. Lutie is shown to have an active role in challenging, engaging with and policing the boundaries that separate (white) employer from (black) employee. Mrs Chandler, in her role as benign, but essentially idle, upper middle-class woman, passes on to Lutie the discarded trappings of her leisured existence which a woman of her position must certainly have, but which she seems to find tedious in the extreme. Lutie receives magazines, books and clothes that she obviously would not otherwise be able to afford. On the one hand Lutie is grateful and quite naive about these gifts from her employer: 'Lutie decided it was almost like getting a college education free of charge. Besides, Mrs. Chandler was really very nice to her. The wall between them wasn't so high' (p. 41). However, Lutie's attitude to the clothes that Mrs Chandler gives her is quite different. Although she receives them with proper gratitude, she mails them off to her father's latest girlfriend, 'taking great ironic pleasure in the thought that Mrs. Chandler's beautiful clothes Designed For Country Living would be showing up nightly at the gin dive at the corner of Seventh Avenue and 110th Street' (p. 41). Lutie emerges as the dialectical reader of the images of whiteness that surround her as she moves around New York. Her idealistic acceptance of the gifts of books is countered by her refusal to accept the clothes Mrs Chandler passes on. This parallels Lutie's identification with the advertisement on the train and her concomitant awareness of her invisibility downtown. Lutie can inhabit this contradictory position because as she observes, 'she had learned all about Country Living' (p. 41):

> She had learned all about it from the pages of the fat sleek magazines Mrs. Chandler subscribed for and never read. *Vogue, Town and Country, Harper's Bazaar, House and Garden, House*

Beautiful. Mrs. Chandler didn't even bother to take them out of their wrappings when they came in the mail, but handed them to Lutie, saying: 'Here, Lutie. Maybe you'd like to look at this.' (p. 41)

Lutie knows about Country Living, of course, in two radically contradictory ways. Her absorption in the consumer fantasies the magazines present and her internalisation of the central tenets of the American Dream are obvious. But so too is her ability to critique this ideological fantasy through a racialised reading of these images, a reading based on her insider knowledge that the gleaming white facade of Country Living presented, symbolically, in the advertisement on the train, has as its cornerstone a black presence. Lutie's ability to read this image as a potential consumer (something which we might otherwise see as deluded fantasy) merely reinforces this presence. Her racialised understanding allows a non-monolithic reading of the Street, and the city, which work so hard to crush the possibilities of subjective agency for African American women. The fact that this agency is marked through Lutie's ability to read images as a potential consumer should not be discounted as merely trivial in terms of the critical exploration of race, gender and class oppression in the novel.

Petry's and Brooks's writing continue the debates we saw in earlier women's texts about the position and subjectivity of African American citizens (particularly, but not exclusively, women) in the modern city. This presentation is sometimes bitter, sometimes idealistic, and frequently heavily ironic and blackly humorous. One might argue that my reading here veers toward a utopian celebration of the engagements with consumer culture and the city in Brooks's and Petry's work. Certainly my rather hopeful analysis doesn't correspond with most critical readings of their work nor is it in line with the writings by their black male contemporaries, especially Wright and Ellison. However, the forms of subjective agency asserted through their writing substantially revise critical understanding of resistance to racist culture or agency within an oppressively racialised city space. Both Petry and Brooks make clear protests against the economic, political and racial disenfranchisement of African Americans within the city space: this places them (rightly) in line with the kind of racial polemic we see in *Native Son*. At the same time their work suggests this racial oppression is never total, or totalisable, in any straightforward way. This is in part because, as feminist critics of their work have been at pains to point out, their understanding of racial oppression is crucially mediated through their experience of gender and sexual identity. In terms of the reading I have been pursuing this experience does not simply add another form of oppression to an already burdensome situation but reshapes fundamentally the experience of oppression, and the forms of resistance and protest which are then elaborated. To be a little less abstract, Petry's and Brooks's work asserts forms of agency we would struggle to recognise as radical. The difficulty with these texts is that they present possibilities (for example, identifying with a white domestic fantasy) which seem on the surface ideologically suspect (at least to the alert, left-inclined critic). Hence, I would argue, the persistent suggestion in critical studies of Petry and Brooks that their critiques of white racism do not go far enough, that their heroines are trapped, duped or insufficiently conscious of the righteous rage they should articulate.[28] This perception fails to note the subtle understanding of the possibilities and pitfalls of urban life and consumer culture that the texts persistently elaborate. But more importantly it fails to pursue the most important implication of their interrogation of urban life, which suggests that the racial place Petry and Brooks's women occupy exceed the usual dimensions of oppositionality.

When we see Lutie gazing at the advertisement the difficulty presented is that any agency she asserts seems in many ways as deeply conservative. Yet this is perhaps the most valuable element of the texts' elaboration of the urban, if the most difficult to write about. I want to challenge the designation conservative even as I introduce it, because with Petry's and Brooks's work it is precisely the polarisation of political positions (black/white, male/female, conservative /radical) which the texts make difficult. But the fact remains that it does seem dubious to suggest that it is the lure of consumer culture that offers some way out for Lutie (and the ending of the novel would not support this). Nevertheless, the text itself insistently reminds us of the difference Lutie's inside knowledge of the consumer world, and her own interest in it, makes. I propose that Lutie's elaboration of desire for things, and a place, may at first seem like a fantasy of whiteness but is instead what we might call the assertion of *modest* agency. Resistance in Lutie's case is the construction of a future that is not a radical alternative to the racist hegemony the novel so strongly protests. Instead it is, in large part, inculcated by and through that hegemonic formation. This does not represent Lutie's duping so much as attest to the inseparability of different forms of identity: racial, class, gendered and sexual, which in its turn assumes the subject's embeddedness in a (racist) culture at the same time as it observes that culture's racist, sexist and classist exclusions. The modesty of Lutie's 'small victories' is in fact a very large claim to insider status in the city space: an immanent claim to knowledge and power in constrained circumstances. Lutie identifies with a dream of white affluence, but her desire for this is presented in racialised form. More importantly, this modest desire represents agency in its refusal of the (segregated) racial place designated for her by the hegemonic white culture that underpins the ideological message of the image.

It seems to me that the complexity of Petry's and Brooks's representations of female subjects in the city has not been explored by critics of their work because the urban scene, and particularly the construction of this space by consumer culture, has rarely been judged as significant. Nor is it an entirely comfortable or rewarding position to make a strong argument for the modesty, or ambivalence, of critical energy in a text. It does, however, do justice to the shifting alignments of racial and gender politics in Petry's and Brooks's writing, and indeed provides a further example of my earlier argument that the difficulty of the intersection – of race, class, gender, sexuality – may just as easily be alternating forms of conservative and radical reaction (as with the passing subjects of Larsen's texts) as it may be a progressively increasing burden of marginalisation. This suggests that the protest both writers produce is ambivalent and contradictory in ways which do not constitute a failure (of racial or feminist consciousness) or a hopeless pessimism. This is made very clear at the end of Brooks's 'Kitchenette Building', where ironic nonchalance replaces pessimistic anger as the poem's speaker queues for the bath. The speaker, standing in for the denizens of the entire building, refuses the possibility of utopian dreams, not because they cannot imagine them (remember, the dream does 'float up') but because the racialised space which they inhabit does not allow them time for such luxuries as radical resistance. Again, this is a modest claim to agency because the assertion of not having time acts as critique of the limitations of the designated racial space and is the perverse articulation of their still active dreaming: dreaming here about not dreaming. This rejects the possibility of standing outside the space in order to gain some kind of autonomy or critical distance (a fantasy of escape from the dimensions of racial and gender subjectivity) which would act as a space of utopian resistance. Brooks's poem here rejects the necessity of this modernist distance, preferring instead the everyday obliquities of the bathroom queue.[29] In both Petry's and Brooks's writing we see an attempt to fashion an everyday critical reading of an urban scene that often violently excludes those it deems its racial or gendered others, but nevertheless calls them as subjects in ways that exceed the racist logic of its exclusionary tactics. In writing modestly of the ambivalent callings of women within the city, both Petry's novel and Brooks's poems exceed the plan of that urban location.

CHAPTER 6

Elegies to Harlem

Nobody says it's pretty here; nobody says it's easy either. What it is is decisive, and if you pay attention to the street plans, all laid out, the City can't hurt you.[1]

As we move toward endings I turn now to two contemporary texts which critically interrogate the Harlem I have been tracing through this study. This last chapter focuses on Isaac Julien's 1989 film *Looking For Langston* and Toni Morrison's 1992 novel *Jazz* as two exemplary urban texts which elaborate the major preoccupations of this text a good deal more elegantly than I would otherwise be able to do.[2] Both texts deal with love and death and mourning and memory. In this sense they share an immediate affinity with the classic passing texts; that is, their narratives are beautiful, but torn and tragic. They also share a preoccupation with passion and the vagaries of desire, presenting meditative treatises on identity; again entirely in line with the conventions of passing fiction. Both texts also share a fascination with beauty as a kind of obsessive haunting, delineating seduction and deception within an urban scene which is itself caught up in a dialectic of beauty and terror.[3] Each text has its faults, and each can be irritating in the manner of avant-gardist enterprises, but they both contain moments of stunning visual delight. This beauty very often derives from the reliance in each text on photography as inspiration for the aesthetic construction of the texts, and specifically both texts are indebted to the work of African American photographer James VanDerZee.[4]

Isaac Julien's film recreates a Harlem of the 1920s in order to intervene in 1980s and 1990s debates on the politics of black identity and representation. Julien's film looks for the always-unspoken sexuality of perhaps the most powerfully iconic figure of the Harlem Renaissance, Langston Hughes, but what it represents, to quote Toni Morrison, is 'the necessity of historical memory ... and the impossibility of forgetting', which it discovers through a meditation on black and white image making.[5] As Kobena Mercer argues, the film focuses on 'who has the right to look by emphasising ambivalent looking relationships, both interracial and intraracial, that complicate the subject/object dichotomy of seeing/being seen; all of which underlines the question of who or what the film is looking for'.[6] It does this in order to begin that which was only implicit in earlier passing texts: the tracing of a sexual politics of African American identity, and specifically the historical exploration of formations of black gay identity and image making. The film derives its visual style and many of its theoretical cues from avant-garde cinema, but in the spirit of a black urban aesthetic it takes its most potent visual images from the Harlem presented in VanDerZee's city photographs. From the scene of a wake which opens the film to the freeze frame of the dancing bohemians which closes it, the film repeatedly recreates 'moving' (in all senses of the word) versions, or critical recreations, of still images by VanDerZee and other avant-garde photographers.[7] This reliance on still photography as aesthetic inspiration (and critical commentary on the process and act of looking) is heightened by the presence within the film of numerous stills as stills, something I will explore in more depth presently. This focus on looking is a keynote in Julien's work, as he says in interview: 'Looking is where the risky business occurs ... which is why cinema and image making become a crucial area in which to open up those questions.'[8]

Jazz too derives much of its power from its self-conscious construction of scenes of heightened visual pleasure, from the interior exploration of the unnamed narrator's pleasure in looking, 'worth the trouble if you're like me – curious, inventive and well informed' (p. 137), to descriptions of the intimate point of connection between the body of a woman and the surface of a building: scenes which map out an architecture of desire,

> sitting on a stoop with a cool beer in her hand, dangling her shoe from the toes of her foot, the man, reacting to her posture, to soft skin on stone, the weight of the building stressing the delicate dangling shoe, is captured. And he'd think it was the woman he wanted, and not some combination of curved stone, and a swinging high-heeled shoe moving in and out of sunlight. He would know right away the deception, the trick of shapes and light and movement, but it wouldn't matter at all because the deception was part of it too. (p. 34)

The desires and obsessions which are mapped out in the novel are repeatedly figured through the medium of a photograph, most notably through Violet and Joe's shared haunting by the picture of Dorcas on their mantelpiece, an image which captures and torments the two central protagonists of the novel. This is merely the most obvious of the images which capture the characters whose fates are revealed in Morrison's mournful recreation of Harlem; images which work as a rich memory-text of Harlem's visual culture. Going against critical opinion on the novel, much of which asserts the centrality of music to the text, it seems to me that Morrison's duplicitous narrator, who leads us and seduces us through the novel, presents a visual panorama around which the ambiguous love story is woven.[9] Morrison has admitted part of the inspiration for the story comes from VanDerZee's photographs, particularly the numerous funeral pictures collected in his *Harlem Book of the Dead*.[10] Indeed, the 'drums' that accompany Morrison's account of the famous July 1917 protest parade (pp. 54–5) and echo through the narrative act as the aural correlative of the many photographs of this parade (including ones by VanDerZee), presenting a contemporary take on this paradigmatic Harlem image. The 1917 march is frequently taken as a starting point for the Harlem Renaissance and photographs of the march, which featured women and children in white gloves, many carrying placards which quoted those sections of the constitution violated by the practice of lynching, have become paradigmatic and deeply powerful representations of the injustices enacted upon African Americans in the 1910s and 1920s.[11] Photographs are thus used in the novel to organise memory and emotion and develop powerful relationships between characters, their urban environment and their history as African Americans.

The texts are curiously bound together in this utilisation of a counter-history of African American photography and they pay homage to the Harlem constructed through the work of VanDerZee. Both texts start with a death and expand outwards from the scene of mourning to recreate the lives of the living and the historical connections between the past and the present. This is made most explicitly clear in *Looking For Langston* where Julien himself is the body in the coffin in the opening scene. The text also stands as elegy to a Harlem, gay Harlem, that has been lost to history, 'history, the smiler with the knife' as Stuart Hall's voice-over comments, and to the men who made up the gay literati, most notably Bruce Nugent – whose 'Smoke, Lilies and Jade' forms the central memory text in the film – but also James Baldwin, whose words are read out by Morrison during the wake and to whom the film is dedicated. We might also add the names of the gay blues singers whose songs make up the soundtrack to the film and Florence Mills whose funeral brought Harlem to a halt, and whose wake, also photographed by VanDerZee, is connotatively connected to the funeral scenes in both texts.[12] There is, of course, the fact that Morrison is one of the voices on Julien's soundtrack so it is entirely possible that she encountered the VanDerZee photographs there and that the shared 'wake' scenes owe more to collaboratively shared passions than mere coincidence.

The obsessive visuality seen in both texts constructs a passing structure akin to that examined earlier in Larsen's work; that is, indeterminate – seductive and dangerous – comments on the politics of identity and the processes of the gaze within urban culture. Both texts perform this politics of identity through their critical appropriation of visual texts, but also as we shall see through their engagement with concepts and proponents of the avant-garde and by setting themselves in critical relation to contemporary debates about African American identity.[13] They serve as apposite final texts for this book since they make it very clear that contemporary debates about sexuality, race, gender and urban identity are too the concerns of the 1920s, and in fact it is the historical dialogue between past and present, particularly in *Looking For Langston*, that allows new and productive commentary on these issues. The passing structure of both novel and film presents an oscillation between different modalities of identity at the same time as they perform an act of beautiful historical recreation, working as, in the words of Kobena Mercer, 'a seductive invitation into the messy spaces in between the binary oppositions that ordinarily dominate representation'.[14] This passing structure suggests that this ambivalent visual field is a necessary component of a politicised relativism, a politics of identity and community which pays attention to postmodern notions of performance and fragmentation whilst holding onto a grounded notion of opposition to dominant cultural representations.

Looking For Langston

In his now classic analysis of racial being, psychoanalysis and existentialism, *Black Skin, White Masks* (1956), Frantz Fanon recounts the cry 'Look, a Negro!' which traumatically fixes his identity as Other – defined in the eyes of the other – through a 'racial epidermal schema' that equates racial being with the colour of the skin.[15] As Mary Ann Doane observes, drawing on Fanon's insights, Otherness – whether racial or sexual – is usually articulated as a problem of the limits of knowledge and hence visibility, recognition, differentiation.[16] Fanon's work on the neuroses that derive from this colonial disequilibrium has been profoundly influential for post-colonial theory (as well as problematic for some feminist and gay theorists) and on the work of Morrison and Isaac Julien, whose most recent film is a biography of Fanon.[17] Julien cites Fanon as inspiration for some of the theoretical work that lies behind the representational energies of *Looking For Langston*. He says in interview with bell hooks:

I think, in trying to transgress, not on one but on several fronts, be they racial, sexual, psychic or social, there's always this unconcealing of ambivalent 'structures of feeling'. And one's ambivalence, I think some of Fanon's work points to this – isn't found so much in polemic, in what one says, as in one's fantasies, in one's desires. (p. 127)

I want to think about what this Fanonian emphasis on ambivalence and the power of the racialised gaze means when sexual as well as racial identity is brought into the frame. Furthermore what happens when difference – racial or sexual – does not materialise on the surface? How does one, for example, 'see' a Negro who is passing, or categorise what one sees when one mode of identity is cut across or troubled by another? How does one discuss the construction of identity, in erotic and racial terms, in the light of passing? In short, how might one discuss identity in the light of the issues raised by this study?

The passing narrative gives us, as we have already seen, a juxtaposition of issues of knowledge, identity and visual verifiability (as well as fear and pleasure in looking). Given this, it is perhaps unsurprising that passing has become an important and fashionable theoretical preoccupation in recent years, since these issues also mark the debates about identity and representation which have been central to cultural and literary studies over the last two decades. The stock figure of the passing novel – the tragic mulatta – is, as much scholarship on Larsen and Fauset demonstrates, judged 'tragic' because she is seen to be caught irresolvably between two cultures. However, as my reading of Larsen's fiction suggests, one might conceive of this irresolvability as the grounds for a productive (if still tragic) interrogation of African American urban identity. In *Looking For Langston* we see this posed in yet another way as the conflictual claims to identity are taken as a necessary prerequisite for the exploration of desire and fantasy and their relationship to the social world and the histories of sexual and racial communities. The problem remains, however, one of how the subject defines itself through and between modalities of racial and sexual subjectivity. Recurrent motifs of passing circulate around the trauma of recognition (echoing Fanonian preoccupations) and, following this, Mary Ann Doane suggests: 'The mulatta, then, always signifies a potential confusion of racial categories and the epistemological impotency of vision.'[18]

Looking For Langston, however, utilises a passing structure to suggest not so much the impotency of vision but a certain insufficiency of vision, because the 'truth' of what is seen is determined from elsewhere. That is, it is determined at least in part by the politics and predilections of the viewer in a formulation which employs the tactics we saw in Irene and Clare's fateful rooftop meeting in Larsen's *Passing*, but here orchestrates the politics of intra- and extra-textual voyeurism. This is a key development, for as Mercer observes: 'In contrast to the claims of academic deconstruction the moment of undecidability is rarely experienced as a purely textual event; rather it is the point where politics and the contestation of power are felt at their most intense.'[19] Accordingly, in *Looking For Langston* the power of the gaze is explored by the characters within the film as the means by which the narrative, such as it is, is propelled forward, and as a means to conduct historical exploration of Harlem and its artists. But, the gaze is also negotiated by the viewer who comes to the film and whose predilections are addressed directly by the enfolding dialogues. Lastly, it is determined by the various visual fields – stereotypes, iconography, regimes of representation – that the images are very self-consciously located within and in relation to. To list these briefly we need to pay attention to the contradictory fields of racial and gay representational practices, issues of eroticism and exoticism, the historical context of the Harlem Renaissance and African American history and its relationship to homosexuality, the practices of avant-garde cinema, as well as a critical relationship to Hollywood representations. Finally the film's images ask to be read in relation to the theoretical practices of contemporary identity politics. It is text as theory, and very good-looking theory too. This constitutes, then, a visual politics of passing.

What must also be emphasised here is that the film also entertains the idea that all of the above may be held in abeyance – forgotten entirely – in the breathtaking pleasure of the deliciously extended look. The film, I can rigorously argue, stands as a piece of theory but it also passes as erotica (and has functioned as such at gay film festivals across the world). It is this doubled status – as work cerebral and also rather more corporeal – that gives the film its status as a theory of identity and positionality which does not dissolve into depoliticised relativism. It forces one to confront the awkward dimensions of one's fantasies and erotic identifications, and affirms the insecurity of identifications – sexual, racial or otherwise. It insists on the legacy of racism in the homosexual or homoerotic imaginary and likewise on the existence of homophobia in the black imaginary. It also insists that these factors are an issue for both black and white, gay and straight viewers (as participants in the politics of looking). As Stuart Hall's history lesson within the film announces:

> Not to discuss the moral significance of Countee Cullen, Langston Hughes, Alain Locke choosing, in the main, others of their own kind to love is to emasculate and embalm their society

as a whole. It erases the image of the two colored sissies kissing and producing poems and paintings for and about one another.

Further, like the beautifully dissected dark-and-light face of Alex (played by Ben Ellison) – one of the keynote images in the film – the negotiation of identity this requires is located in the movement between two discursive and representational regimes: as a process of passing identification.

Looking For ... or At?

We see this process of passing identification most clearly in one of the film's central scenes that I want to examine now in some detail. The opening of the film presents a wake (troping on VanDerZee's famous funeral pictures) with the body of Isaac Julien in the coffin surrounded by a group of mourners who are dressed as Harlem literati. This ceremony takes place in the upstairs of a night-club that recreates the Cotton Club as gay night-spot. The film then moves to a history lesson about Harlem, the Harlem Renaissance and homosexuality, which counterpoints a reading by Stuart Hall with archival footage of 'sissy' artists, and we then return to the Cotton Club, where the major fictional episodes in the film take place. As with so many important moments in the film we start from a still image, of the 'jazzers' in the club, nostalgically evoking a Harlem scene only too familiar in its night-time allure. As we close in on the still and the jazzers start to move, this familiarity is confirmed and critically destabilised as it becomes clear all the dancing couples are same-sex. The scene begins, then, by situating itself in relation to – taking its visual language from – a number of clearly recognisable cultural discourses: stereotypes of Jazz Age Harlem, the chiaroscuro light of early black-and-white cinema, avant-garde cinema and photography.[20] On the soundtrack Bessie Smith sings 'Freakish Man', conjoining the blues as the paradigmatic African American expressive form with the history of homosexuality.

The camera draws in to a close-up of the face of Alex lit to divide precisely his face along its vertical axis, giving us a perfectly realised image of passing identity – between black and white, gay and straight – and we move from his face through a series of profoundly extended glances to the exploration of a triangulated scene of desire. The scene gives us Alex staring at a black man called Beauty and the jealous reaction of the white lover with whom he sits. As Alex and Beauty exchange glances, the white lover bangs his champagne bottle on the table to discipline Beauty and reclaim his erotic attention. The slowness of shot movement and the construction of mise-en-scène and lighting mark the film's debt to avant-garde cinema. The film cuts from the shot of Alex's face divided into black and white to Beauty's face framed through an iris shot. This works in a very complex way to reverse the coding of colour (and race) associated with this sort of shot. Common in silent films, this shot is used to particular effect in D.W. Griffith's *Birth of a Nation* (1915) where, as Richard Dyer points out, it works to emphasise the whiteness of the film's heroine Lillian Gish.[21] Further, the usage of this kind of shot and lighting schema by Griffith marks the construction of what Manthia Diawara calls 'the grammar book of Hollywood representation of black manhood and womanhood'.[22] Whiteness becomes more-than-white, a cinematic as well as racial ideal which must be defended from the assault of darkness (in *Birth of a Nation*, the black and mulatto characters who appear as monstrous presences and move in and out of the dark edges of the frame).[23] This shot sets Julien's camerawork in relation to this tradition and works a transformation upon it.

As the iris frames Beauty's face he is lit so as to lighten his skin, making him appear almost white. Yet at the same time the camera dwells sensuously on Beauty's lips, an obviously provocative strategy given the stereotypes of thick Negro lips. There is a disjunction between the lightening of the epidermal signifiers of blackness and the hyper-valorisation of other corporeal signifiers of race, which mirrors the doubled discourse of identity that underpins this scene. As a scene of racial recognition ('Look, A Negro!', to use Fanon again) the shot flirts with some pernicious stereotypes, but from another perspective this kind of 'look' becomes the inscription of homosexual desire as the camera dwells on Beauty's lips as a site of erotic pleasure. The look is a seduction that draws the viewer into a passing structure which problematises simplistic conceptions of identity. Each interpretation inhabits the other, something that is only emphasised by 'Freakish Man' on the soundtrack, underlining the contention that the construction of race in this scene has also to be read through the construction of homosexual desire.[24] This re-coding of racial representation is also extended to the white man in this scene as we see his face lit so as to drain the colour from his face. Normative traditions of cinematic lighting are revealed in their racial specificity as white skin is quite clearly the marked exception rather than the normative centre of the film. Thus, the dubious racial motives for this man's participation in this scene of desire and his imperious attitude are mirrored by the formal organisation of shot and scene, at the same time as he is allowed to articulate his homosexuality by jealously competing for Beauty's attention.

In a scene a little later this exchange of glances is recapitulated to explore the disjunction between discourses of black pride (in their New Negro and post-1960s black power versions) and those of homosexuality. If the previous scene flirted with a racist homoerotic this scene deals with homophobia within black cultural discourses. Placing the articulation of black pride (a song 'Beautiful Black Man' by Blackberri) against the visual exchange of looks between Beauty's white lover, Alex, and a third unnamed 'dark' black man, the scene allows the viewer to draw out suggestive analogies. Although the song to the 'Beautiful Black Man' would be appropriate to the articulation of both forms of 'pride' (as it is obviously intended to be) it is also a fact that the rhetoric of black pride – in the 1920s as now – has tended to articulate a positively homophobic stance, as Stuart Hall's early commentary points out: 'Homosexuality was considered an affront to the race so it had to be kept a secret, even if it was a widely shared one.'[25] Once again the scene is characterised by a seductive doubleness which allows a pleasure in looking but suggests at the same time a rather more uncomfortable 'other' scene writ within the desiring exchange. The scene is again one where two (potential) lovers compete for the right to look at the desired object. The beloved in this sequence is shown to have the (nascent) ability to refuse the objectifying gaze of the white looker/lover. This suggests that there are in fact two orders of looking being negotiated in the exchange of glances; one consensual and erotic that is valorised in the sequence, and one commodifying and objectifying that is critiqued.

The scene starts with the injunction 'Look at me' on the soundtrack, and as the 'beautiful black man' walks into the club the aggressive gaze of the white man attempts to transfix and shame the black man. Another order of looking is suggested, however, by the sideways looks of the light-skinned Alex at the face of the dark man. The close-ups of his steady gaze work to suggest a meditation on the power of looking as his own face is examined in detail as he looks with desire at another man, and the narcissism of desire is elaborated as the camera acts as a mirror to his own beauty. His 'looks' appear to be supported by the soundtrack that calls for the black man to look up, to return his glance and 'be proud of his race', but his staring is a sexual invitation as well. Julien trades here on the characteristic rhetoric of the New Negro in the service of a politics of sexuality that inhabits the inside of the racial discourse the soundtrack pronounces. A language of race typically associated with the New Negro documents examined in the first chapter (and which also find their way as artefacts into the historical section of *Looking For Langston*) is here doubled to mark sexuality's manifest absence in these originary texts and to suggest the erotic instability of identity within the fantastic and spectacular urban scene that forms the film's visual content.

As the scene develops the look of the white man that attempts to objectify the black man is returned, refused and critiqued. He feels the power of the gaze turned upon him as he becomes the observed, in a contrary movement to the shaming of the black man that is protested in the soundtrack. In an even more pronounced manner than the earlier scene as blackness is lit for maximum sensuous effect, whiteness is presented as a deathly pallor in a witty reversal of the supposed hyper-visibility of blackness.[26] His vampire-like appearance stands as a visual metaphor for the draining and demeaning order of looking associated with him. He is also, we should note, presented as a gay stereotype – with kiss curl, cigarette holder and foppish demeanour – and we should view this exaggerated nature of his white gayness as a risky fetishisation in the same vein as the focus on Beauty's Negroid lips in the earlier scene. While it makes possible the doubled racial and sexual vocabulary we see at play in this scene, it also moves deliberately close to dangerous stereotypes of gayness, pointing again to the powerful organising energies of social stereotyping. The exchange of sexually charged looks between Alex and the other black man becomes the means by which certain kinds of voyeurism and racial and sexual objectification are critically explored. It is the means by which we experience the pleasures of voyeurism (having our critical cake and eating it) as a passing both/and formulation.

The film is also, as critics have noted, peopled largely by light-skinned black men, something Julien claims is dictated by the racial aesthetic of the 1920s, but can also be seen as provocatively linked to the construction of the Cotton Club as gay space in the film. Julien comments on the difficulties the prevalence of light-skinned bodies has caused for reception of the film by some black audiences. He says:

> I think there's a matter of historical specificity that we tried to preserve: the kind of black men who would have been at the centre of the Bohemian life style would have tended to be black middle-class Americans, and because of certain structures in that society, they were more or less light-skinned ... But also I think behind those kind of accusations there lies something else, which is a kind of closure around racial representations and anything that aims to be slightly ambivalent. For example, when you hear the slogan: 'Black men loving Black men is the revolutionary act of the 80s' everyone knows we're talking about dark-skinned black men. And again, I sense this closure, this essentialism, in that statement that I feel is problematic. (pp. 128–9)

One might argue that the film shows black men passing as white in order to identify as homosexual or at least that related category, the bohemian. The film flirts with this suggestion, ultimately to undermine it, as a critical commentary on the seductions of avant-gardism and to point up the whiteness of stereotypes of bohemianism and modernism that the film takes on. At the same time it emphasises the ambiguous address of the film because the seductive valorisation of avant-gardist style is part of the film's homoerotic challenge to certain tendencies within black cultural discourses. As Julien comments:

I think it's the kind of transgression which some black audiences are interested in not seeing, not looking at – because within the act of looking, their own insecurities start to unravel. There's also this invitational mode of address which I try to circulate in the images in my films, where they're caught up with the seduction and then it's interrupted, to a certain extent, by these representations. (p. 132)

That it is the politics of the gaze at issue is made more explicit by the following scene. In this the white man walks through a darkened extension of the night-club, caressing suspended images of naked black men by Robert Mapplethorpe. These are the most explicit images of nudity in the whole film and they address directly the commodification and exoticisation of African American culture and black male sexuality which are the implicit background to the earlier night-club scenes – concerns common to the film's historical subject and its contemporary moment. These are images of the black man as sex and, as the Essex Hemphill poem 'And His Name Is Mandingo' on the soundtrack make clear, as stereotype. The white man consumes the images here voyeuristically, touching and dismissing the nude bodies offered up, mirroring the sexual transaction that concludes this scene. This kind of looking is presented as aggressive and commodifying, and this way of looking is strongly separated from the erotic exchange of glances in the earlier scene. The disjunctive relationship between images and soundtrack again works to make it clear that refusal of this order of looking is possible as the voice runs an ironic commentary on the white man's progress through this hall of images. The sequence is also insistent in its critique of a particular kind of looking, not the look or presence of the white man in itself, something which is a central concern for Julien's project. As he explains: 'Because of the historical inscription of male bodies in photography and in art in general, I was always worried about trying not to show the black male body in a particular construction that could be consumed for an unquestioning white gaze. I was worried about that gaze' (p. 128).

The complexity of this engagement with looking can be seen in the way the film itself spends some time moving across these images, exploring them in detail to suggest that there could be a kind of gaze which would not turn these body images into appropriable commodities. It also admits that despite the commodifying potential of the images they are the source of (homo-) erotic pleasure in looking and that this is part of their function within the film. This is confirmed by the treatment of the same white man in other sections of the film where he does not engage in this kind of peepshow, but instead is shown positively as part of the 'scene' documented in the film. My emphasis here is on the contradictory doubleness of looking and identity which is at the heart of Julien's stylised recreation of Harlem, a doubleness which stresses the interconnected histories of racial and sexual identity as a shared feature of the 1920s and the 1980s, something underlined by the textual embedding of Bruce Nugent's 'Smoke, Lilies and Jade' (as one of the very few 'out' Harlem Renaissance texts) as the central erotic fantasy in the film. The film looks back to Harlem, not as utopian space but rather for the usefully 'messy ambivalence' (to use Kobena Mercer's phrase) around issues of race and sexual identity that one sees in the writers and cultural producers of the Harlem Renaissance.

Bitch or Dumpling Girl

To turn back now to Toni Morrison's *Jazz*, a text equally reliant on still photography for inspiration and aesthetic power, one finds that the field of vision proves to be equally deceptive. As with *Looking For Langston* the text opens with a funeral, which is disrupted by Violet's attempts to slash the face of the 'bitch or dumpling girl' (p. 106) Dorcas who has been murdered (in loving destructiveness) by Violet's husband Joe Trace. This scene, which makes reference again to the funereal tradition of VanDerZee's photography, sets the novel on a course of mourning, but also searching, for the something lost that could explain the drive to murder, passion and desire. While this something lost is not ever straightforwardly recovered for the characters in the text, it is made clear that the project of understanding is bound up with the slippery truth(s) attributed to the visual. Thence, we come to know Violet and Joe and their violent history through their contradictory obsessions with a photograph of the dead girl Dorcas. Photography, the visual pleasure of architecture and urban space, and exploration of the deceptions of visual perception through the figure of the curious and voyeuristic narrator, constitute the text's dynamic relationship to modernism and postmodernism, and to its historical subject, Harlem and the Harlem Renaissance; it also marks the limits of its project (at least in relation to *Looking For Langston*). It goes some way to explain the peculiar absence in the novel of actual Harlem places, jazz joints, famous buildings, events or people. Instead what we have is a love story, and a deliberately abstract aesthetic appreciation of urban space and its parameters.[27] The love triangle plot of the novel is recounted on the first page by the narrator, and her gossipy voice tells us the story of the whole book, betraying the ending and her own incapacity as narrator at the beginning of the tale. The gender of the narrator is never actually specified and critics have argued over whether one can or should decide either way. Andrea O'Reilly suggests the sound which starts the novel, 'Sth', is a characteristically feminine expression, the sound of thread being licked before it is passed through the eye of a needle, or as others have observed that typically Africanist female sound, the sucking of the teeth. The ordinary intimacies of the narratorial voice suggest femininity to me, though at other points the voyeuristic tendencies and modernist wonder at the city would ordinarily connote masculinity. The complex pleasure with which these different modes are adopted and interrogated is perhaps the most beguiling feature of the novel.[28] The text then elaborates the story of Joe, Violet and Dorcas as a narrative of Harlem and desire and identity, weaving this story as a dynamic interrogation of the power and ambiguity of the image. As Joe and Violet tiptoe out in the dark to stare at the photograph of Dorcas on their mantelpiece which Violet has taken from Dorcas's Aunt Alice Manfred, the picture which torments their sleepless nights appears to shift under their respective gazes. For Joe, 'it is the absence of accusation that wakes him from his sleep hungry for her company ... Her face is calm, generous and sweet' (p. 12). But for Violet the face is very different; powerful in a way which suggests the ability to reverse the relationship between subject and object so that the photograph may possess the perceiver with a kind a kind of visual haunting: 'The girl's face looks greedy, haughty and very lazy. The cream-at-the-top-of-the-milkpail face of someone who will never work for anything ... An inward face – whatever it sees is its own self. You are there, it says, because I am looking at you' (p. 12). This photograph of Dorcas becomes, through a process of introjection, the outward trace of a horribly intimate history of love and loss for Violet. The woman who stole her husband becomes the daughter who Violet (and Joe) lost (through abortion or miscarriage, the issue is deliberately confused) in their everyday dash to become 'City People'. After the fact the photograph comes to stand for the traumatic loss of a history which never happened.[29]

> The scheming bitch ... Or mama's dumpling girl? Was she the woman who took the man, or the daughter who fled the womb? Washed away on a tide of soap, salt and castor oil ... Or was it

the city that produced a crooked kind of mourning for a rival young enough to be a daughter? (p. 109)

Violet's identification with and against the image of Dorcas as both daughter and rival (with its deliberately provocative psycho-analytic resonances) is another example of a passing structure, and it is no accident that this at first appears to be a story of a dark woman's fury at a rival light enough to pass. In the end though Morrison takes the tragic elements of the classic passing narrative to present a story of country folk passing as urbanites, and it is the deceptions and seductions of the city, not the temptation to pass as white within it, which are presented as the greatest threat to a racial authenticity that Morrison (unlike, I think, Isaac Julien) wishes to defend against the depredations of a delightful, beautiful, but ultimately predatory urban modernity:[30]

> How soon country people forget. When they fall in love with the city it is forever and it is like forever ... There in the city they are not so much new as themselves: their stronger riskier selves ... what they start to love is the way a person is in the city ... Little of that makes for love but it does pump desire. (pp. 33–4)

The reader's deceitful guide to the seductions of the city is Morrison's consummately brilliant narrator, and it is her modernist city passion I want to concentrate on for a moment. The pain and confusion and extreme ambiguity of desire associated with Violet and Joe Trace are held against the insistent, confident, all seeing, *nosy* voice of the narrator who sings a modernist paean of praise to the city, and to her own all-encompassing interpretative passion. This voice, the lyrical centre of the novel, develops a powerful seductive effect on the reader that I would compare with the risky gorgeousness of the chiaroscuro history presented in *Looking For Langston*:

> I'm crazy about this city ... A city like this makes me dream tall and feel in on things. Hep. It's the bright steel rocking above the shade below that does it. When I look over strips of green grass lining the river, at church steeples and into the cream-and-copper halls of apartment buildings, I'm strong. Alone, yes, but top-notch and indestructible – like the City in 1926 when all the wars are over and there never will be another one. The people down there in the shadow are happy about that. At last, at last, everything's ahead. The smart ones say so and the people listening to them and reading them agree: Here comes the new. (p. 7)

This exultant voice steals centre stage in the novel and carries a force which is both stirring and hypnotic but is also the novel's most problematic feature. The sheer urban savvy of the narratorial voice attempts to close down the interpretative indecision that we saw earlier associated with Violet's relationship to her own past (as Violet, or Violent). In her desire to capture the city's essence and sing its praises the narrator falls into a celebratory modernism which is very close to Ann Douglas's 'terrible honesty': the characteristic white modernist attitude in the 1920s.[31] The city in this rendition is characterised by its lack of ambiguity: 'What it is is decisive' (p. 7), and although it is the fate of the narrator to realise that she has fallen in love with the city and missed the action within it entirely, the decisive brilliance of this writing is not so easily undermined.

As the novel moves toward its end (which is also its beginning, in that it is the section which Morrison wrote first) the knowing narrator of the glittering city becomes increasingly disillusioned with her own interpretative powers, particularly when it comes to ascribing meaning to the novel's miscegenation story and its white/black hero Golden Gray: 'What was I thinking of? How could I have imagined him so poorly? Not noticed the hurt that was not linked to the color of his skin, or the blood that beat beneath it' (p. 160). In fact, as Peter Brooker points out, Morrison suggests a whole other interpretative angle on racial conjoining with her symbolically named passing character.[32] But in describing a genealogy of black–white relations the narrator becomes confused, frustrated with her own desire to see things as categorically black and white; while the story of Wild, Joe Trace's mother (who, it seems likely, is also Beloved, pregnant with Paul D's child) and her connection to Golden Gray, the (black) white child who owned True Belle's heart and possessed the mind of her grand-daughter Violet, goes beyond these opposed polarities tracing a complex pattern of desire and loathing that the narrator simply cannot get to grips with: 'I have been careless and stupid and it infuriates me to discover (again) how unreliable I am' (p. 160).[33] It is also clear that the history hunted down by Joe Trace and Violet is part of a longer, more complex, history (of African Americans and their experience of modernity) which *Jazz* takes on as a sequel to *Beloved* (1987) and of which *Paradise* (1997) is the third section.[34] The city becomes both the site of the destruction of the rememory that haunts Sethe, and also its apotheosis through the haunting of Wild/Beloved's son Joe Trace by his mother's reincarnation, the bitch/dumpling girl Dorcas: a girl young enough to be his daughter. The convoluted chronology of all this suggests the extreme unreliability of testimony and memory in the novel, perhaps the only way to recover a traumatic history in its pain and poignant energy. But at the same time this unreliability is repeatedly forsaken in the luxuriant pleasures of city sights, which are not simply Joe and Violet's experience but also that of the narrator who gives us their experience. It is this that provides the key to the novel's oddly elegiac tone, and is, whether Morrison intends it or not, the key feature of the novel's aesthetic ambitions.

The narrator is not so much unreliable, as belatedly coming up against the deceptiveness of the visual field that she so confidently declares she can read in the early sections of the novel ('sth, I know that woman' (p. 3)). She is forced to admit that for her interpretation is a matter of positionality and power (as in so many of the instances examined in this chapter): 'It was loving the City that distracted me and gave me ideas. Made me think I could speak its loud voice and make that sound human. I missed the people altogether' (p. 220). The narratorial conviction of the outcome of the 'scandalizing threesome' (p. 6) on Lenox Avenue, 'that the past is an abused record with no choice but to repeat itself at the crack' (p. 220), is undermined by the shifting perceptions of the images and encounters that structure this Harlem world. In its repetitions the story of 'who shot whom' (p. 6) turns out very differently, an effect which follows the 'ambivalent unconcealings' of fantasy and desire that one sees in *Looking For Langston*.

In the end however, the novel is rather less challenging than the film (though more personally pleasurable) in that it remains wedded to a modernist aesthetic whose redemptive focus is ultimately individualist. The pleasure the narrator takes in her own beautiful experiences is mirrored by the pleasure the text takes in its own language: a heady seduction which seems in the end to override the narrator (or Morrison's) cautionary admonitions about believing the city's (or the text's) hype. This pleasurable complicity between reader and text is interesting in that it takes one back to the seductions of the gaze explored in *Looking For Langston* and reminds one of the dangerous pleasures of the politics of identity – what Kobena Mercer calls the 'dark side of desire and identification'.[35]

We see this most clearly in the closing love song of the novel, which follows the narrator's interpretative disclaimers to authority after the story of Violet, Joe and Felice does not repeat that of Joe, Violet and Dorcas but instead finds itself some kind of future (beyond the seductive malevolence of Beloved's spirit) in the confidently striding figure of Felice who claims the city as her own, 'her speed may be slow, but her tempo is next year's news' (p. 222). Finding herself islanded by her smug superiority and entirely superseded by the agency of the characters who peopled her cityrama, the narrator retires from prying and in doing so is intended to teach us a lesson about historical uncertainty and the unpredictability of human desire; a lesson which would set the text on a similar track to *Looking For Langston*. Ultimately though this does not happen, for even as the narrator insists upon her wrong-headedness and the incapacity of her view ('I missed it altogether'

(p. 220)) for this reader at least the intensely subjective, passionate swan song with which she closes the novel makes one feel that the modernist pretensions of the narrator were spot on after all. It is the most stunning piece of prose from an author who specialises in the painfully beautiful, and reading it recapitulates the modernist city epiphanies of the earlier sections of the novel:

> *That I have loved only you, surrendered my whole self reckless to you*
> *and nobody else. That I want you to love me back and show it to me.*
> *That I love the way you hold me, how close you let me be to you. I*
> *like your fingers on and on, lifting, turning. I have watched your face*
> *for a long time now, and missed your eyes when you went away from*
> *me. Talking to you and hearing you answer – that's the kick …*
> … If I were able I would say it. Say make me, remake me. You are free to do it and I am free to let you because look, look. Look where your hands are now. (p. 229)

Despite the delight I take in reading this passage, if I remove my hands from the book (or somewhere slightly lower given the sensuousness of the passage) I find this closure to the novel difficult. This paragraph traces again the soaring splendour of the 'I'm crazy about this city' sections of the text and tells us that despite the narrator's protests we were right to love it, and more to the point we were right to love the narrator that gave it to us in this fashion. The 'experience' of the novel becomes ultimately the fleshly contract between reader's hands and the pages of the text. Whilst this might be nicely postmodern it is also individualist in a way that rather undermines the tracing of a community's history beyond the 'abused record' of exploitation and exclusion: a community story which bears testament to this and to the singing pleasures of the 'Harlem' experience. In fact, history (in the form of Harlem in its specifics) and community (in the form of Joe, Violet and Felice) disappear into the self-absorbed song of book to reader and back again. Most problematically (noted by some black feminist analyses) the woman whose yellow pock-marked face, *whose photograph*, occasioned all this love and trouble – Dorcas, the true passing heroine of the novel – is decisively removed from the picture, a sleight of hand which is deeply satisfying in its push toward closure but a slight to a murdered girl nevertheless, as well as a typical fate for a passing woman.[36]

On the other hand, the more fluid both/and formulation of *Looking For Langston* leaves us with an evaporated image of community, which is there in raucous celebration but is also, as powerfully, not there as the thugs break into a scene which is gone already and was never really there except in its evocation of a community in process. Eschewing the seductiveness of the stable image, 'look where your hands are now', for the indeterminacy of the (passing) gaze *Looking For Langston* presents an avant-gardist meditation on identity without falling into modernist solipsism. In the terms this book has worked with *Looking For Langston* develops a representation of city life that can embrace the striving toward urbanity as the construction of community in terms both social and political. The thugs breaking in to the suddenly empty night-club represent, after all, not the postmodern instability of history but its brutal suppression by the forces of the dominant culture. But the aesthetic celebration of community that makes up the filmic text also suggests that in this passing structure we will find the practice of urbanity embedded in the striving toward being urbane. In uniting these oft-opposed meanings of the practice of urban life the film returns to Harlem not to rewrite its history but to explore the ambivalences that are integral to the various Harlems traced throughout this text.

Conclusion

There are many different pathways this book might have taken through the diverse figurations of twentieth-century urban African American writing, and many different authors whose work might lay claim to inclusion in such a project. The selectivity of any attempt to cover such a diverse field is always the most onerous element of the work. I end with *Looking For Langston* and *Jazz* not as representative contemporary texts so much as texts that reflect on the issues of urbanity, identity and representation, which have been central to the readings of all the texts that make up this study. That they should present their meditations on race and identity as city texts is no surprise given that the city, urbanism and urbanity have been key issues for debate throughout the 1990s. This is even more strongly the case as we enter a new century, and critical and cultural theorists, sociologists and cultural geographers ponder the question of what will be the future of the city in the new millennium. This project has its autobiographical impetus in my own life as an urban girl and city lover, but it finds its wider context and greater inspiration from this critical and cultural work on the city as a site of representation, imaginary space and social location.

It is as part of the exploration of what the city means, as image and as cultural location, for its diverse communities that I would locate this book. As *Looking For Langston* and *Jazz* prove this question is bound up with the meanings of race, history and identity in an unequal social world, and the city that each text uncovers demonstrates that the issues remain unanswered in the present as they are in the 1920s world each text creates. If the 'looking for' of Isaac Julien's title stands for anything it must surely be the multiple meanings of urban identity that he discovers in the search for the elusive Langston. Likewise, Morrison's text resists its city location whilst finding in it both a language of desire and, for Joe and Violet, a rhythm of urban being that reconciles their past with the future embodied in the slow-fast pace of Felice.

These texts are not unique, however. In fact if this study demonstrates anything it is that these contemporary texts find their best contexts in the writings of the period they seek to recreate. The same can be said of the contemporary urban theorising that inspired my interest in African American urban writing. If we are currently concerned with the fate of the cities and its citizens then we are only as engaged with these questions as the writers and thinkers from the first decades of the twentieth century. That African American writers have not always been seen as part of these debates speaks volumes about the fate of black peoples in these city spaces, as it does about our understandings of the shaping of modernity and the place of race within this. Despite the experience of African Americans in the city, and I would not want to write of this as a successful 'refuge' narrative, it has been the city that has been the testing ground for African American modernity just as assuredly as the city has served this role for so-called mainstream culture. The philosophical, literary and cultural debates that have structured African American discussion of the meanings of racial being in America are inextricably bound up with the meanings of city life and urbanity for African Americans: whether this has been told as a story of heaven or a story of hell. This is not, though, to end with a suggestion that the urban African American story is the only one to be told. Even if this were true, the texts and issues dealt with here trace only one part of a much more complex story – a narrative of African American experience in modernity outside the Northern urban centres as well as within them. The racial aesthetic traced here maps out some of the dimensions of this larger experience. In their engagement with new conditions of urban living and new forms of social organisation, their embrace of the technological innovations of modernity, and in their spirited embrace of the everyday Bang/Crash experience of the American city all the writers featured herein take the city as the keynote of their aesthetic aspirations. This goes beyond addressing the city as subject matter in their writing, and it goes beyond simply an urban sensibility, to present forms of writing and analysis that produce and are produced by urban African American experience. I suggest the very complexity of the city as representational object in African American writing gives us compelling evidence of a racialised aesthetic that draws its energy from the competitive conversations, debates and arguments that have structured African American urban experience, community and writing.

Notes

Introduction

1. Toni Morrison, *Jazz* (New York: Alfred A. Knopf, 1992), p. 24; and 'City Limits, Village Values: Concepts of the Neighbourhood in Black Fiction' in Michael C. Jaye and Ann Chalmers Watts (eds), *Literature and the American Urban Experience* (New Brunswick: Rutgers University Press, 1981), p. 39.

2. The quotations are taken from 'City of Refuge' (1925) and 'The South Lingers On' (1925); rpt in *City of Refuge: The Collected Stories of Rudolph Fisher*, ed. John McCluskey Jr (Columbia, London: University of Missouri Press, 1987), p. 4; p. 30.

3. Texts that deal with the city and its relationship to African American writing include Jaye and Watts (eds), *Literature and the American Urban Experience*; Yoshinobu Hakutani and Robert Butler (eds), *The City in African American Literature* (London, Toronto: Associated University Presses, 1995); and Charles Scruggs, *Sweet Home: Invisible Cities in the Afro-American Novel* (Baltimore: Johns Hopkins University Press, 1984). Scruggs's text covers similar terrain to this study, but his approach diverges from my own in significant ways. Concentrating on those male authors central to the racial protest tradition of urban writing – Wright, Ellison, Baldwin – he sidelines the issues of gender and sexuality that are so central to this study. His focus is on the mythic cities these works project as alternatives to the grim urban contexts of his authors. He ends with discussion of Morrison's *Beloved*: a rather strange choice as an urban novel.

4. This message is conveyed in the novel with only partial success. I argue in Chapter 5 that the novel's supposed warning about the dangers of city life is undermined by the seductiveness of the textual evocation of the city.

5. Paul Gilroy, *The Black Atlantic: Modernity and Double Consciousness* (London, New York: Verso, 1993).

6. See Scruggs, *Sweet Home*, pp. 13–37 for a fuller discussion of nineteenth- and early twentieth-century urban writings. The distinction between specific urban place and generalised moral space is his and refers in particular to the absence of a detailed urban map or texture he notes in texts prior to the beginning of the twentieth century; see pp. 17–18.

7. Carlo Rotella, *October Cities: The Redevelopment of Urban Literature* (London, Los Angeles: University of California Press, 1998).

8. Scruggs, *Sweet Home*, pp. 4–5.

9. The debate about the politics of white feminist readings of black texts has been a powerful one within black and white feminist

communities. For key interventions that have influenced my own thinking see Elizabeth Abel, 'Black Writing, White Reading: Race and the Politics of Feminist Interpretation', *Critical Inquiry*, Vol. 19 (Spring 1993), pp. 470–98; Hazel Carby, 'The Multicultural Wars' in Gina Dent (ed.), *Black Popular Culture* (Seattle: Bay Press, 1992), pp. 187–99; Patricia Hill Collins, 'The Social Construction of Black Feminist Thought', *Signs: Journal of Women in Culture and Society*, Vol. 14 (Summer 1989), pp. 745–73; Margaret Homans, '"Women of Color": Writers and Feminist Theory', *New Literary History*, Vol. 25, No. 1 (Winter 1994), pp. 73–94; bell hooks, 'Critical Interrogation: Talking Race, Resisting Racism', *Inscriptions*, Vol. 5 (1989), pp. 159–62; Valerie Smith, 'Black Feminist Theory and the Representation of the "Other"' in Cheryl Wall (ed.), *Changing Our Own Words: Essays on Criticism, Theory and Writing by Black Women* (London: Routledge, 1990), pp. 38–57; Michele Wallace, 'Who Owns Zora Neale Hurston? Critics Carve Up the Legend' in her *Invisibility Blues: From Pop to Theory* (London: Routledge, 1990), pp. 172–86.

10. Examples of this work would include Beatrix Colomina (ed.), *Sexuality and Space* (New York: Princeton Architectural Press, 1992); Elizabeth Grosz, *Space, Time and Perversion: Essays on the Politics of Bodies* (New York, London: Routledge, 1995); Michael Keith and Steve Pile (eds), *Place and the Politics of Identity* (London: Routledge, 1993); Steve Pile, *The Body and the City: Psychoanalysis, Space and Subjectivity* (London: Routledge, 1996).

11. Scruggs, *Sweet Home*, pp. 4–5.

12. The phrase is taken from Wright's famous 1937 essay, 'Blueprint for Negro Writing', *New Challenge*; rpt in Addison Gayle (ed.), *The Black Aesthetic* (Garden City: Doubleday, 1971), pp. 10–16.

13. See Jervis Anderson, *This Was Harlem: A Cultural Portrait, 1900–1950* (New York: Farrar, Straus and Giroux, 1981); Nathan Huggins, *Harlem Renaissance* (London, Oxford, New York: Oxford University Press, 1971); David Levering Lewis, *When Harlem Was In Vogue* (New York, Oxford: Oxford University Press, 1982).

14. The definitive statement of the Black Arts movement would be Addison Gayle's *The Black Aesthetic* (1971).

15. This position has been challenged forcefully by George Hutchinson in his *The Harlem Renaissance in Black and White* (Cambridge, Mass., London: Harvard University Press, 1995), who suggests that this view of the period is based on an unsatisfactory understanding of the institutional contexts of Harlem Renaissance literary production and improper historisisation of the relationships between black and white intellectuals in the period.

16. See Henry Louis Gates Jr, 'Criticism in the Jungle' in his *Black Literature and Literary Theory* (New York, London: Methuen, 1984), pp. 1–24.

17. For some key moments and interventions in these debates see Michael Awkward, 'Appropriative Gestures: Theory and African American Literary Criticism' in Linda Kaufman (ed.), *Gender and Theory: Dialogues on Feminist Criticism* (New York: Basil Blackwell,

1989), pp. 235–46; Michael Bérubé, *Public Access: Literary Theory and American Cultural Politics* (London, New York: Verso, 1994); Hazel Carby, 'The Multicultural Wars'; Barbara Christian, 'The Race For Theory' in Kaufman (ed.), *Gender and Theory*, pp. 225–35; Ann DuCille, *The Coupling Convention: Sex, Text and Tradition in Black Women's Fiction* (New York, Oxford: Oxford University Press, 1993), pp. 3–12; Henry Louis Gates Jr, *Loose Canons: Notes on the Cultural Wars* (New York, Oxford: Oxford University Press, 1992); David Theo Goldberg (ed.), *Multiculturalism: A Critical Reader* (Oxford: Blackwell, 1994).

18. Baker revises, or tropes, upon his own earlier Black Arts-inspired work – particularly in *Afro-American Poetics: Revisions of Harlem and the Black Aesthetic* (Madison: University of Wisconsin Press, 1988). He perceives a reorientation of concerns in his own work that is sometimes a little hard to discern. Indeed I would suggest it is more interesting to explore the continuities that persist despite his embrace of apparently very different critical paradigms.

19. See *Workings of the Spirit: The Poetics of Afro-American Women's Writing* (Chicago: University of Chicago Press, 1991), p. 25.

20. For black feminist critique of the work of Houston A. Baker and Henry Louis Gates Jr, see Mae G. Henderson, 'Response to "There Is No More Beautiful Way: Theory and Poetics of Afro-American Women's Writing" by Houston Baker' in Houston A. Baker and Patricia Redmond (eds), *Afro-American Literary Study in the 1990s* (Chicago, London: University of Chicago Press, 1989), pp. 155–63; see also the bad-tempered exchanges between Joyce A. Joyce on one side and Baker and Gates on the other in *New Literary History*, Vol. 18 (Winter 1987), pp. 335–84.

21. For discussion of the usages of this idea in feminist study of African American literature see Margaret Homans, '"Women of Color"'.

22. Hazel Carby, 'The Multicultural Wars', p. 191–3.

23. Hazel Carby, *Race Men* (Cambridge, Mass., London: Harvard University Press, 1998), p. 5.

24. See in particular Hazel Carby, *Reconstructing Womanhood: The Emergence of the Afro-American Women Novelist* (New York, Oxford: Oxford University Press, 1987), the still definitive analysis of the literary production and social activism of African American women from Reconstruction to the middle of the 1920s.

25. Carby, *Race Men*, pp. 1–6.

Chapter One: New Negroes, New Spaces

1. See James Weldon Johnson, 'Harlem: The Culture Capital' in Alain Locke, *The New Negro* (1925; rpt, New York: Atheneum, 1968), p. 301.

2. Arna Bontemps, one of the foremost chroniclers of Harlem literary life, recorded his sense of the dynamism of Harlem in the 1920s, which had drawn him all the way from California: 'In some places, the autumn of 1924 may have been an unremarkable season. In Harlem it was like a foretaste of paradise. A blue haze descended at

night and with it strings of fairy lights on the broad avenues. From the window of a small room in an apartment on Fifth and 129th Street I looked over the rooftops of Negrodom and tried to believe my eyes. What [a] city! What a world! ... full of golden hopes and romantic dreams.' Preface to *Personals* (London: Paul Bremen, 1963), p. 4.

3. Rudolph Fisher, 'City of Refuge', *Atlantic Monthly*, Vol. 135 (1925), pp. 178–87. Rpt in *City of Refuge: The Collected Stories of Rudolph Fisher*, ed. McCluskey, pp. 3–16. All further page references to Fisher's work will be to this edition and incorporated in the text.

4. See Locke, *The New Negro*, p. 6: 'In Harlem, Negro life is seizing upon its first chances for group expression and self-determination. It is – or promises to be – a race capital.' The term race capital becomes a widely used one in writings on Harlem from the mid-1920s. On the concept of a race capital and its links to ideas of urban civility see Scruggs, 'City Cultures' in his *Sweet Home*, pp. 38–67.

5. Gilroy, *The Black Atlantic*. See in particular pp. 41–71, pp. 187–223.

6. For analyses of the role of race in the construction of 'America' and concomitant debates over citizenship and national identity, see Walter Benn Michaels, *Our America: Nativism, Modernism, and Pluralism* (Durham: Duke University Press, 1995); Lauren Berlant, 'National Brands/ National Body: *Imitation of Life*' in Hortense J. Spillers (ed.), *Comparative American Identities: Race, Sex and Nationality in the Modern Text* (New York, London: Routledge, 1991), pp. 110–40; Hortense J. Spillers, 'Introduction: Who Cuts the Border? Some Readings on "America"' in *Comparative American Identities*, pp. 1–25; Robyn Wiegman, *American Anatomies: Theorizing Race and Gender* (Durham, London: Duke University Press, 1995).

7. For contemporary critical accounts which address the cultural significance of the Harlem Renaissance phenomenon and its relationship to debates about modernity and modernism in the US context see Houston A. Baker, *Modernism and the Harlem Renaissance* (Chicago: University of Chicago Press, 1987); Benn Michaels, *Our America*, pp. 85–94; Ann Douglas, *Terrible Honesty: Mongrel Modernism in the 1920s* (London: Picador, 1996), pp. 73–107; pp. 303–45; Hutchinson, *The Harlem Renaissance in Black and White*.

8. The 1997 *Rhapsodies in Black* exhibition at the Hayward Gallery, London, clearly revealed the extent to which Harlem artists both drew on modernist motifs and critically reformulated them to suit the new urban context of Harlem. See David A. Bailey's introduction to the exhibition book and essays by Richard J. Powell, 'Re/Birth of a Nation' and Henry Louis Gates Jr, 'Harlem on our Minds' in David A. Bailey (ed.), *Rhapsodies in Black: Art of the Harlem Renaissance* (London: Hayward Gallery, 1997), pp. 10–13; pp. 14–33; pp. 160–7.

9. See Huggins, *Harlem Renaissance*, pp. 84–136; Bruce Kellner, '"Refined Racism": White Patronage in the Harlem Renaissance" in Victor A. Kramer (ed.), *The Harlem Renaissance Re-Examined* (New York: AMS Press, 1987), pp. 93–106; Levering Lewis, *When Harlem Was In Vogue*, pp. 240–81.

10. See Lillian Faderman, *Odd Girls and Twilight Lovers* (Harmondsworth: Penguin, 1992), pp. 66–8; Eric Garber, '"A Spectacle in Color": The Lesbian and Gay Subculture of Jazz Age Harlem' in Martha Baum Duberman, Martha Vicinus and George Chauncey Jr (eds), *Hidden From History* (New York: New American Library, 1989), pp. 318–31; Gregory Woods, 'Gay Re-readings of the Harlem Renaissance Poets' in Emmanuel Nelson (ed.), *Critical Essays: Gay and Lesbian Writers of Color* (New York: Haworth, 1993), pp. 25–41.

11. The literature on black authenticity and the black vernacular is extensive. For key interventions see Houston A. Baker Jr, *Blues, Ideology and Afro-American Culture* (Chicago, London: University of Chicago Press, 1984); Henry Louis Gates Jr, *The Signifying Monkey* (New York, Oxford: Oxford University Press, 1980); Paul Gilroy, *Small Acts* (London: Serpent's Tail, 1993); bell hooks, *Yearning: Gender and Cultural Politics* (London: Turnaround Press, 1991); Isaac Julien, '"Black Is, Black Ain't": Notes on De-Essentializing Black Identities' in Dent (ed.), *Black Popular Culture*, pp. 255–63; Kobena Mercer, *Welcome to the Jungle* (New York, London: Routledge, 1994), pp. 233–58.

12. See Kevin Robins, 'Prisoners of the City: Whatever Could a Postmodern City Be?' in Erica Carter (ed.), *Space and Place: Theories of Identity and Location* (London: Lawrence and Wishart, 1993), pp. 303–30; Michael Walzer, 'The Pleasures and Costs of Urbanity' in Phillip Kasinitz (ed.), *Metropolis: Centre and Symbol of Our Times* (London: Macmillan, 1995), pp. 320–30; Iris Marion Young, 'City Life and Difference' in Kasinitz (ed.), *Metropolis*, pp. 250–70.

13. See Robert E. Park, Ernest W. Burgess, Roderick D. McKenzie, *The City* (1925; rpt Chicago, London: University of Chicago Press, 1967); Louis Wirth, 'Urbanism as a Way of Life' (1938) in *On Cities and Social Life: Selected Papers* (Chicago, London: University of Chicago Press, 1964), pp. 60–83.

14. See Louis Wirth, 'Urbanism as a Way of Life', pp. 71–7. See also Iris Marion Young: 'By "city life" I mean a form of social relations which I define as the being together of strangers.' 'City Life and Difference', p. 264.

15. Park, 'The City: Suggestions For The Investigation of Human Behaviour In The Urban Environment' in Park, Burgess and McKenzie, *The City*, p. 1.

16. For an analysis of the changing meanings attached to the term urbanity and the sense of a contemporary crisis of urbanity, see Robins, 'Prisoners of the City', pp. 314–15.

17. Chicago Commission on Race Relations, *The Negro in Chicago: A Study of Race Relations and a Race Riot* (1922; rpt New York: Arno Press, 1968). See in particular the summary report, pp. 595–651.

18. See *The Negro In Chicago*, pp. 640–51.

19. On Park see Hutchinson, *The Harlem Renaissance in Black and White*, pp. 50–60; Scruggs, *Sweet Home*, pp. 50–4. For discussion of Charles S. Johnson's influence on the New Negro movement see Hutchinson,

pp. 173–80; Levering Lewis, *When Harlem Was In Vogue*, pp. 88–9; pp. 125–9.

20. Locke, *The New Negro*. All further references will be incorporated in the text.

21. *Survey Graphic*, Vol. VI, No. 6 (March 1925), Harlem Number.

22. These positions belong to Henry Louis Gates Jr, 'The Trope of the New Negro and the Reconstruction of the Image of the Black' in Philip Fisher (ed.), *The New American Studies: Essays From Representations* (Berkeley, Los Angeles, Oxford: University of California Press, 1991), pp. 319–45; Baker, *Modernism and the Harlem Renaissance*; Levering Lewis, *When Harlem Was In Vogue*; Hutchinson, *The Harlem Renaissance In Black and White*; Huggins, *Harlem Renaissance*.

23. Hutchinson, *The Harlem Renaissance in Black and White*, p. 16.

24. Recent provocative reassessments of *The New Negro* which have been important to this study include Hutchinson, *The Harlem Renaissance in Black and White*, pp. 387–433; Benn Michaels, *Our America*, pp. 85–94; Scruggs, *Sweet Home*, pp. 38–67.

25. See Hutchinson, *The Harlem Renaissance in Black and White*, pp. 389–95 on the development of *The New Negro* from the Civic Club dinner. For an account of the dinner see 'The Debut of the Younger School of Negro Writers', *Opportunity*, Vol. 2, No. 5 (May 1924), pp. 143–4. See also Patrick J. Gilpin, 'Charles S. Johnson: Entrepreneur of the Harlem Renaissance' in Arna Bontemps (ed.), *The Harlem Renaissance Remembered* (New York: Dodd, Mead, 1972), pp. 224–50; Levering Lewis, *When Harlem Was In Vogue*, p. 93.

26. Hutchinson, *The Harlem Renaissance in Black and White*, p. 390; pp. 394–5, n. 523.

27. Ibid. p. 400.

28. See Hutchinson for an excellent summary of scholarly work on *The New Negro*, particularly 'Introduction' and 'Producing *The New Negro*', pp. 1–28; pp. 387–434; see also Scruggs, *Sweet Home*, pp. 56–7. For responses contemporary to *The New Negro* see John E. Bassett, *Harlem In Review: Critical Reactions to Black American Writers, 1917–1939* (London, Toronto: Associated University Presses, 1992), pp. 60–1.

29. See *Survey Graphic* Vol. IV, pp. 692–4; pp. 713–15; pp. 682–3; pp. 711–12; p. 684.

30. See Locke, 'The New Negro' and 'Negro Youth Speaks', pp. 3–16, pp. 47–53; J.A. Rogers, 'Jazz At Home', pp. 216–24; James Weldon Johnson, 'Harlem: The Culture Capital', pp. 301–11; Melville J. Herskovits, 'The Negro's Americanism', pp. 353–60; Elise Johnson McDougald, 'The Task of Negro Womanhood', pp. 369–82. All page references refer to *The New Negro*.

31. As a magazine of social work, *Survey Graphic* had run special issues on cultural movements in a number of different countries including Ireland, Russia and Mexico as well devoting issues to ethnic and racial groups within the US.

32. Hutchinson's analysis of 'City of Refuge' is one of the few which notes the innovativeness of the story. See *The Harlem Renaissance in Black and White*, pp. 403–4.

33. *The New Negro*, p. 226; p. 227; p. 225; pp. 214–15; pp. 216–24.
34. This attack starts with Langston Hughes, *The Big Sea: An Autobiography* (New York, London: Alfred A. Knopf, 1940) and has come to be a largely uninvestigated truism of Harlem Renaissance study. Hutchinson's *The Harlem Renaissance in Black and White* dislodges some of the more persistent myths about white influence on the Harlem phenomenon, but he does not explore the importance of ideas of urbanity which are the basis of my analysis here.
35. *Fire!! A Quarterly Devoted To the Younger Negro Artist*, Vol. 1, No. 1 (November 1926).
36. For a detailed study of Wallace Thurman's life and writing see Eleonore Van Notten, *Wallace Thurman's Harlem Renaissance* (Amsterdam: Rodopi, 1994); see also David Wadden, '"The Canker Galls ..." or the Short Promising Life of Wallace Thurman' in Kramer (ed.), *The Harlem Renaissance Re-Examined*, pp. 201–21.
37. Quoted in Hughes, *The Big Sea*, pp. 235–6.
38. *Fire!!*, p. 20; pp. 25–8. 'Elevator Boy' upset many since it appeared to lack any sense of a respectable American work ethic. Benjamin Brawley, the embodiment of conservative middle-class African America, thundered, 'the running of an elevator is perfectly honorable employment and no one with such a job should leave it until he is reasonably sure of getting something better.' 'The Negro Literary Renaissance', *Southern Workman*, Vol. 56 (April 1927), p. 183.
39. Aaron Douglas designed a number of modernist-Africanist covers for *Opportunity* starting in December 1925 (Vol. 3, No. 12) and running through 1926 to July 1927 (Vol. 5, No. 7).
40. See Hutchinson, *The Harlem Renaissance in Black and White*, pp. 394–5 for details of this controversy. See also Jeffrey C. Stewart, *To Color America: Portraits by Winold Reiss* (Washington, DC: Smithsonian Institute Press, 1989) pp. 50–4.
41. For Douglas's drawings see *The New Negro*, p. 54; p. 56; p. 112; p. 128; p. 138; p. 152; p. 196; p. 198; p. 216; p. 228; p. 270.
42. See Albert C. Barnes, 'Negro Art and America', pp. 19–28; Locke, 'The Legacy of the Ancestral Arts', pp. 254–70; Arthur Schomburg, 'The Negro Digs Up His Past', pp. 231–7.
43. See Hutchinson, *The Harlem Renaissance in Black and White*, pp. 398–9 for more on Douglas's embrace of white modernist ideas and African traditions.
44. See for example the work of William H. Johnson, Archibald J. Motley or Edward Burra. Their work is reproduced and discussed in Mary Schmidt Campbell (ed.), *Harlem Renaissance: Art of Black America* (New York: Studio Museum in Harlem and Abradale Press, Harry N. Abrams, Inc., 1987), pp. 105–54. See also Bailey (ed.), *Rhapsodies in Black*, pp. 111–17.
45. Aaron Douglas, 'Three Drawings', *Fire!!*, pp. 29–32.
46. Bruce Nugent, 'Drawings', *Fire!!*, p. 4; p. 24.
47. See Abby Arthur Johnson and Ronald Maberry Johnson, *Propaganda and Aesthetics: The Literary Politics of Afro-American Magazines in the Twentieth Century* (Amherst: University of Massachusetts Press, 1979), pp. 82–4 for details of the responses by Graves and Brawley.

48. *Fire!!*, p. 47.
49. In general the younger reviewers and writers liked the magazine but Du Bois, though gracious about its publication, let it be known that he was upset by its tone, and Alain Locke disapproved of its deliberate decadence. See Johnson and Johnson, *Propaganda and Aesthetics*, pp. 77–84 for full details of African American critical response to *Fire!!*
50. 'Smoke, Lilies and Jade', *Fire!!*; rpt in Nathan Huggins (ed.), *Voices From the Harlem Renaissance* (New York: Oxford University Press, 1976) pp. 99–110. All further references will be to this edition and incorporated in the text.
51. Quoted in Johnson and Johnson, *Propaganda and Aesthetics*, p. 83.
52. Benjamin Brawley, 'The Writing of Essays', *Opportunity*, Vol. 4, No. 9 (September 1926), p. 284.
53. Isaac Julien's 1989 film *Looking For Langston*, which will be examined in the final chapter, still remains the most comprehensive, if elliptical, examination of the sexuality of major Harlem Renaissance figures. It is fitting that Nugent's text is taken as inspiration for a sexual fantasy within the film.

Chapter Two: Space, Race and Identity

1. Hughes, *The Big Sea*, p. 240.
2. For details of contemporary reviews see the introduction to *City of Refuge*, xi–xxxix. *Atlantic Monthly* published 'City of Refuge' and 'Ringtail', Vol. 135 (1925), pp. 652–60; 'The Promised Land', Vol. 139 (1927), pp. 37–45; 'Blades of Steel', Vol. 140 (1927), pp. 183–92. *McClure's Magazine* published 'The Backslider' and 'Fire By Night', Vol. 59 (1927), p. 16, p. 64, p. 102, p. 104. *Story* published 'Miss Cynthie', Vol. 4 (1933), pp. 112–23. Fisher also published in *The Crisis*, *Opportunity*, *Negro News Syndicate* and *American Mercury*.
3. See McCluskey, 'Introduction' to *City of Refuge*, pp. xi–xxxix.
4. For essays on Fisher see John McCluskey Jr, '"Aim High and Go Straight": The Grandmother Figure in the Short Fiction of Rudolph Fisher', *Black American Literature Forum*, Vol. 15, No. 2 (Summer 1981), pp. 55–9; and 'Healing Songs: Secular Music in the Short Fiction of Rudolph Fisher', *CLA Journal*, Vol. 26, No. 2 (December 1982), pp. 191–203. See also Margaret Perry, 'A Fisher of Black Life: Short Stories by Rudolph Fisher' in Kramer (ed.), *The Harlem Renaissance Re-Examined*, pp. 253–63; Eleanor Q. Tignor, 'The Short Fiction of Rudolph Fisher', *The Langston Hughes Review*, Vol. 1, No. 1 (Spring 1982), pp. 18–24 and 'Rudolph Fisher: Harlem Novelist', *The Langston Hughes Review*, Vol. 1, No. 2 (Fall 1982), pp. 13–22. There is a short section on *The Walls of Jericho* in Levering Lewis, *When Harlem Was In Vogue*, p. 230 and he is discussed briefly in Huggins, *Harlem Renaissance*, pp. 118–21 but is not treated as anything more than a minor literary talent.
5. Zora Neale Hurston sent a telegram to Fisher's wife that read: 'THE WORLD HAS LOST A GENIUS. YOU HAVE LOST A

HUSBAND AND I HAVE LOST A FRIEND.' Quoted in McCluskey, 'Introduction', p. xxxix.

6. Levering Lewis draws attention to the death of Fisher and Wallace Thurman in the same month as a point of closure for the Renaissance. See *When Harlem Was In Vogue*, pp. 304–5.

7. Rudolph Fisher, 'Blades of Steel', *Atlantic Monthly*, Vol. 140 (1927) pp. 183–92; rpt. in *City of Refuge*, pp. 132–44. All further references will be to the reprint and incorporated in the text.

8. 'Miss Cynthie', *Story*, Vol. 4 (1933), pp. 112–23 and 'Guardians of the Law', *Opportunity*, Vol. 19 (1933), pp. 82–90; rpt in *City of Refuge*, pp. 68–78; pp. 60–7.

9. For example, Mouse Uggams in 'City of Refuge' is gifted with urban savvy that manifests itself in his ability to outtalk the naive Gillis.

10. 'Miss Cynthie', *City of Refuge*, p. 68.

11. 'The Promised Land', *City of Refuge*, p. 58.

12. 'Fire By Night', *City of Refuge*, p. 120.

13. See McCluskey, 'Introduction', p. xxi, and his 'Healing Songs: Secular Music in the Short Fiction of Rudolph Fisher'.

14. 'Common Meter', *Negro News Syndicate*, (February 1930); rpt in *City of Refuge*, pp. 145–57.

15. Rudolph Fisher, *The Walls of Jericho* (1928; rpt London: X-Press, 1995). All references will be to the reprint and incorporated in the text.

16. 'High Yaller', *The Crisis*, Vol. 30–31 (1925) pp. 281–6, pp. 33–8; rpt in *City Of Refuge*, pp. 81–97.

17. 'The Caucasian Storms Harlem', *American Mercury*, Vol. 11 (August 1927), pp. 393–8.

18. 'The Caucasian Storms Harlem', p. 394.

19. *The Conjure Man Dies* (1932; rpt Ann Arbor: University of Michigan Press, 1992). All references will be to the reprint and incorporated in the text.

20. McCluskey argues that too often the scenes featuring Bubber and Jinx come across as contrived set-pieces and veer too close to the racist representations of the comic darky, embodied in the period by the highly successful radio duo Amos and Andy; see McCluskey, 'Introduction', *City of Refuge*, p. xxix. I read their vernacular play rather differently, as one of a number of different strategies for reading urban culture, which are played off against one another in the novel.

21. 'John Archer's Nose', published posthumously in *Metropolitan Magazine*, Vol. 1 (1935), pp. 10–82; rpt in *City of Refuge*, pp. 158–94.

22. The phrase is Amiri Baraka's, from the poem 'Return of the Native' in *The Selected Poetry of Amiri Baraka/ LeRoi Jones* (New York: Morrow, 1979), p. 101.

23. See Douglas, *Terrible Honesty*, pp. 48–9 on the penchant for ingesting goat and monkey glands in 1920s New York. The practice was supposed to increase sexual potency and lengthen the life. Humorously, given the conjunction between conjure and psycho-analysis in Fisher's novel, Freud is reputed to have considered undergoing a form of the monkey gland treatment.

24. See Wiegman, *American Anatomies*, pp. 43–78.

25. In a radio interview in 1933 Fisher was asked if he intended always to write of Harlem. In reply he stated: 'I intend to write of whatever interests me. But if I should be fortunate enough to become known as Harlem's interpreter, I should be very happy.' Quoted in McCluskey, 'Introduction', p. xxxix.

Chapter Three: Passing and the Spectacle of Harlem

1. Thadious M. Davis, *Nella Larsen: Novelist of the Harlem Renaissance* (Baton Rouge: Louisiana University Press, 1994).

2. Nella Larsen, *Quicksand* (1928) and *Passing* (1929). Reprinted as *Quicksand and Passing*, ed. and intro. Deborah E. McDowell (London: Serpent's Tail, 1986); all further references will be to the reprint and incorporated in the text.

3. See for example, Baker, *Workings of the Spirit*; Robert Bone, *The Negro Novel in America* (New Haven: Yale University Press, 1958); Sterling Brown, *The Negro in American Fiction* (Albany: J.B. Lyon, 1937); Hiroko Sato, 'Under the Harlem Shadow: A Study of Jessie Fauset and Nella Larsen' in Bontemps (ed.), *The Harlem Renaissance Remembered*, pp. 63–89; Amritjit Singh, *The Novels of the Harlem Renaissance: Twelve Black Writers, 1923–1933* (University Park, London: Pennsylvania State University Press, 1976).

4. First theorised within legal studies and drawn on extensively by feminist and African American critics, see Kimberle Crenshaw, 'Demarginalising the Intersection of Race and Sex: A Black Feminist Critique of Antidiscrimination Doctrine, Feminist Theory and Antiracist Politics', *University of Chicago Legal Forum* (1989), pp. 139–67; Judith Butler, 'Passing, Queering: Nella Larsen's Psychoanalytic Challenge' in her *Bodies That Matter: On the Discursive Limits of 'Sex'* (New York, London: Routledge, 1993), pp. 167–85; Valerie Smith, 'Reading the Intersection of Race and Gender in Narratives of Passing', *Diacritics*, Vol. 24, No. 2 (Summer 1994), pp. 43–57.

5. See 'Freedom for the Second Sex' in George E. Mowry (ed.), *The Twenties: Ford, Flappers and Fanatics* (Englewood Cliffs, New Jersey: Prentice-Hall, Inc., 1963), pp. 173–86; Ann Douglas, 'White Manhattan' in her *Terrible Honesty*, pp. 31–72.

6. For an analysis of popular fears about new women and their connection with anxieties about the city see Michael Rogin, 'The Great Mother Domesticated: Sexual Difference and Sexual Indifference in D.W. Griffith's *Intolerance*' in Christoph K. Lohmann (ed.), *Discovering Difference: Contemporary Essays in American Culture* (Bloomington, Indiana: Indiana University Press, 1993), pp. 148–88.

7. The most famous example of this would be D.W. Griffith's *Intolerance* (1915) where New York is presented as a modern day Sodom, and where an equation is made between the freedom to move around the city and promiscuity. For more on the debates around birth control and its connections with race science see David

M. Kennedy, *Birth Control in America: The Strange Career of Margaret Sanger* (New Haven: Yale University Press, 1970).

8. For discussion of the connection between race science (particularly comparative anatomy) and definitions of the citizen and modernity see Wiegman, 'Sexing the Difference' in her *American Anatomies*, pp. 46–69. For more on the popular impact of Freud's work see Douglas, *Terrible Honesty*, pp. 115–29.

9. On the body, reproduction and national identity see Laura Doyle, *Bordering on the Body: The Racial Matrix of Modern Fiction and Culture* (New York, Oxford: Oxford University Press, 1994), pp. 10–34.

10. On the establishment of ideas of racial being and the means by which they are both contradicted and secured through a logic of gender difference see Wiegman, *American Anatomies*, pp. 56–69. For more on how the aftermath of slavery and the developing creed of racial improvement position African American women see Hazel Carby 'On the Threshold of a Woman's Era: Lynching, Empire, and Sexuality in Black Feminist Theory' in Henry Louis Gates Jr (ed.), *"Race", Writing and Difference* (Chicago: University of Chicago Press, 1985), pp. 301–16.

11. See Levering Lewis, *When Harlem Was In Vogue*, pp. 174–97; Anderson, *This Was Harlem*, pp. 213–24. Hutchinson's *The Harlem Renaissance in Black and White* presents a counter-argument to the widely accepted conclusion that Harlem was indeed split along genteel versus sensationalist lines and that all white influence was pernicious, though he has little time for Van Vechten.

12. See W.E.B. Du Bois, 'The Browsing Reader', *The Crisis* (June 1928) p. 202.

13. Locke, 'Negro Youth Speaks', *The New Negro*, pp. 47–53. Langston Hughes, 'The Negro Artist and the Racial Mountain', *The Nation* (23 June 1926), pp. 692–4. Hughes's famous assertion runs: 'We younger Negro artists who create now intend to express our individual dark-skinned selves without fear or shame. If white people are pleased we are glad. If they are not, it doesn't matter. We know we are beautiful. And ugly too. The tom-tom cries and the tom-tom laughs. If colored people are pleased we are glad. If they are not, their displeasure does not matter either. We build our temples for tomorrow.'

14. See 'The Negro In Art', *The Crisis* (April 1926), pp. 278–80; (May 1926), pp. 35–6; (June 1926), pp. 71–3; (August 1926), pp. 193–4; (September 1926), pp. 238–9.

15. Flyleaf to the Knopf first edition of *Quicksand* by Nella Larsen, copy held in the Schomburg Centre for the Study of Black Culture, New York Public Library. The flyleaf is written in the third person by Larsen.

16. For more on Madame C.J. and A'Leila Walker see Anderson, *This Was Harlem*, pp. 92–8; pp. 225–31. Toni Morrison references this cultural phenomenon in *Jazz* when she makes Joe Trace a beauty product salesman.

17. George Schuyler, *Black No More* (1932; rpt London: X-Press, 1998), page references will be to the reprint and incorporated in the text.

Other literary examples are too numerous to mention here but one can see this obsession extending (at least) from Charles Chesnutt's *The House Behind the Cedars* (1890) through articulation in passing novels, to the scathing critique of Wallace Thurman's *The Blacker The Berry* (1929).

18. Wallace Thurman, *Infants of the Spring* (1932; Boston: Northeastern University Press, 1992).

19. George Schuyler, 'Negro Art Hokum', *The Nation* (June 16, 1926), pp. 662–3.

20. See Charles S. Johnson's editorials, 'On Women's Brains', *Opportunity*, Vol. 1, No. 4 (April 1923); 'Another Vexation For the Biologists' and 'The Dramatist Turns Biologist', *Opportunity*, Vol. 2, No. 6 (July 1924); 'Faces', *Opportunity*, Vol. 6, No. 1 (January 1928); and the article, 'Mental Measurements of Negro Groups', *Opportunity*, Vol. 1, No. 2 (February 1923), pp. 21–4; Alexander A. Goldenweiser, 'Racial Theory and the Negro', *Opportunity*, Vol. 1, No 9 (August 1923), pp. 229–31; Melville Herskovits, 'The Racial Hysteria', *Opportunity*, Vol. 2, No. 5 (June 1924), pp. 166–8; and his *The American Negro: A Study in Racial Crossing* (New York: Alfred A. Knopf, 1928); Alain Locke, 'The Problem of Race Classification', *Opportunity*, Vol. 1, No. 9 (September 1923), pp. 261–4.

21. Albert Sidney Beckham, 'Applied Eugenics', *The Crisis*, Vol. 28 (August 1924), pp. 177–8.

22. Cited in Levering Lewis, *When Harlem Was In Vogue*, p. 193.

23. See bell hooks, 'Sexism and the Black Female Slave Experience' and 'Continued Devaluation of Black Womanhood' in her *Ain't I A Woman: Black Women and Feminism* (London: Pluto Press, 1982), pp. 15–50; pp. 51–86; Valerie Smith, 'Split Affinities: The Case of Interracial Rape' in Marianne Hirsch and Evelyn Fox-Keller (eds), *Conflicts in Feminism* (New York, London: Routledge, 1990) pp. 271–87; Wiegman, *American Anatomies*, pp. 56–62.

24. On the cost of genteel conformism for African American women writers see Carby, *Reconstructing Womanhood*, pp. 163–75; Ann DuCille, 'Blues Notes on Black Sexuality: Sex and the Texts of Jessie Fauset and Nella Larsen' in John C. Fout and Maura Shaw Tantillo (eds), *American Sexual Politics: Sex, Gender and Race Since the Civil War* (Chicago, London: University of Chicago Press, 1993), pp. 193–219.

25. See Anderson, *This Was Harlem*, pp. 27–9, pp. 334–8, pp. 339–46. See also Levering Lewis, *When Harlem Was In Vogue*, pp. 122–5 on Jessie Fauset as an example of the sexually conservative African American elite.

26. For more on the cultural significance of passing, and the anxieties it produces see Werner Sollors, *Neither Black Nor White Yet Both* (New York, Oxford: Oxford University Press, 1997), pp. 246–84, and Samira Kawash, *Dislocating the Color Line: Identity, Hybridity, and Singularity in African American Literature* (Stanford, California: Stanford University Press, 1997), pp. 125–8.

27. See Kawash, *Dislocating the Color Line*, 'the passing theme foregrounds ... the collapse of the continuity between representation

and identity, appearance and being, as they are supposedly determined along the color line' (p. 134).

28. See Rogin, 'The Great Mother Domesticated'.
29. On passing women see Cheryl Wall, *Women of the Harlem Renaissance* (Bloomington: Indiana University Press, 1995), pp. 85–138.
30. See Debra Silverman, 'Nella Larsen's *Quicksand*: Untangling the Webs of Exoticism', *African American Review*, Vol. 27, No. 3 (Fall 1993) pp. 599–614.
31. Mary Helen Washington, 'Nella Larsen: Mystery Woman of the Harlem Renaissance', *Ms Magazine* (December 1980) pp. 44–50. Of the many recent articles on Larsen, see in particular Pamela E. Barnett, '"My Picture Of You Is, After All, the True Helga Crane": Portraiture and Identity in Nella Larsen's *Quicksand*', *Signs: Journal of Women in Culture and Society*, Vol. 20, No. 3 (Fall 1995), pp. 575–600; David L. Blackmore, '"That Unreasonable Restless Feeling": The Homosexual Subtexts of Nella Larsen's *Passing*', *African American Review*, Vol. 26, No. 3 (Fall 1992), pp. 475–91; Butler, 'Passing, Queering: Nella Larsen's Psychoanalytic Challenge' in her *Bodies That Matter*, pp. 167–86; Carby, 'The Quicksands of Representation: Rethinking Black Cultural Politics' in her *Reconstructing Womanhood*, pp. 163–75; Martha J. Cutter, 'Sliding Significations: Passing as a Narrative and Textual Strategy in Nella Larsen's Fiction' in Martha J. Ginsberg (ed.), *Passing and the Fictions of Identity* (Durham, London: Duke University Press, 1996), pp. 75–100; DuCille, 'Blues Notes on Black Sexuality' in Fout and Tantillo (eds), *American Sexual Politics*, pp. 193–219; Mary Esteve, 'Nella Larsen's "Moving Mosaic": Harlem, Crowds, and Anonymity', *American Literary History*, Vol. 9, No. 2 (Summer 1997), pp. 268–86; Jeffrey Gray, 'Essence and the Mulatto Traveller: Europe as Embodiment in Nella Larsen's *Quicksand*', *Novel: A Forum on Fiction*, Vol. 27, No. 3 (Spring 1994), pp. 257–70; Beverley Haviland, 'Passing from Paranoia to Plagiarism: The Abject Authorship of Nella Larsen', *Modern Fiction Studies*, Vol. 43, No. 2 (Summer 1997), pp. 295–318; Ann Hostetler, 'The Aesthetics of Race and Gender in Nella Larsen's *Quicksand*', *PMLA*, Vol. 105 (Spring 1995), pp. 35–46; Jonathan Little, 'Nella Larsen's *Passing*: Irony and the Critics', *African American Review*, Vol. 26, No. 1 (Spring 1992), pp. 173–82; Kimberley Monda, 'Self-Delusion and Self-Sacrifice in Nella Larsen's *Quicksand*', *African American Review*, Vol. 31, No. 1 (Spring 1997), pp. 23–39; Claudia Tate, 'Death and Desire in *Quicksand*, by Nella Larsen', *American Literary History*, Vol. 7, No. 2 (Summer 1995), pp. 234–60. See also the full-length study of Larsen's work, Jacquelyn Y. McLendon, *The Politics of Color in the Fiction of Jessie Fauset and Nella Larsen* (Charlottesville and London: University of Virginia Press, 1995).
32. Deborah McDowell, Postscript to *Quicksand and Passing*, pp. 249–75, and '"That Nameless ... Shameful Impulse": Sexuality in Nella Larsen's *Quicksand* and *Passing*' in her *The Changing Same: Black Women's Literature, Criticism and Theory* (Bloomington: Indiana University Press, 1995), pp. 78–100.

33. Davis, *Nella Larsen*, p. 10.
34. Carl Van Vechten stands as common link between these figures. He acted as literary sponsor to Fisher and Larsen, was closely involved with Nugent and Thurman (in both literary and social circles) and was the primary conduit – through his famed parties – for actual and literary encounters between white modernist writers such as Stein and African American authors. See Davis, *Nella Larsen*, pp. 60–77, and Bruce Kellner, *Carl Van Vechten and the Irreverent Decades* (Norman: University of Oklahoma Press, 1968), pp. 107–17.
35. Quoted in Silverman, 'Nella Larsen's *Quicksand*, p. 610.
36. Larsen, Flyleaf to *Quicksand* (1928).
37. On the formal sophistication of Larsen's writing see Little, 'Nella Larsen's *Passing*' and Cutter, 'Sliding Significations'. For essays and books which discuss the complexity of passing as a phenomenon see Ginsberg (ed.), *Passing and the Fictions of Identity*; Kawash, *Dislocating the Color Line*; Harryette Mullen, 'Optic Whiteness: Blackness and the Production of Whiteness', *Diacritics*, Vol. 24, No. 2–3 (Summer–Fall 1994), pp. 71–89; Amy Robinson, 'It Takes One To Know One: Passing and Communities of Common Interest', *Critical Inquiry*, Vol. 20 (Summer 1994), pp. 715–36; Smith, 'Reading the Intersection of Race and Gender in Narratives of Passing'; Sollors, *Neither Black Nor White Yet Both*.
38. 'Semi-anonymous urban space' is Rachel Bowlby's phrase, quoted from her conference paper, 'The Last Shopper', presented at the *Urban Space and Representation* conference, University of Nottingham, 16 May 1998.
39. For a useful analysis of Larsen's engagement with modernism and the development of crowd psychology and other forms of early urban sociology see Esteve, 'Nella Larsen's "Moving Mosaic": Harlem, Crowds, and Anonymity'.
40. For an analysis of the importance of portraiture in the novel see Barnett, 'My Picture Of You Is, After All, the True Helga Crane'; Monda, 'Self-Delusion and Self-Sacrifice in Nella Larsen's *Quicksand*'.
41. For more on the construction of the black woman as primitive within a still more primitive scene see Silverman, 'Nella Larsen's *Quicksand*'. Silverman continues: 'While Stein's heroine keeps notions of female exoticism and sexual availability intact, Larsen challenges these and the already written scripts of black female desire ... Larsen works against the exotic primitivism that is in Stein's text and becomes a familiar trope in modernist literature' (p. 607).
42. Carby, 'The Quicksands of Representation', p. 170.
43. See Andrea D. Barnwell, 'Like the Gypsy's Daughter: Or Beyond the Potency of Josephine Baker's Eroticism' in Bailey (ed.), *Rhapsodies in Black*, pp. 82–9. Cheryl Wall also discusses the signif- icance of Baker as a commodified image of black female sexuality and draws interesting comparisons between her career and Larsen's work; see *Women of the Harlem Renaissance*, pp. 103–11.
44. A study that pursues these insights has yet to be written, though one finds very useful analysis of African American women and psycho-

analysis in Elizabeth Abel, Barbara Christian and Helene Moglen (eds), *Female Subjects in Black and White: Race, Psychoanalysis and Feminism* (Berkeley, Los Angeles, London: University of California Press, 1997); see particularly Barbara Johnson, 'The Quicksands of the Self: Nella Larsen and Heinz Kohut', pp. 252–65.

45. See, for example, Helga's experience on the streets of Chicago where she does not suffer from her racial designation but from being recognised as the wrong kind of woman (a prostitute): a typical fate for the 'new woman'.

46. For discussion of shot structure in classic Hollywood and its relationship to the construction of femininity in film see Mary Ann Doane, *Femmes Fatales: Feminism, Film Theory, Psychoanalysis* (New York: Routledge, 1991), pp. 1–45.

47. See Laura Mulvey, *Visual and Other Pleasures* (New York: Routledge, 1994), pp. 10–35, and Doane, *Femmes Fatales*, for discussion of the male gaze and Hollywood cinema.

48. On the problem of passing and vision see Lauren Berlant, 'National Brands/National Body: *Imitation of Life*' in Spillers (ed.), *Comparative American Identities*, pp. 110–40, and Robinson, 'It Takes One To Know One'.

49. Butler, *Bodies That Matter*, p. 169.

50. Ibid.

51. On the unreliable narrator in *Passing* see Little, 'Nella Larsen's *Passing*: Irony and the Critics'.

52. *Passing* is the most overdetermined of passing texts; Werner Sollors calls it 'a virtual encyclopaedia on the theme', *Neither Black Nor White Yet Both*, p. 276.

53. Mary Ann Doane, 'Technology's Body: Cinematic Vision in Modernity', *Differences: A Journal of Feminist Cultural Studies*, Vol. 5, No. 2 (Summer 1993), p. 9.

54. See 'Dark Continents: Epistemologies of Racial and Sexual Difference in Psychoanalysis and Cinema' in *Femmes Fatales*, pp. 209–48.

55. Ibid, p. 214.

Chapter Four: Women in the City of Refuge

1. See Gloria T. Hull, *Color, Sex and Poetry* (Bloomington: Indiana University Press, 1987), and 'Under the Days: A Study of Angelina Weld Grimké's Poetry', *Conditions Five* (Autumn 1979), p. 15–25.

2. Wall, *Women of the Harlem Renaissance*, pp. 1–32.

3. The ignorance of Bonner's work in most analyses of Harlem Renaissance literature is made all the more poignant by the 1986 republication of her collected work, a volume whose flyleaf asserts that the edition will change Harlem scholarship and introduce Bonner's work to a general readership. That this text is now out of print speaks volumes about the fate of African American women writers even in these days of reconstructed canons and multicultural anthologies. Bonner is generally known as the author of 'On Being Young – A Woman – and Colored', a 1925 essay which was reprinted

in Mary Helen Washington (ed.), *Invented Lives: Narratives of Black Women, 1860–1960* (New York: Anchor, 1987). Essays on her work are rare; see Lorraine Elena Roses and Ruth Elizabeth Randolph, 'Marita Bonner: In Search of Other Mothers' Gardens', *Black American Literature Forum*, Vol. 21, No. 1–2 (Spring–Summer 1987), pp. 165–83; Sharon Dean and Erlene Stetson, 'Flower-dust and Springtime: Harlem Renaissance Women', *Radical Teacher*, Vol. 18 (1980), pp. 1–8.

4. See Marita Bonner, *Frye Street and Environs: The Collected Works of Marita Bonner*, ed. and intro. by Joyce Flynn and Joyce Occomy Stricklin (Boston: Beacon Press, 1986). Further references to Bonner's stories will be in the text and from this edition except where otherwise indicated.

5. Fauset called *Rachel* 'a play as terrible, as searching and as strong as anything produced by the continental European dramatists.' See *The Crisis*, Vol. 21 (1920), p. 64.

6. Grimké had a number of poems published in *Opportunity* in the early 1920s including 'The Black Finger', *Opportunity*, Vol. 1, No. 11 (November 1923), p. 343; 'Little Grey Dreams', *Opportunity*, Vol. 2, No. 1 (January 1924), p. 20. The number of her poems published in Countee Cullen (ed.), *Caroling Dusk: An Anthology of Verse by Negro Poets* (London, New York: Harper and Bros, 1927) and Robert T. Kerlin (ed.), *Negro Poets and Their Poems* (Washington: Associated Publishers, 1923) speak to a substantial reputation in her own time. Her short stories and plays are reprinted in *The Selected Works of Angelina Weld Grimké*, ed. Carolivia Herron (New York: Oxford University Press, 1991). Grimké's plays have received some critical attention, often in comparison with those of Marita Bonner, see Doris E. Abrahamson, 'Angelina Weld Grimké, Mary T. Burrill, Georgia Douglas Johnson and Marita O. Bonner: An Analysis of Their Plays', *Sage*, Vol. 2, No. 1 (Spring 1985), pp. 9–13; Helene Keyssar, 'Rites and Responsibilities: The Drama of Black American Women' in Enoch Brater (ed.), *Feminine Focus: The New Women Playwrights* (New York, Oxford: Oxford University Press, 1989) pp. 32–46.

7. Bonner published essays and short stories in *The Crisis* magazine, 'On Being Young – A Woman – and Colored' (December 1925); 'Nothing New' (November 1926); 'One Boy's Story' (November 1927); 'Drab Rambles' (December 1927). The remainder of her published output appears in *Opportunity* between 1926 and 1941. She was awarded *The Crisis* literary prize for 'On Being Young' and picked up two *Opportunity* prizes, for the three-part story 'A Possible Triad on Black Notes', published in the magazine in July, August and September of 1934 and for the two-part 'Tin Can', published July and August 1934.

8. For more on the S Street Salon see Hull, *Color, Sex and Poetry*, pp. 165–6; Wall, *Women of the Harlem Renaissance*, p. 10. As Hull makes clear it is likely that Grimké's relationships with the poets Clarissa Scott Delany, Georgia Douglas Johnson and Mary Burill were sexual as well as literary, and it is certain that Johnson's salon was an important meeting place for those artists and authors in the

Harlem Renaissance who for at least part of their lives pursued same-sex relationships.

9. See Levering Lewis, *When Harlem Was In Vogue*, p. 127.

10. See Wall, *Women of the Harlem Renaissance*, pp. 1–84.

11. Details of the relationships between Jackman and Cullen and Hughes and Locke appear in some form in most histories of Harlem, even though the sexual dimension is not always stressed or examined, in particular see Levering Lewis, *When Harlem Was In Vogue*, p. 76, pp. 81–8. On gay rent parties see Faderman, *Odd Girls and Twilight Lovers* and Garber, '"A Spectacle in Color"'.

12. Wall, *Women of the Harlem Renaissance*, p. 10.

13. On A'Leila Walker see Anderson, *This Was Harlem*, pp. 225–31; on Fauset's editorship of *The Crisis* see Wall, *Women of the Harlem Renaissance*, pp. 43–57; pp. 61–64; pp. 72–3.

14. See 'The Ebony Flute', which ran from September 1926 to May 1928 in *Opportunity*, Vol. 4, No. 9 to Vol. 6, No. 5.

15. To this one might add the extensive role played by women like Ernestine Rose who was librarian at the 135th Street library (later the Schomburg), or Regina Andrews (who was Rose's assistant at the 135th Street Library and a close friend of Fauset and Bennett) whose massive collection of photographs and papers are now housed at the Schomburg Center for Research into Black Culture, New York.

16. Marcy Knopf (ed.), *The Sleeper Wakes: Harlem Renaissance Stories By Women* (London: Serpent's Tail, 1993).

17. See Bruce Kellner (ed.), *The Harlem Renaissance: A Historical Dictionary for the Era* (Westport, Conn., London: Greenwood Press, 1984), pp. 144–5 for Grimké's biography.

18. 'The Closing Door', *The Birth Control Review*, Vol. 4 (Nov–Dec 1920); rpt in Knopf (ed.), *The Sleeper Wakes*, pp. 124–45. All further references will be to this reprint and incorporated in text. There are two other versions of this story extant, 'Goldie', *Atlantic Monthly* (1920) and 'Blackness' (previously unpublished): both are reprinted in the *Selected Works of Angelina Weld Grimké*, ed. Herron.

19. On the multiple connections between racism and sexual exploitation through US history see Carby, *Reconstructing Womanhood*; hooks, *Ain't I A Woman?*; Smith, 'Split Affinities'.

20. For discussion of the politics of *The Birth Control Review* in relation to the content of Grimké's story see Hull, *Color, Sex and Poetry*, p. 129 and Carolyn M. Dever, 'Voluntary Motherhood: Angelina Weld Grimké and *The Birth Control Review*', cited in David A. Hedrich Hirsch, 'Speaking Silences in Angelina Weld Grimké's "The Closing Door" and "Blackness"', *African American Review*, Vol. 26, No. 3 (Fall 1992), p. 463.

21. The letter accompanied 'Goldie', which with 'Blackness' constitute alternative versions of 'The Closing Door'. The first version of this story was Grimké's play *Rachel*, first performed in 1916 and published in 1920, which was more straightforwardly propagandist in its intentions. The repeated reworking of the central lynching motif seems to suggest the difficulty Grimké had in dealing with this subject, and her determination to tell this story.

22. Hirsch, 'Speaking Silences in Angelina Weld Grimké's "The Closing Door" and "Blackness"', pp. 459–74.

23. Undated letter from Angelina Weld Grimké to the editors of *Atlantic Monthly* (1920) cited in Hull, *Color, Sex and Poetry*, pp. 129–30.

24. Smith, 'Split Affinities', pp. 271–87. See also Hortense J. Spillers, 'Mama's Baby, Papa's Maybe', *Diacritics*, Vol. 17, No. 2 (Summer 1987), pp. 67–80.

25. Hirsch states: 'If the word does not bring transcendence in Grimké's text, the repossession and translation of the word by her narrators ... try to give voice to silenced African Americans; and at the same time, by withholding information, these narrators attempt to deprive the reader from being able to master their blackness.' 'Speaking Silences', p. 472.

26. 'One Boy's Story', *The Crisis* (November 1927); rpt in *Frye Street and Environs*, pp. 78–91. References will be to the reprint and incorporated in the text.

27. See Anderson, *This Was Harlem*, pp. 88–9; p. 105, and Levering Lewis, *When Harlem Was In Vogue*, pp. 9–10.

28. Hirsch, 'Speaking Silences', p. 466.

29. Gilroy interprets accounts of Garner's trial thus: 'Margaret's lawyer ... told the court that she and the other fugitives "would all go singing to the gallows", rather than be returned to slavery. The association of this apparent preference for death is highly significant. It joins a moral and political gesture to an act of cultural creation and affirmation' (p. 68). See also pp. 64–71.

30. 'Living Memory: a Meeting With Toni Morrison' in Gilroy, *Small Acts*, p. 179.

31. Hughes, *The Big Sea*, p. 124.

32. Marita Bonner, 'On Being Young – A Woman – and Colored', *The Crisis* (December 1925); rpt in *Frye Street and Environs*, pp. 3–8. All further references will be to the reprint and incorporated in the text.

33. All Bonner stories discussed from here on are reprinted in *Frye Street and Environs*. Page references will be to the reprint and incorporated in the text.

34. Gates, 'The Trope of the New Negro and the Reconstruction of the Image of the Black'.

35. Richard Wright, 'Blueprint for Negro Writing', *New Challenge* (1937); rpt in Gayle (ed.), *The Black Aesthetic*, pp. 10–16.

36. This common phrase is first presented in Hughes, *The Big Sea*.

37. See Werner Sollors, *Beyond Ethnicity: Consent and Descent in American Culture* (New York, Oxford: Oxford University Press, 1986), pp. 20–39; Michael Omi and Howard Winant, 'Ethnicity' in their *Racial Formation in the United States: From the 1960s to the 1990s* (New York, London: Routledge, 1994), pp. 14–23.

38. See Joyce Flynn, Introduction to *Frye Street and Environs*, p. xvi.

39. See Levering Lewis, *When Harlem Was In Vogue*, pp. 282–5; St. Clair Drake and Horace Clayton, *Black Metropolis: A Study of a Negro Life in a Northern City* (New York: Harcourt, Brace, 1945).

Chapter Five: Consumer Desire and Domestic Urbanism

1. Gwendolyn Brooks, *A Street in Bronzeville* (New York: Harper & Row, 1945); rpt in *The World of Gwendolyn Brooks* (New York: Harper & Row, 1971), pp. 1–59. All further references will be to this edition and incorporated in the text. Ann Petry, *The Street* (1946; rpt London: Virago Press, 1986). All further references will be incorporated in the text.

2. Hazel Carby makes this point at the end of her chapter on Larsen, see *Reconstructing Womanhood*, p. 175.

3. See Brooks's autobiography for details of her personal and literary history, *Report From Part One* (Chicago: Broadside Press, 1972). See also George Kent, *A Life of Gwendolyn Brooks* (Lexington: University of Lexington Press, 1990).

4. Maria K. Mootry and Gary Smith (eds), *A Life Distilled: Gwendolyn Brooks, Her Poetry and Fiction* (Urbana: University of Illinois Press, 1987).

5. See Barbara Johnson, 'Apostrophe, Abortion, Animation', *Diacritics*, Vol. 16, No. 1 (Spring 1986), pp. 29–39; Hortense J. Spillers, 'Gwendolyn the Terrible: Propositions on Eleven Poems' in Mootry and Smith (eds), *A Life Distilled*, pp. 224–38 and 'An Order of Constancy: Notes on Brooks and the Feminine' in Henry Louis Gates Jr (ed.), *Reading Black, Reading Feminist* (New York: Meridian, 1990), pp. 244–71.

6. See Barbara Christian, *Black Women Novelists: The Development of a Tradition* (Westport, Conn.: Greenwood Press, 1980) and 'Nuance and the Novella: A Study of Gwendolyn Brooks's *Maud Martha*' in Mootry and Smith (eds), *A Life Distilled*, pp. 239–53; Mary Helen Washington, '"Taming All That Anger Down": Rage and Silence in Gwendolyn Brooks's *Maud Martha*' in Gates (ed.), *Black Literature and Literary Theory*, pp. 249–62 and 'Plain, Black, and Decently Wild: The Heroic Possibilities of Maud Martha' in Elizabeth Abel, Hirsch, Elizabeth Langland (eds), *The Voyage In: Fictions of Female Development* (Hanover, NH: University of New England for Dartmouth College, 1983), pp. 270–86.

7. Richard Wright, *Native Son* (New York: Harper & Row, 1940). All further references will be incorporated in the text.

8. Robert Bone, *The Negro Novel in America* (New Haven: Yale University Press, 1958); Addison Gayle, *The Way of the New World: The Black Novel in America* (Garden City: Doubleday, 1976).

9. The title of Wright's 1937 essay published in *New Challenge*. This essay crystallises many of the criteria for 'race writing' which underpin modes of African American literary history I work against in this book.

10. Bone, *The Negro Novel*, p. 73.

11. Maria Lauret, *Liberating Literature: Feminist Fiction in America* (London, New York: Routledge, 1994) pp. 40–2. The significant stylistic differences between *The Street* and *Native Son* are demonstrated by Bernard Bell, *The Afro-American Novel and its Tradition* (Amherst: University of Massachusetts Press, 1987), pp. 178–83.

12. This point is argued forcefully by Barbara E. Johnson, 'The Re(a)d and the Black' in Gates (ed.), *Reading Black: Reading Feminist*, pp. 145–54, though she examines how this conception of black masculinity depends on (the erasure of) the black female reader of this textual identity. See also Maria K. Mootry, 'Bitches, Whores and Woman Haters: Archetypes and Topologies in the Art of Richard Wright' in Richard Macksey and Frank E. Moorer (eds), *Richard Wright: A Collection of Critical Essays* (Engelwood Cliffs, NJ: Prentice Hall, 1984), pp. 44–59.

13. On the concept of life practices see Michel de Certeau, 'Walking in the City' in his *The Practices of Everyday Life* (Berkeley: University of California Press, 1984) John Fiske, 'Cultural Studies and the Culture of Everyday Life' in Lawrence Grossberg, Cary Nelson, Paula Treichler (eds), *Cultural Studies* (New York, London: Routledge, 1992), pp. 154–64.

14. David Theo Goldberg, *Racist Culture: Philosophy and the Politics of Meaning* (Oxford: Blackwell, 1993). See in particular Chapter 8, 'Polluting the Body Politic: Race and Urban Location', pp. 185–205.

15. On 'structural containment' see Goldberg, *Racist Culture*, pp. 187–92.

16. See Walter Benjamin, 'Paris: Capital of the Nineteenth Century', rpt in Kasinitz (ed.), *Metropolis*, pp. 46–57; Georg Simmel, 'The Metropolis and Mental Life', rpt in Kasinitz, pp. 30–45.

17. The opening up of the private realm to debates over the meaning of race and femininity is congruent with the examples we saw earlier in Larsen, Grimké and Bonner.

18. See Gilbert Osofsky, *Harlem: The Making of a Ghetto* (New York, Hagerstown, San Francisco, London: Harper and Row Publishers, 1963) and Drake and Clayton, *Black Metropolis*.

19. See Goldberg, *Racist Culture*, pp. 185–205 for a discussion of periphractic space. The term refers to the marginalising, or peripheralising, of spaces along racial lines which makes those spaces identified as racial or ethnic enclaves peripheral to (in economic, cultural or political terms) the city as a whole, despite their (frequent) geographical location in the centre of the city. Thus non-white spaces are identified and rendered central but marginalised within the politico-geographical dimensions of the city.

20. Gwendolyn Brooks's 1960 collection of poems, *The Bean Eaters* (New York: Harper and Row, 1960) also focuses very interestingly on this topic.

21. Goldberg, *Racist Culture*, pp. 185–205.

22. Gloria Wade-Gayles, *No Crystal Stair: Visions of Race and Sex in Black Women's Fiction* (New York: Pilgrim Press, 1984), pp. 45–67.

23. See Berlant, 'National Brands/National Body'; Donald Bogle, *Toms, Coons, Mulattoes, Mammies and Bucks: An Interpretative History of Blacks in American Film* (New York: Viking, 1973); Gerda Lerner (ed.), *Black Women in White America: A Documentary History* (New York: Panther, 1972).

24. Wade-Gayles, *No Crystal Stair*, p. 55.

25. For discussion of the Sapphire stereotype see bell hooks *Ain't I A Woman*, pp. 85–6; Jean Carey Bond and Pat Peery, 'Is the Black

Male Castrated?' in Toni Cade Bambara (ed.), *The Black Woman: An Anthology* (New York: Signet, 1970), pp. 113–18.

26. Gayle Wurst, 'Ben Franklin in Harlem: The Drama of Deferral in Ann Petry's *The Street*' in Gert Buelens and Ernst Rudin (eds), *Deferring a Dream: Literary Subversions of the American Columbiad* (Basel, Boston, Berlin: Birkhauser, 1994), pp. 1–23; Christian, *Black Women Novelists*, pp. 62–8.
27. For more on this see James Snead, *White Screens, Black Images: Hollywood from the Dark Side* (New York, London: Routledge, 1994), pp. 67–80.
28. See in particular Washington, 'Plain, Black, and Decently Wild: The Heroic Possibilities of Maud Martha'.
29. See Hortense J. Spillers, '"The Permanent Obliquity of an In(pha)llibly Straight": In the Time of the Daughters and the Fathers' in Wall (ed.), *Changing Our Own Words*, pp. 127–49.

Chapter Six: Elegies to Harlem

1. Toni Morrison, *Jazz*, p. 8. All further references will be incorporated in the text.
2. *Looking For Langston*, dir. Isaac Julien, 1989.
3. On haunting in Morrison's work see Peter Nicholls, 'The Belated Postmodern: History, Phantoms and Toni Morrison' in Sue Vice (ed.), *Psychoanalytic Criticism: A Reader* (Cambridge: Polity Press, 1995), pp. 50–74.
4. For details of VanDerZee's photographs and career see Deborah Willis Braithwaite, *VanDerZee: Photographer, 1886–1983* (New York: Harry N. Abrams, Inc., Publishers in association with the National Portrait Gallery, Smithsonian Institute, 1993).
5. 'Living Memory: a Meeting With Toni Morrison' in Gilroy, *Small Acts*, p. 179.
6. Mercer, 'Reading Racial Fetishism' in *Welcome to the Jungle*, p. 209.
7. Notably Robert Mapplethorpe's black nudes, Carl Van Vechten's portraits of Harlem literati, and Georges Platt Lynes's homoerotic photography.
8. bell hooks, 'States of Desire: Interview with Isaac Julien' in Isaac Julien and Colin MacCabe, *Diary of a Young Soul Rebel* (London: BFI Publishing, 1991), p. 127. All further references will be incorporated in the text.
9. See Peter Brooker, 'Black and White Notes: Toni Morrison's *Jazz*' in his *New York Fictions: Modernity, Postmodernism and the New Modern* (London, New York: Longman, 1996), pp. 200–13; Henry Louis Gates Jr, 'Review of *Jazz*' in Henry Louis Gates and Anthony Appiah (eds), *Toni Morrison: Critical Perspectives* (New York: Amistad, 1993), pp. 52–5; Richard Hardack, 'Double-Timing and Double Consciousness in Toni Morrison's *Jazz*', *Callaloo*, Vol. 18, No. 2 (Spring 1995), pp. 451–71; Deborah E. McDowell, 'Harlem Nocturne', *The Women's Review of Books*, Vol. IX, No. 9 (June 1992), pp. 4–5; Alan Rice, 'Jazzing It Up A Storm: The Execution and Meaning of Toni Morrison's Jazzy Prose Style', *Journal of American*

Studies, Vol. 28, No. 3 (Winter 1994), pp. 423–32; and Eusebio L. Rodrigues, 'Experiencing *Jazz*', *Modern Fiction Studies*, Vol. 39, No. 3–4 (Fall–Winter 1993), pp. 733–54.

10. James VanDerZee, Camille Billops and Owen Dodson, *The Harlem Book of the Dead: Photographs by James VanDerZee* (Dobbs Ferry, New York: Morgan and Morgan, 1978).

11. For reproductions of some of these photographs see Allon Schoner (ed.), *Harlem On My Mind: Cultural Capital of Black America* (New York: Random House, 1969), p. 42.

12. See *VanDerZee: Photographer*, p. 17 for the pictures VanDerZee composed of Mills's wake.

13. See in particular Henry Louis Gates Jr, 'Looking for Modernism' in Manthia Diawara (ed.), *Black American Cinema* (New York, London: Routledge, 1993), pp. 200–7, and 'The Black Man's Burden' in Dent (ed.), *Black Popular Culture*, pp. 75–84.

14. Mercer, 'Reading Racial Fetishism', p. 209.

15. Chapter 5, 'The Fact of Blackness' in *Black Skin: White Masks* (1956: rpt London: Pluto Press, 1986), p. 109; p.112.

16. Doane, *Femmes Fatales*, p. 212.

17. See Gwen Bergner, 'Who Is That Masked Woman? Or, The Role of Gender in Fanon's *Black Skin: White Masks*', *PMLA*, Vol. 10 (1995), pp. 75–88; and Doane, *Femmes Fatales*, pp. 216–27, for details of some of the difficulties Fanon's work raises for feminist and queer theorists.

18. Doane, *Femmes Fatales*, pp. 234.

19. Mercer, 'Reading Racial Fetishism', pp. 202.

20. For more on Julien's usage of avant-garde techniques in relation to sound, narrative and mise-en-scene see Manthia Diawara, 'The Absent One: The Avant-Garde and the Black Imaginary in *Looking For Langston*' in Marcellus Blount and George P. Cunningham (eds), *Representing Black Men* (New York, London: Routledge, 1996), pp. 205–24.

21. Richard Dyer, 'Into the Light: The Whiteness of the South in *The Birth of a Nation*' in Richard H. King and Helen Taylor (eds), *Dixie Debates: Perspectives on Southern Culture* (London: Pluto Press, 1996), pp. 171–5.

22. Manthia Diawara, 'Black American Cinema: The New Realism' in his *Black American Cinema*, p. 3.

23. See Richard Dyer, *White* (London: Routledge, 1997), pp. 82–144; Snead, *White Screens: Black Images*, pp. 37–46.

24. One could also assert the reverse, in that the film makes reference to and visually quotes from gay avant-garde cinema – particularly Bunuel's *Un Chien Andalou* (1928), Cocteau's *Sang d'un Poete* (1930) and Genet's *Un Chant D'Amour* (1950) – and re-codes the racial exoticism which can seen to work in these texts. For more on this see Diawara, 'The Absent One', pp. 211–16.

25. The homophobia of black nationalist discourses is a current as well as a historical issue; see Carby, *Race Men*, particularly pp. 1–6; Paul Gilroy, 'Climbing the Racial Mountain: a Conversation with Isaac Julien' in *Small Acts*, pp. 166–72. There are many other examples one could point to: the virulently homophobic pronouncements in

parts of the key document of the Black Arts movement, Gayle's *The Black Aesthetic* (1971); notorious pronouncements by black Muslim leaders like Elijah Muhammad; the anti-feminist, anti-lesbian ranting in Ishmael Reed's *Reckless Eyeballing* (1990); to the at best combative attitude to homosexuality one finds in Spike Lee's movies.

26. See Dyer, *White*, pp. 89–144 on the problems in lighting black and white skin simultaneously.

27. The absence of any actual jazz places is noted in Peter Brooker's perceptive essay on *Jazz* in his *New York Fictions*, p. 200. It is, in part, the lack of any actual jazz in the novel that leads me to be suspicious of the analogies made by critics between Morrison's writing style and jazz music.

28. Andrea O'Reilly, 'Mother-Love, Healing and Identity in Toni Morrison's *Jazz*', *African American Review*, Vol. 30, No. 3 (Fall 1996), pp. 367–80.

29. For more on functioning of historicity and the employment of tropes of 'belatedness' in Morrison's writing see Nicholls, 'The Belated Postmodern', pp. 50–74.

30. As I discussed in my introduction Morrison's attitude to the city is deeply contradictory; see 'City Limits, Village Values: Concepts of the Neighbourhood in Black Fiction' in Jaye and Watts (eds), *Literature and the Urban Experience*, pp. 35–44. One should also note the repeated motif in her fictions of a city character who has to relearn the older wisdom of the country, or as it often figured, of Africa, for example Jadine in *Tar Baby* (1980) or Milkman Dead in *Song of Solomon* (1977).

31. See Douglas, *Terrible Honesty*, pp. 3–72.

32. Brooker, *New York Fictions*, pp. 207–8.

33. For details on the connections between *Beloved* and *Jazz* see O'Reilly, 'Mother Love: Healing and Identity in Toni Morrison's *Jazz*' and Nicholls, 'The Belated Postmodern'.

34. Morrison argues that because of the impact of slavery African Americans experience the conditions of modernity very differently. In fact she goes so far as to suggest that their experience of a characteristically postmodern condition substantially predates that of white Americans. She says: 'It's not simply that human life originated in Africa in anthropolological terms, but that modern life begins with slavery ... From a woman's point of view, in terms of confronting the problems of where the world is now, black women have had to deal with "postmodern" problems in the nineteenth century and earlier. These things had to be addressed by black people a long time ago. Certain kinds of dissolution, the loss of and the need to reconstruct a certain kind of stability. Certain kinds of madness, deliberately going mad, as one of the characters says in the book [*Beloved*] "in order not to lose your mind." These strategies for survival made the truly modern person. They're a response to predatory Western phenomena. You can call it an ideology and an economy, what it is is a pathology.' 'Living Memory', p. 178.

35. Mercer, 'Reading Racial Fetishism', p. 219.

36. See McDowell, 'Harlem Nocturne' for an argument along these lines.

Index